D1142073

KA 0144395 X

MEDIEVAL CLASSICS

GENERAL EDITORS

V. H. Galbraith and R. A. B. Mynors

REGVLARIS CONCORDIA

THE MONASTIC AGREEMENT

Regularis Concordia

Anglicae Nationis Monachorum Sanctimonialiumque

Thomas Nelson and Sons Ltd

London Edinburgh Paris Melbourne Toronto and New York

The Monastic Agreement

of the Monks and Nuns of the English Nation

Translated from the Latin with Introduction
and Notes by
Dom Thomas Symons
of Downside Abbey

Thomas Nelson and Sons Ltd
London Edinburgh Paris Melbourne Toronto and New York

THOMAS NELSON AND SONS LTD

Parkside Works Edinburgh 9
3 Henrietta Street London WC2
312 Flinders Street Melbourne C1
5 Parker's Buildings Burg Street Cape Town

THOMAS NELSON AND SONS (CANADA) LTD
91-93 Wellington Street West Toronto 1

THOMAS NELSON AND SONS
19 East 47th Street New York 17

SOCIÉTÉ FRANÇAISE D'EDITIONS NELSON
25 rue Henri Barbusse Paris V^e

First published 1953

Edwardi Cuthberti Butler Abbatis Memoriae

CONTENTS

ACKNOWLEDGEMENT

This book owes its beginnings to the inspiration of the late Abbot Cuthbert Butler; its development to the advice, assistance and encouragement of the late J. Armitage Robinson, D.D.; and its completion to Dom David Knowles and the Editors of the series, Professor R. A. B. Mynors and Professor V. H. Galbraith, who have laid themselves out to help me in every way: I owe them more than I can say. I have also to thank Sir Frank Stenton for some valuable criticisms; the Right Rev. Christopher Butler, Abbot of Downside, for permission to make use of articles that have already appeared in the *Downside Review*; Dom Joseph Marshall for helping me with the proofs; Mr. J. P. T. Bury, Librarian of Corpus Christi College, Cambridge, for allowing me to examine MS CCCC 190; and Messrs. Nelson, the Publishers, for their skill, patience and courtesy.

Worth Priory
Feast of St Dunstan, 1952

Dom Thomas Symons

Corripiet me iustus in misericordia et increpabit me

REFERENCES EMPLOYED THROUGHOUT

To the Latin Text: figures for section and line
To Martène (*De Ant. Eccl. Rit.* and *De Ant. Monach. Rit.*) : the *Editio novissima*, Venice, 1783
All Scriptural references are to the Vulgate

SIGNS USED IN THE APPARATUS TO THE TEXT

The symbol + denotes an addition; *om.* denotes an omission. A group of two or more words omitted or altered is indicated by square brackets, thus: [ ] *om.*, or [ ] followed by the alternative reading.

T = Cotton MS Tiberius A 3 ff. 3*a*–27*b*
F = Cotton MS Faustina B 3 ff. 159*a*–198*a*
F_2 = Cotton MS Tiberius A 3 f. 177 *a* and *b*
AE = MS CCCC 265 ff. 237 ff.
T (gloss) = the interlinear Anglo-Saxon glosses of T

ABBREVIATIONS USED IN INTRODUCTION AND NOTES IN TEXT

*AE	Aelfric's *Letter to the Monks of Eynsham*, ed. Bateson in *Obedientiary Rolls of St Swithun's Winchester* (Hampshire Record Society, 1892), Append. vii. 174 ff.
**Aix Capit.*	The Capitula of Aix, C.M. iii. 115 ff.
BCS	W. de G. Birch, *Cartularium Saxonicum*, 3 vols.: cited by number
C.M.	Dom Bruno Albers, *Consuetudines Monasticae*, 5 vols.
DR	Downside Review
EHR	English Historical Review
HBS	The Henry Bradshaw Society Publications
H.E.	*Historia Ecclesiastica*
**Eins*	C.M. v. 73 ff.
**Farfa*	C.M. i. 1 ff.
**Fleury*	C.M. v. 137 ff.
**Gelas*	H. A. Wilson, *The Gelasian Sacramentary* (Oxford 1894)
**Greg*	H. A. Wilson, *The Gregorian Sacramentary* (HBS 1915)
JTS	Journal of Theological Studies
**Jumièges*	H. A. Wilson, *The Missal of Robert of Jumièges* (HBS 1896)
**Leofr* (A) and *Leofr* (C)	F. E. Warren, *The Leofric Missal* (Oxford 1883)
**Liber Vitae*	W. de G. Birch, *Newminster and Hyde Abbey* (Hampshire Record Society, 1892) pp. 11 ff.
**Memorials*	Stubbs, *Memorials of St Dunstan* (RS 1874)

**Monastic Order*	Dom D. Knowles, *The Monastic Order in England* (Cambridge 1940)
Opp. Hist.	Plummer, *Baedae Opera Historica*, 2 vols. (Oxford 1896)
*OQ	*Ordo Qualiter*, C.M. iii. 26 ff.
*OR I	*Ordo Romanus Primus* (and Appendix), *PL* lxxviii. 937 ff. and 959 ff.
PL	Patrologia Latina
Ratoldus	The Missal of Ratoldus Abbot of Corbie (cited from Martène, *De Ant. Eccl. Rit.*, and from Menard's notes to his edition of the Gregorianum, *PL* lxxviii)
RS	Rolls Series
Rule	*Benedicti Regula*, ed. Butler (Freiburg im Breisgau 1912 and 1927): cited by ch. and line
**Sources*	Symons, *Sources of the Regularis Concordia* (DR 1941; Jan. pp. 14 ff., April pp. 143 ff., July pp. 264 ff.)
**Times of St Dunstan*	J. Armitage Robinson, *The Times of St Dunstan* (Oxford 1923)
**Trèves*	C.M. v. 7 ff.
**Ulrich*	Consuet. Clun. Ant., *PL* cxlix. 635 ff.
**Verdun*	C.M. v. 113 ff.
**Vita Ethelwoldi*	*Vita Ethelwoldi auctore Aelfrico*, Stevenson, Chronicon Monasterii de Abingdon (RS 1858), ii. 255 ff.
**Vita Oswaldi*	*Vita Oswaldi auctore anonymo*, Raine, Historians of the Church of York (RS 1879), i. 399 ff.
**Warnfrid*	*Pauli Warnefridi in Sanctam Regulam Commentarium* (Monte Cassino 1880)
**Wulfstan Collectar*	W. H. Frere, *The Leofric Collectar*, ii. (HBS)

* Cited by page or column only

From the Cotton MS Tiberius A 3 folio 2b

(By courtesy of the British Museum)

INTRODUCTION

I

THE ENGLISH MONASTIC REVIVAL OF THE TENTH CENTURY

THE consuetudinary or code of monastic law known to us as the Regularis Concordia forms a landmark in the religious history of this country. Coming down to us from that great period of national prosperity, the reign of Edgar (959–975), when the political union of England had been in some sort achieved, it marks the final settlement, as it were, of the Benedictine revival in which a spiritual movement that had been gathering strength for well-nigh a hundred years found its highest expression.

We must remember that the England of the great days of Wilfred and Benet Biscop, of Aldhelm, Venerable Bede and Boniface had all but passed away under the pressure of the Viking raids. When the turning point came and the tide of invasion that had overflowed the whole country, save only the more remote parts of Mercia and a little corner of Wessex, was stemmed at Ethandune in 878, Alfred had to lay anew the foundations of national life.

A prime necessity was the education of the younger generation. Yet it would appear that Alfred could find no teachers in Wessex; indeed his own words [1] would lead us to suppose that few men south of the Humber and none south of the Thames could so much as understand a Latin Service Book. Help came from the unravished portions of Mercia, from Wales and from abroad ; and Alfred was able to gather round him as advisers and teachers Werferth the Bishop of Worcester, Plegmund and Werwulf, the Welsh Asser, Grimbald

[1] But see F. M. Stenton, *Anglo-Saxon England* (Oxford 1947), p. 268: '. . . it is probable that Alfred, writing in 894, heavily over painted the depression of English learning in 871.' See p. xiii below.

of St Bertin's in Flanders and Abbot John the Old Saxon from Corvey. Of this group of new men only Asser and the foreigners, Grimbald and John, were monks. This is not surprising; for Saxon monasticism, already weakened by the growth of an abuse later forbidden under the name of *saecularium prioratus*[1]—the overlordship of laymen over monasteries—had been brought to the lowest possible condition by the Danish invasions. Most of the monasteries were destroyed; some are commonly supposed to have come into the possession of secular clerks; a very few, among them St Augustine's, Canterbury, may have survived to carry on something of their traditional way of life.

The decline of monasticism seems to have been such that the very words ' abbot ' and ' monk ' are rarely found in documents of the period; while Asser has only the most contemptuous references to Wessex monasticism: ' Many monasteries,' he says, ' there are; but in none of them is the monastic rule kept properly (*ordinabiliter*).'[2] This may serve to explain why Alfred, who recognised the importance of monasticism, made no attempt to reform one of the old monasteries. Instead, he established two new foundations, one at Athelney with a community of foreigners under John the Old Saxon, another at Shaftesbury for women, under his second daughter Aethelgeofu. No real success seems to have attended the Athelney venture: the hoped-for revival was not to come until an Englishman and English monks should show the way.

Under Edward the Elder (899–924) Alfred's projected foundation of the Newminster at Winchester was proceeded with, Grimbald becoming its first head. According to Florence of Worcester a house for women also, the Nunnaminster,

[1] See Proem (10, 1 f.). This abuse was of long standing. See, e.g., a letter of St Boniface to Archbishop Cuthbert (Tangl, *S. Bonifatii et Lulli Epp.* in *Mon. Germ.* 8vo no. 26, p. 169) and, with special reference to Northumbria, Bede's *Letter to Egbert* (*Opp. Hist.* i. 413 ff.). In 803 the Council of Cloveshoe passed an Act forbidding the election of laymen as lords over ' regular ' monasteries. Abbot Muca of Glastonbury was one of the signatories to this Act.

[2] W. H. Stevenson, *Asser's Life of King Alfred*, p. 80 f.

was established in the same city by Ealhswith, the Queen Mother. New episcopal sees were founded for Wessex: Ramsbury, Wells and Crediton.

In 924 Athelstan came to the throne. Under his rule the prestige of the country was immensely advanced both at home and abroad. Foreign princes sought his friendship, received his sisters in marriage, and found at his court a refuge from the troubles of their own countries. One religious house, Middleton (Milton Abbas), owed its foundation to him; another, Crediton, received gifts from him; while many churches were enriched by him with books and relics.

The close political connections between this country and the Continent in the reign of Athelstan had their counterpart in an increase of ecclesiastical intercourse just about the time when a great monastic reform was beginning to spread throughout the Burgundian and Lotharingian lands. Thus in 929 Bishop Cenwald of Worcester heads a mission to the monasteries of Germany; in this reign or in the next, refugee monks from St Bertin's in Flanders are given a place in the monastery of Bath[1]; the priest Godescalc,[2] evidently a foreigner, appears at Abingdon. Coincident with this intercourse or, more probably, following on it, can be remarked indications of a revival of interest in monasticism. It looks very much as though Archbishop Athelm and Bishop Cenwald[3] were monks: Aelfheah, Bishop of Winchester, certainly was. The title 'abbot' occurs with greater frequency in charters, and if we cannot be sure that these abbots were monks, it is at least likely that they were ecclesiastics.[4]

[1] *Folcwini Gesta Abbatum S. Bertini*, Pertz *Mon. Germ.* xiii. 628.

[2] For Godescalc see F. M. Stenton, *Early History of Abingdon*, p. 38. For other foreign ecclesiastics living in English religious houses about this time see F. M. Stenton, *Anglo-Saxon England*, p. 438.

[3] The tradition that Cenwald was a monk (see Flor. Wig. s.a. 957) may help to explain the attestation *Kenwald monachus* (for *Kenwald episcopus*) in four charters: BCS 883, 909, 911, 937.

[4] In the St Gall Confraternity Book, from which we know of Bishop Cenwald's visit there, Kenod and Albrich, two of the abbots who attest Athelstan's charters, are entered as abbots; while Cudret, identified by Stubbs with the Cuthred of the ancient list of Glastonbury abbots, appears without title. See p. xix *n.* 1 below.

We must now turn our attention to a young boy from the West Country, as yet only the *puer strenuus*,[1] who was beginning to attract the notice of Athelstan's court, but at no very distant period to be at the right hand of kings and an outstanding personality in Church and State.

It was in or about the year 909, at Baltonsbury, a village to the south east of Glastonbury that St Dunstan was born.[2] His parents, Heorstan and Cynethrith, were people of rank and importance, one of them at least being in some way related to the Royal House of Wessex. His paternal uncle Athelm was the first bishop of the newly-founded See of Wells from 909 until his translation to Canterbury in 923; two of his kinsmen became bishops, Aelfheah the Bald (Winchester, 934–951) and Kynesige (Lichfield, 934–964); another of his relatives, the Lady Ethelfleda, was niece to King Athelstan.

The boy grew up under the shadow, as it were, of the ancient sanctuary which lay close to his father's lands. About the year 923, when his uncle Athelm left Wells for Canterbury and Dunstan was about fourteen, his parents allowed him to take the tonsure, and he was admitted to membership in the community of Glastonbury.[3]

There must have been something remarkable about a place that could inspire a boy of birth and worldly prospects to associate himself with its fortunes; something must have still survived of its ancient religious spirit and traditions. But we know little of the Glastonbury of Dunstan's boyhood. It

[1] '. . . oritur puer strenuus.' See the *B Life* of Dunstan (*Memorials*, p. 6).

[2] A prime authority for the life of St Dunstan is the *Vita auctore B*, written about the year 1000; next in value comes the slightly later *Vita auctore Adelardo*. These and other Lives and documents are printed in Stubbs, *Memorials*. For a study of St Dunstan's early career see *English Monastic Reform of the Tenth Century* in DR 1942, pp. 6 ff., 196 ff. and 268 ff.

[3] 'Videntes itaque parentes praenominati tantam sui excellentiam filii, dignam sibi clericatus imposuere tonsuram officii inque famoso Glestoniensis ecclesiae sociaverunt coenobio' (*Memorials*, p. 10); 'Natus ergo puer Dei, sacro est lavacro intinctus, et Glestoniae divino servitio mancipatus . . .' (*ibid.* 54). See DR Jan. 1942, pp. 16 f. and 22 *n.*

was called the *regalis insula*[1]; it possessed a long line of abbots[2]; a religious community was still settled there; Ina's church was standing; there was a library; there was a place set apart for burials. Last and not least Glastonbury was a place of pilgrimage and numbers of people, Irish and other, journeyed thither for the sake of devotion.[3] There was a tradition of learning at Glastonbury, and the young Dunstan profited from the books of the Irish pilgrims and of 'other prudent men'[4] and perhaps from the teaching of the Saxon Wulfred, a deacon of Glastonbury, his *prelatus* and familiar friend. No doubt Dunstan was influenced also by his uncle Athelm, as he certainly was by his kinsman Aelfheah the Bald, monk and bishop: both of these men seem to have been members of the Glastonbury community.

Shortly after taking the tonsure, Dunstan spent about a year with Archbishop Athelm, who introduced him to King Athelstan. In January 926 the archbishop died, and for the next seven years or so Dunstan was mainly occupied with his studies at Glastonbury. That he was also in touch with the court is clear, but his relations with the royal household were probably limited to the occasions when the king was in the neighbourhood of the 'royal island.' There followed a crisis in his career. His other-worldliness and love of study brought him into conflict with his companions of the court. They accused him of dealing in the black arts and, having secured his banishment from their society, set upon him, threw him into a muddy pool and trampled on him. It must have been

[1] Possibly it was in the king's hands as Bath was and as were Abingdon in the reign of Edred and Ely in that of Edgar. Alternatively the expression *regalis insula* may merely commemorate the tradition that Glastonbury was in a sense a royal foundation. That the abbacy was in the gift of the king in Edmund's reign is proved by his appointment of Dunstan. It has been suggested that Cuthred and Ecwulf, who immediately precede Dunstan in the ancient list of abbots, were laymen—king's thanes.

[2] See J. Armitage Robinson, *The Saxon Abbots of Glastonbury* (Somerset Historical Essays, Oxford 1921), pp. 26 ff.

[3] The visits of the Irish and other pilgrims can have been no new thing in Dunstan's boyhood. Long before his time it is likely that members of the Glastonbury familia had learned from Irish teachers.

[4] *Memorials*, p. 11

at this point that he began to think of marriage. As he hesitated between marriage and the religious life there came upon him the illness which was to prove the turning point in his life. Almost at death's door, he sent for Bishop Aelfheah, who had constantly admonished him to become a monk, promised to obey him and received from him the monastic habit. This would have been about the year 934.

Until the end of Athelstan's reign Dunstan seems to have lived at Glastonbury, often however spending considerable periods with Bishop Aelfheah, by whom he was ordained priest in or about 939, the last year of Athelstan's reign.

One of the first acts of the new king, Edmund, was to give Dunstan a place in the royal household. But the old jealousies revived, and it was not long before Edmund, at the instance of Dunstan's enemies, deprived him of all honours and dignities and sent him into banishment. On the following day, however, Edmund narrowly escaped death while hunting. In the stress of the moment, he called to mind the injury that he had done to Dunstan and vowed to repair it if his life was spared. This vow he carried out at once. The court was at Cheddar at the time, and on his return to the royal residence the king sent for Dunstan and presently set off with him to Glastonbury, a few miles distant. There he placed Dunstan in the abbot's chair and bade him rule over the ancient sanctuary. On the strength of a charter[1] in which Dunstan appears for the first time as abbot, we may place this appointment in the year 940.

Dunstan's promotion to Glastonbury, sudden as it may seem to us, can have been no unconsidered whim on Edmund's part. We have already drawn attention to a revival of interest in monasticism during the reign of Athelstan, and have suggested that there were some in the English Church who were working and praying for its restoration. Aelfheah's action, for instance, in persuading Dunstan to become a monk, must have been prompted by considerations that went far

[1] BCS 752: Edmund's grant of land at Christian Malford in Wiltshire to 'my faithful abbot Dunstan' in 940. See DR April 1942, p. 221 f., and F. M. Stenton, *Anglo-Saxon England*, p. 440 and *n*.

beyond the furtherance of his young kinsman's personal welfare.[1] It may well be that English churchmen were already contemplating the possibility of doing for the decayed English monasticism something of the sort that was being done for the monastic life abroad. The close relations between England and the Continent in Athelstan's reign make it certain that the overseas movements of reform were a matter of common knowledge in this country. It is not unlikely that Glastonbury may already have been regarded by some as the place where a beginning might be made and Dunstan as the man to whom the work might be entrusted.

When Dunstan took charge of the place in which he had received his education and spent the greater part of his life, he at once attracted disciples. Of high birth and handsome presence,[2] intellectually gifted,[3] and of marked holiness of life,[4] his renunciation of the world had already excited admiration, and now that he was an abbot men were eager to follow his example. The type of man drawn to Glastonbury and the training received there may be judged by the number of Dunstan's pupils who in course of time attained to high positions in the English Church. We have no record of what the Glastonbury observance under Dunstan was really like,

[1] A somewhat similar view was put forward long ago by Bishop Stubbs when he wrote that 'there had taken place, probably under the influence of Elphege the Bald, a strong tendency towards pure Benedictinism' (*Memorials*, p. lxxxv).

[2] Abbo of Fleury, in a celebrated acrostic, addresses Dunstan as 'angelicam qui fers faciem' (*Memorials*, p. 410); in a letter from one of Dunstan's friends we find the following:

> 'Carne es sic pulcher, sic pulcher acumine sensus
> Alter te nullus pulchrior esse queat' (*ibid.* p. 371);

the author of the later Life of Ethelwold speaks of Dunstan as *angelicus* (*PL* cxxxvi. 101). In the miniature found in Cott. MS Tib A 3 (see p. lv below) the artist has evidently striven to depict Dunstan as tall and handsome.

[3] Dunstan's learning, often mentioned in the *B Life*, is witnessed to by many of his friends, among them, Abbo of Fleury.

[4] Of Dunstan's holiness of life the late E. Bishop wrote: 'The institution of his religious cult immediately after his death, its almost universal diffusion throughout the country among his contemporaries, is a fact of the highest significance' (*English Hagiology*, Dublin Review xiii 1885, p. 142).

but from the express statement of his first biographer[1] we know that the Rule of St Benedict was followed; and from the one detail that has been preserved to us,[2] we may gather that it was followed strictly. Possibly the life was not very different from that prescribed in the *Ordo Qualiter*,[3] a Benedictine writing of the eighth century. It is unlikely that anything was known of such accretions to the Rule as already obtained in reformed houses abroad; for there was as yet no direct outside influence at work in England. But the want, if want there was, of detailed and ceremonious observance affords no indication that the early reform at Glastonbury[4] differed essentially from those of twenty or thirty years later when Continental ideas were exercising a direct influence in this country. Particular devotional practices, ritual splendour and the like have always been dependent on the fashion of the day, and our early authorities for this period lend no support to the view that any essential change in the character of its monasticism took place at Glastonbury at some further stage of the movement.

Dunstan's main work during this period was, naturally, concerned with Glastonbury itself—reorganising the life and enlarging the monastic buildings, thus fulfilling the dream of his childhood. It would seem nevertheless that his position as abbot of Glastonbury carried with it responsibilities of quite another nature. Adelard's statement that Edmund was 'guided by Dunstan and made glorious through his counsel,'[5] must not be unduly pressed; but there is some foundation for

[1] *Memorials*, p. 25. Note also the words which the *B Life* puts into Edmund's mouth at the installation of Dunstan as abbot: 'quicquid tibi . . . ad *sacrae regulae* supplementum . . . defuerit, ego . . . supplebo' (*ibid.*).

[2] *Loc. cit.* p. 28. There we are told that Dunstan placed his brother Wulfric in charge of the external affairs of Glastonbury 'ne vel ipse vel quispiam ex monastica professione *foris vagaretur*' (cf. *Rule* lxvi, 15–16: 'ut non sit necessitas monachis *vagandi foris*').

[3] See below, p. xlviii.

[4] The *B Life* represents Dunstan in exile at St Peter's, Ghent, then in the first fervour of reform, as looking back with regret on the excellence of the life at Glastonbury (*Memorials*, p. 35).

[5] *Loc. cit.* p. 56

it—witness the story in the *B Life*, of Dunstan's presence at the royal residence at Pucklechurch at the time of the mysterious happenings that culminated in Edmund's murder.[1] Evidently Dunstan, who held some position at court at the very beginning of Edmund's reign, was again among the number of the king's advisers as abbot. It would seem safe to say that, for all his preoccupation with the reform of his monastery, Dunstan had, towards the close of Edmund's reign, entered on that career of statesmanship which was to reach its zenith in Edgar's reign.

The new king, Edred (946–955), brother of the murdered Edmund, showed himself well-fitted, in spite of continual and severe bodily weakness, to carry on the great traditions of the previous reigns. Abbot Dunstan was his right hand man, and to him at Glastonbury was committed a large part of the royal treasure. So great was the king's affection for Dunstan that, the *B Life* tells us, 'scarce one of the chief men was preferred to him.' Dunstan's love for Edred was no less great; and it was probably his devotion to his 'dearest king' that caused him to refuse the episcopate in this reign.[2]

We must now return to the monastic reform, soon to receive a fresh impulse with the restoration of the ancient monastery of Abingdon by Ethelwold, the greatest of Dunstan's disciples.

Of the early life of Ethelwold we know only the meagre details supplied by his biographer, Aelfric.[3] His parents lived at Winchester in the days of Edward the Elder and must have been persons of consequence for, like Dunstan, the young Ethelwold spent part of his youth at Athelstan's court. The king commended him to Aelfheah the Bald who ordained him

[1] *Loc. cit.* pp. 44 ff.

[2] It is not clear whether Edred intended to promote Dunstan to Crediton or Winchester or, indeed, if he did not make two separate offers, one on the death of Aelfheah the Bald in 951, the other on the death of Ethelgar of Crediton in 953. The *B Life* is our authority for the offer of Crediton, Adelard for that of Winchester. Names apart, it looks very much as though both writers had got hold of the same story.

[3] *Vita Ethelwoldi auctore Aelfrico*, written about the year 1004.

and Dunstan to the priesthood together. Later, Ethelwold followed his friend to Glastonbury and there received from him the monastic habit. After some time Ethelwold manifested a desire to go beyond the seas for the sake of perfecting himself in the virtues of the monastic state. The fame of the great Continental reforms—of Cluny under St Odo, of Ghent under Gerard of Brogne, most of all of Fleury—would seem to have fired his imagination. But he was not allowed to fulfil his desire. When the loss that his departure would mean to the country was represented to Edred, he at once made over to Ethelwold the old monastery of Abingdon, then a poor and neglected establishment with most of its possessions in the king's hands. We need not doubt that it was Dunstan who advised, as we know he approved,[1] such an outlet for the capabilities of his disciple. Thus it was that about the year 954 the pupil took with him from Glastonbury five young men to spread from a new centre the flame kindled by the master some fourteen years before. In a short time Ethelwold gathered together a community, organised the discipline of the house and projected the new monastic buildings: the king had already given him, in addition to the monastery itself, the royal property at Abingdon. We do not know how far the work progressed in this reign or whether it was interrupted by the troubles that followed on Edred's death. At all events the church, Aelfric tells us, was not completed until the reign of Edgar. There is nothing to show that Ethelwold was able at once to introduce at Abingdon anything of the Continental observance that had so greatly impressed him. It is more likely that he had to wait for this until the restoration of peace, and that direct connections between Abingdon and Continental monasticism are to be referred to Edgar's reign.

The example set by Glastonbury and Abingdon must have put new life into the communities of the few ancient houses in which something of the old monastic tradition may

[1] *Op. cit.* p. 257: 'permittente Dunstano'

yet have survived.[1] But the moment had not come for further reforms. In 955 came the untimely death of Edred and with it a partial set-back to the movement. The new king, Eadwig, was under the domination of those who resented the power of Dunstan and the old Queen Mother, Eadgifu. On his coronation day, the story goes, Eadwig left the hall where the bishops and nobles were assembled and betook himself to the company of two high-born ladies, Æthelgifu and her daughter. It was Abbot Dunstan and his kinsman, Bishop Kynesige of Lichfield, who went at the request of Archbishop Oda to insist on the young king's return; and it was on Dunstan and the Queen Mother that the anger of Eadwig and the two women fell. The estates of Eadgifu were confiscated while Dunstan had to flee the country and take refuge at the monastery of St Peter at Ghent, then in the hey-day of its reform.

Eadwig's mismanagement of affairs soon led to a revolt in Mercia and to the choice of his younger brother, Edgar, to rule the country north of the Thames. Edgar at once recalled Dunstan, appointing him to the vacant see of Worcester and, shortly after, to that of London as well. On Eadwig's death in 959 Edgar became king over the whole country and in 960, on the death of Aelfsige of Canterbury and the retirement of Brihthelm, Dunstan succeeded as archbishop. He made the customary visit to Rome and received the pallium from Pope John XII.

The opening years of the reign saw the beginning of an extension of the movement of reform. As need arose, episcopal sees were filled by monks; secular clerks were removed from some of the old religious foundations and their place taken by monks; religious houses were established or restored all over

[1] e.g., possibly St Augustine's Canterbury (see *Times of St Dunstan*, p. 116). For the names of Abbot Eadhelm (? and some of the community of that house) in 958 see BCS 1010. In 949 and 951 Abbots Eadhelm and Dunstan attest charters together (BCS 880, 890). For a reference to an abbot at Canterbury in Athelstan's time see F. Liebermann, *Gesetze der Angelsachsen*, p. 159: 'In Cantuaria septem monetarii sunt : regis quattuor, episcopi duo, abbatis unus.' For Evesham see *Times of St Dunstan*, pp. 36–40.

the country by the united efforts of Dunstan, Ethelwold and a new leader, Oswald. Behind the movement was the royal support. It is from this period that we may date the beginnings of effective external contacts with the reformed monasticism of the Continent.

Dunstan's share in the active promotion of the monastic reform is witnessed to by the *B Life* where we are told that he 'went about the country visiting the monasteries in his care.'[1] This may be taken as a general indication that Dunstan was responsible for and took an immediate interest in the restoration of certain monasteries; for it can hardly be supposed that he would have felt it necessary to visit in so authoritative a manner houses restored by Ethelwold or Oswald. Moreover, in the passage just referred to, the *B Life* goes on to relate how, when Dunstan was visiting the brethren of Bath, the provost of Glastonbury came to take counsel with him on the affairs of that house, as was his custom.[2] Here we have evidence both of Dunstan's superintendence of his old monastery for at least some time after his consecration as archbishop, and of his care for the monastery of Bath.

This pre-Conquest tradition of Dunstan's relations with certain monasteries, Glastonbury and Bath in particular, gives some colour to the statement of his later biographers, Osbern, Eadmer and William of Malmesbury, that the saint applied the legacy of the Lady Ethelfleda to the endowment of five monasteries, all of which he kept under his own rule.[3] Moreover, it furnishes us with a key to the interpretation of later traditions of his reforming connections with Malmesbury and Westminster. The details of the Malmesbury story[4] may not all be of equal value, but that that house was restored in Dunstan's time is clear, and the tradition that it owed its restoration to Dunstan himself was never contested. For Westminster we have the statement of William of Malmesbury

[1] *Memorials*, p. 46. See also *Vita Ethelwoldi*, p. 262

[2] He is mentioned as *pontifex, episcopus* (*Memorials*, p. 47).

[3] *Loc. cit.* pp. 89, 178, 301

[4] William of Malmesbury, *Gesta Pontificum* (RS), p. 404 f. and *Gesta Regum* (RS) i. 173; *Memorials*, p. 301 f.

that Dunstan founded a monastery there for twelve monks,[1] and the evidence of a charter of *c.* 971 in which Westminster is handed over to Dunstan for reform.[2] St Augustine's, Canterbury, too, would naturally have come under Dunstan's special notice, and it is significant that Abbots Sigeric of St Augustine's and Cyneweard of Milton (Abbas) are both said to have been monks of Glastonbury. As for the presence of monks at Christ Church, Canterbury, during Dunstan's archiepiscopate, we may recall that the *B Life*, relating the story of a vision in which the saint was taught a new anthem, goes on to say that Dunstan, on awakening, called together his household both *monks* and clerks.[3] From the same authority we have also the significant fact that the archbishop shortly before his death lay down to rest after the midday meal 'according to the summer custom'[4]—an allusion to the monastic siesta prescribed by the Concordia in accordance with the Rule. It may be that at Christ Church under Dunstan there was quietly taking place a change comparable to that effected at Worcester by Oswald.[5]

The history of Ethelwold's reforming activities rests for the most part on the evidence of his biographer and pupil, Aelfric. The restoration of Abingdon has already been mentioned. Special interest attaches to this monastery on account of the tradition that men were attracted to it by the fame of its 'stricter' observance, that monks were brought from Corbie to instruct the community in the chant, and that Ethelwold sent one of his monks, Osgar, later Abbot of Abingdon, to study the observance of Fleury.

In 963 Ethelwold was consecrated to the bishopric of Winchester. In the two following years clerks were removed from the Old and New Minsters there and their place taken by monks from Abingdon. Ethelwold appointed Ethelgar, who

[1] See J. Armitage Robinson, *Saxon Bishops of Wells* (Brit. Acad. Supplementary Papers iv. 1919), p. 67

[2] BCS 1048; cf. *Crawford Charters*, p. 90

[3] *Memorials*, p. 41

[4] *Loc. cit.*, p. 52

[5] See *The Introduction of Monks at Canterbury*, JTS July 1926, pp. 409 ff.; and *Monastic Order*, p. 696 f.

had been under Dunstan at Glastonbury, as abbot of the Newminster, keeping the monastery of the Cathedral Church, the Old Minster, under his own rule. A third Winchester reform was that of the Nunnaminster where Etheldreda was made abbess.

The expulsion of clerks from their houses has often been brought forward as an instance of the 'harshness' of Ethelwold's [1] reforming zeal; but if Aelfric's oft-quoted picture of the clerks of the Old Minster [2] be a fair one, the measure was inevitable at Winchester. It is true that the principal critics of the clerks, Aelfric and the anonymous biographer of Oswald, wrote forty years or more after the event, that their criticism mainly concerns the clerks of Winchester, that there is no suggestion of parallel happenings at Canterbury or Worcester and that the Chronicle (A), our only really contemporary evidence,[3] is content to record, under the year 964, that King Edgar 'drave out the priests from the Old and New Minsters, from Chertsey and from Milton and introduced monks.' Yet even when all allowance has been made, it is difficult to see how the evidence against the clerks can be altogether discounted; and in an age of new ideals there could be no compromise with a decadent condition of things.

Ely, Medeshampstead (or Burgh, later known as Peterborough) and Thorney, under Abbots Brihtnoth, Aldulf and Godeman, close Aelfric's list of foundations made by Ethelwold.

Oswald's [4] work as a monastic reformer had the foreign element in it from the start. After his experience of a Winchester *monasterium* of clerks, he went abroad and became a monk at Fleury. There he stayed until recalled by his uncle,

[1] The *Liber Eliensis* (ed. D. J. Stewart, 1848), p. 160 f., says that clerks expelled from Ely complained to the king not against Ethelwold but against Dunstan.

[2] Very similar to Aelfric's, and possibly related to it, is the description given in the Laws of Ethelred; see Wilkins, *Concilia*, i. 288 f., and F. Liebermann, *Gesetze der Angelsachsen*, i. 248 ; cf. also *Liber Vitae*, p. 7.

[3] The Proem to the Concordia speaks of the 'abominations' of the clerks, but it is doubtful if this can be considered as impartial evidence.

[4] Our chief authority here is the *Vita Oswaldi auctore anonymo*. For the authorship of this work see *Monastic Order*, p. 494 and *n*.

Archbishop Oda, in 958. On his arrival in England he found that Oda had passed away. In 961, through Dunstan's influence, he became Bishop of Worcester and began to take a leading part in the monastic movement. Westbury-on-Trym was his first foundation; but it is Ramsey in Huntingdonshire that must be looked upon as the centre of his reforming activities, and thither monks were transferred from Westbury (*c.* 968–970). Winchcombe was colonised from Ramsey shortly before 972. A little later Oswald introduced monks at his own cathedral see of Worcester, the change from a secular to a monastic condition being brought about gradually. According to his anonymous biographer Oswald had under his rule ' within the confines of the Hwiccas ' seven monasteries:[1] Worcester, Winchcombe and Pershore are doubtless among these.

Of reformed houses of women there is scant record. But references to abbesses and nuns in the Concordia, in the early lives of Dunstan, Ethelwold and Oswald, in the *Liber Vitae* of the Newminster, in the old Anglo-Saxon tract called *The Resting Places of the Saints*, and elsewhere make it quite clear that active participation in the work of reform was not confined to the monks.[2] Among the principal houses of nuns restored before the close of the century may be mentioned the Nunnaminster, Romsey, Wilton, Wareham, Wherwell, Shaftesbury, Reading, Horton, Berkeley, Exeter, and St Mildred's, Thanet.

To return to our story: by about the year 970 a number of foundations were well in hand; and the time had come when the leaders would have to pull the whole movement together. This brings us to the Council of Winchester and the drawing up of a monastic code that should bind together Glastonbury, Abingdon, Ramsey and the other houses. The

[1] *Vita Oswaldi*, p. 439

[2] There exists a fragment of an Anglo-Saxon translation of the Concordia in which the word ' abbess ' has been inserted as an alternative to ' abbot ' (Bateson, *Rules for Monks and Canons*, EHR ix. 707). A translation of the Rule, in all likelihood for the use of nuns, was made by St Ethelwold (*Times of St Dunstan*, p. 121 f.).

full title of this code shows it to have been in the nature of an agreement, a settlement of differences (*concordia*) drawn up on lines in accordance with the Rule (*regularis*), as well as something of national importance in a united England (*Anglicae nationis*). Our sole evidence for this Council[1] and for the condition of things that led up to it is the account given in the Proem to the Concordia itself. The exact date is uncertain, but may be placed between the years 965 when Aelfthryth—mentioned in the Concordia as caring for the nuns—became Edgar's queen and 975, the year of Edgar's death, say 970.

After an introductory account of the reform, the Proem tells how the king summoned a Synodal Council at Winchester. A number of bishops, abbots and abbesses were present, Archbishop Dunstan being mentioned by name as insisting on certain provisions governing the relations between monks and nuns. A letter written by Edgar to the assembly, urging the need of unity, was received with enthusiasm; regulations were drawn up; by royal command a book of customs—the Regularis Concordia—was compiled from various sources; and the Assembly vowed to carry out its precepts.

The work of the Council here summarised suggests that, in the opinion of leading men, all was not well with the reform. In the letter put forward in the king's name the monasteries are represented as united in the observance of St Benedict's Rule but not in the manner of that observance (*consuetudinis usu*); the monks are exhorted to 'agree peaceably together . . . lest the divergent use of one Rule and one country bring their holy conversation into disrepute'; obedience is insisted on; all are to do alike.

From warnings such as these we may gather that the houses of the reform needed some bond of union. When we call to mind that the life at Glastonbury seems not wholly to

[1] For the suggestion that the great Easter gathering narrated in the *Vita Oswaldi* (p. 425) was actually the occasion of this Council, see *Monastic Order*, p. 42. The *Liber Eliensis* (p. 161), speaking of the expulsion of clerks from Ely, says that Dunstan on that occasion went to Winchester 'coacto concilio.'

have satisfied Ethelwold, that later, relations with Continental monasticism had been established, that the work of Oswald lacked the English background which was the basis of the Dunstan-Ethelwold side of the movement—then we begin to understand: the fame of the great abbeys of the Continent, of their elaboration of ritual and devotional practice, had begun to stir the English monks, and one house was striving to outdo another in the practice of special devotions introduced from abroad. A limit to this had to be imposed, 'and here,' to quote an acknowledged authority on the period, 'perhaps we may trace the moderating strength of the great archbishop . . . the words of warning are said to have come from the letter of the king; but the king's speech is the speech of his chief minister.' [1]

With the loyal acceptance of the ruling of the Council the crisis passed and the crowning stage of the movement was reached. Its results were lasting. Troublous times lay ahead; but the Benedictinism revived by St Dunstan had come to stay, and it remained a vital force right up to the advent of the Normans.

In 975, two years after his solemn coronation at Bath, King Edgar the Peaceful died; he was buried at Glastonbury, where Edmund his father lay. The succession of the elder son, Edward, was secured by Dunstan who, with Oswald—now Archbishop of York—crowned him at Kingston. Three years later Edward was murdered, his half-brother Ethelred became king, and a period of national decline set in. From the confused history of these years the fact emerges that the kingdom was rent by dissension within while from without a renewal of the Danish invasions was only a question of time. According to the anonymous biographer of Oswald the ecclesiastical reforms of Edgar seem to have been made an occasion of party warfare, the monastic party being persecuted for a time and monks being expelled by the ealdorman Aelfhere from some of the Mercian monasteries. The story is,

[1] *Times of St Dunstan*, p. 155

however, highly coloured, and only one abbot is mentioned as having been driven from his abbey—Germanus of Winchcombe. On the other hand the great fenland abbeys, Ramsey, Peterborough, Ely and others rested secure under the protection of the powerful nobles, Ethelwine 'the friend of God,' Aelfwold and Brihtnoth. More than one synod was held for the purpose of restoring peace, but it is probable that the Mercian monasteries continued to suffer until the death of Aelfhere in 983.

Meanwhile Dunstan was ageing. For the last decade of his life he seems to have been no longer in favour at court and to have had little or no further real share in public affairs.[1] Grieved as he must have been at his powerlessness to avert the ruin of much that he had striven for,[2] the archbishop may well have rejoiced in a retirement that left him free to attend to pastoral duties only and that enabled the contemplative side of his character to assert itself yet more strongly. It was about this time that Dunstan consecrated Ethelwold's new church at Ely as well as the restored church of the Old Minster. In 984 Ethelwold died at Beaddington, and two years later the great archbishop himself passed away.

On the feast of the Ascension Dunstan celebrated Mass; at the Gospel, at the blessing and — his *vale ultimum* — at the Agnus Dei 'he preached,' says Adelard,[3] 'as he had never preached before . . . . After the Mass he was present with the brethren in the refectory and then, during the hour of the monastic siesta, he was seized with his last illness. He spent the whole of Friday and the following night in the contemplation of heavenly things . . . . Early on Saturday, when the Office of Matins was over, he sent for the brethren and commending to them his spirit, he received from the heavenly

[1] See *Monastic Order*, p. 54; for another judgment see F. M. Stenton, *Anglo-Saxon England*, p. 444.

[2] 'The disasters of the Kingdom began again when Ethelred the "Redeless" ceased to enjoy the "rede" or counsel of Dunstan' (Trevelyan, *History of England*, p. 94).

[3] *Memorials*, p. 65 f.

table the Viaticum of Christ's Sacrament. Then with thanksgiving he broke out into the words of the Psalmist: The merciful and gracious Lord hath made a remembrance of His works, He hath given meat to them that fear Him. With this verse on his lips he rendered his soul into the hands of his Creator.' It was the 19th of May, 988, and Dunstan was in or near his seventy-ninth year.

Oswald was the last of the three great leaders to go. Old and infirm as he was, he still kept up his Lenten practice of washing the feet of twelve poor men daily. On the third Sunday in Lent of the year 992 Oswald, then staying at Worcester, was feeling unusually well, and on the day following was able to attend the Divine Office with the brethren. He then carried out his customary Maundy at the close of which, in the attitude of prayer, he passed away.

Each of the three leaders, Dunstan, Ethelwold and Oswald, is represented as founding or restoring monasteries and as keeping certain houses under his personal care. The place of honour in the triumvirate naturally belongs to Dunstan, with whom at Glastonbury the active work of reform began, and under whom as archbishop it was brought to completion. But there is no need to exalt one leader at the expense of another: they were all working to one end; and the picture drawn for us by the authors of the early lives of the three saints is one of a great work carried out in a great way by great men. If, on the one hand, from Glastonbury went forth 'a column of monastic religion throughout the English land,' on the other, Ethelwold is the 'Father of monks,' while Oswald is the 'pious Father of the monastic order.' If discretion be assigned to Dunstan and zeal to Ethelwold, it need not imply in the one weakness [1] nor in the other overbearingness. Differences there must have been; but the mutual friendship and common interests of the three remained unimpaired. It is delightful to read of the English Dunstan's affection for the half-Danish

[1] Four times in the *B Life* the word *constantia* is applied to Dunstan; Aelfric, in his *Life of St Swithun* (ed. Skeat, p. 470), describes Dunstan as 'the resolute.'

Oswald and of his care for Ethelwold whom he twice persuaded to relax his austerities for his health's sake. From more than one intimate glimpse one might almost gather that the position of disciple and master was never wholly altered, and that Ethelwold remained, even in later life, under the spiritual direction, as it were, of the *magnificus vir* Dunstan.[1]

[1] His friends have left on record something of their feeling for him, the affection and veneration of which help us to understand how truly Dunstan was the grand figure of his day. To them he is the 'Mons immobilis,' 'Columna Dei' (*Adelard*); 'Columna immobilis,' 'Magnificus vir' (*Vita Ethelwoldi*); 'Decus omnis patriae' (*Vita Oswaldi*); 'Dunstan amande valde,' 'Summe sacer' (Abbo of Fleury); 'Alme Dunstane,' 'Dunstane noster.' Later, he is the 'Gemma Anglorum' (*Liber Eliensis*).

II

ORGANISATION AND LIFE

Of the consuetudinaries of the tenth and early eleventh centuries the Regularis Concordia, itself probably the oldest of them all, gives the most complete and intimate account of the duties of the monastic life. To us, its want of logical order, its repetitions, redundancies and silences, its inflated style, are often baffling; but such faults are common to documents of its type, which assume in those for whom they were written a working knowledge of existing custom. The following pages will give some idea of the organisation of a monastery and of the life of a monk according to the prescriptions of the Concordia.

When the Concordia was put forward at the Synodal Council of Winchester, the assembled abbots and abbesses, we are told, vowed solemnly to abide by its rulings. There was no machinery to ensure obedience: instructions that novelties should not be introduced into the monastic life without reference to authority are laid down in the Concordia, but that code itself allows for variation in minor points; and some thirty years after the Winchester settlement, Aelfric—of all people—was content to draw up a mere abridgment of the Concordia [1] for his monks of Eynsham. Thus there was no cast-iron uniformity, no centralisation of government. True, the monasteries are represented in the Concordia as being dependent for their well-being on the royal power; but this was doubtless a manner of speaking; for, necessary as the royal support and favour were, the monastic movement was actually in the hands of Dunstan and the other leaders, the houses of the reform constituting, for a time, three groups under the predominating influence of Dunstan, Ethelwold and Oswald respectively. Apart, then, from this loose form of control, each monastery enjoyed a practical independence

[1] See below, p. lvi

which, in course of time, tended to become more and more marked.

At the head of the monastic community was the abbot. Each house elected an abbot from—normally—among its own members, 'according to the Rule,'[1] with the advice and consent of the king. The abbot held the place of Christ and was the *pater spiritualis* of his monks. In matters of moment he would take counsel of the brethren as ordered by the Rule.[2] In the work of governing his house he was assisted by various officers. It had been St Benedict's idea that, where the community was a large one, there should be deans, each in charge of a group of ten or more monks, though in certain cases he allowed the abbot to appoint a provost instead, as a kind of second in command. As a working arrangement, the distribution of executive authority among several deans does not seem to have found much favour in Benedictine monasteries; but there is plenty of evidence, in the documents of the eighth and early ninth centuries, for the presence of a provost and deans, one of whom was styled the *senior decanus*. In the tenth century we find only one dean, still sometimes called the *senior decanus*, and sometimes a provost as well. In *Verdun* the provost ranks next to the abbot while the dean comes third.[3] This is what we find in the Concordia. Later the meaning of the word 'provost' was to become extended while, in some monasteries, the dean was known as the prior. The word 'prior' was originally used of the 'superior' and might thus denote the abbot. It is frequently used in the Concordia in this sense of 'superior'; sometimes it refers definitely to the abbot and once definitely to the senior officer of the house. But the order, provost, dean, of the Concordia does not seem

[1] cf. *Rule*, lxiv [2] *Ibid.*, iii and lxv, 34

[3] p. 128 f. But in a list of officials at Fleury in the time of Abbot Wlfald (943–962) the dean is placed before the provost (*Vita Oswaldi*, p. 423). In the *B Life* it is the provost who discusses the affairs of Glastonbury with Dunstan (*Memorials*, p. 47); there too, Dunstan's pupils are spoken of in the following order: 'praepositi videlicet, decani, abbates, episcopi' (p. 26). 'Ælfric praepositus' is in the *Liber Vitae* (p. 32) among deceased brethren of the New Minster, but there is nothing to show his position relative to the dean.

to have been universal in English monasteries of the tenth and eleventh centuries: more often than not the dean appears as the senior officer.

Other officers were heads of departments and, with the exception of the cellarer, had no general authority. Curiously enough the cellarer, to whose duties a whole chapter of the Rule is devoted, does not appear in the Concordia. The sacrist had the charge of the church and of the church services: later in English monastic uses he appears as *secretarius*. The *magister*, or *custos*, had the care of the children who were being trained for the monastic life. The *cantor* is mentioned several times and was evidently a person of importance. The only other officer referred to by name in the Concordia is the *circa* who was in immediate charge of the discipline of the cloister, under the dean. That there were other monks in posts of subordinate authority is suggested by the use, in the Concordia, of general terms such as *priores*, *quilibet prior*.

We do not possess a plan of an English monastery of the tenth century; but we know from the Concordia that there would have been the *oratorium* or church, in which all assembled at stated times for the daily round of prayer and praise; the refectory where all fed together; the dormitory where all slept together; the cloister in which the monks read and studied together; a room set apart for the daily Chapter or meeting of the community; a 'suitable place' with a fire where all could carry out the full claustral observance in the cold of winter; the *coquina* (kitchen) and *pistrinum* (bakehouse); the guesthouse, infirmary and *auditorium*.

The framework of the monastic life was constituted by the great body of prayer comprising the Divine Office, St Benedict's *Opus Dei*: the night Office (Nocturns, the modern Matins) and the seven day hours, Matins (the modern Lauds), Prime, Tierce, Sext, None, Vespers and Compline. The Concordia recalls the instructions of the Rule [1] on the carrying out of this paramount duty, but beyond this it does little more

[1] xix, 11

than mention the different portions of the Office as they occur in the ordinary course of the monk's duties.

To the daily Office as arranged and prescribed by St Benedict the Concordia adds a number of devotional practices: two extra Offices, Of All Saints and Of the Dead; the *Trina oratio* (thrice daily); psalms and prayers for the Royal House (after each Office except Prime); the Gradual and Penitential psalms; two Litanies (one after Prime, the other before the Principal Mass on weekdays). There were, moreover, the daily Morrow and Principal Masses, private Masses, the Chapter, the daily Maundy of the Poor.[1] Some of these observances are found very early in Benedictine history; all, with the exception of the prayers for the Royal House and a few other peculiarly English usages, were in substantial agreement with the accepted monastic practice of the day.

A word must be said about the two extra Offices. The Office of the Dead consisted of Nocturns [2] (invariably styled 'Vigils' in the Concordia), Matins and Vespers; that of All Saints consisted of Matins and Vespers only. In the Summer period (Lent to November 1st) Matins Of All Saints and Of the Dead were placed after Nocturns and Matins of the day, Vespers Of All Saints and Of the Dead after Vespers of the Day with Vigils of the Dead after the second meal (*cena*) or, when there was no second meal, immediately after the three Vesper Offices. In the Winter period (November 1st to Lent) on ferial days Vigils and Matins Of the Dead together with Matins Of All Saints were said in the interval between Nocturns and Matins of the day, and Vespers Of All Saints and Of the Dead after Vespers of the day. On Sundays and feasts of twelve lessons the same order was kept except that Vigils were after the second meal (*cena*). From Maundy Thursday to Saturday in Easter week both Offices, and thence to the Octave of Pentecost that Of the Dead only, were omitted.[3]

[1] For these devotions see J. B. L. Tolhurst, *The Monastic Breviary of Hyde Abbey*, vi (HBS).

[2] Probably one nocturn only, i.e., three psalms and three lessons.

[3] For the Offices Of the Dead and Of All Saints see *DR*, October 1932, pp. 449 ff., and January 1933, pp. 137 ff.

Between the hours devoted to prayer the monk's day was filled up by some form of work or reading. This was in accordance with the Rule. But there was a considerable difference here between the life arranged by St Benedict and that of a tenth century monastery. Thus the Lenten horarium of the Rule provides *lectio*, or reading, between Nocturns and Matins, an interval of roughly one hour, and between Matins and Tierce, a period of some four hours broken only by Prime. The second of these two periods is not mentioned in the Concordia; the first is prescribed 'according to the Rule,' but is largely taken up by devotions for the king, queen and benefactors, Vigils and Matins Of the Dead and Matins Of All Saints. Then the horarium of the Rule for the period from October 1st to Lent prescribes *lectio* between Matins and Tierce (interrupted only by Prime), some two and a half hours, and between the one meal *ad nonam* until Vespers, rather more than an hour. Both these times for reading appear in the Concordia, but the first does not begin until after the long devotions that followed Prime; the second, however (in which work is mentioned as an occasional alternative to reading), may have been as long as in the Rule. Again, the summer horarium of the Rule (Easter to October 1st) makes no provision for the hour between Matins and Prime which may have been devoted to *meditatio;* but there was *lectio* between Tierce and Sext for about two and a half hours. So also in the Concordia we find *meditatio* between Matins and Prime, but only after the brethren have changed into their day shoes, washed and said the *Trina oratio*.

It was the same with work. In the winter period the Rule prescribes one period of work: between Tierce and None (broken by Sext); an average working period of just over five hours. The corresponding Concordia period for work only began when the Morrow Mass and Chapter, which followed Tierce, were finished, and ceased at Sext, which was immediately followed by the Principal Mass and

None.[1] The Rule arranges for two periods of work in summer (Easter to October 1st): one, from Prime till Tierce, the other from None till Vespers. The Concordia gives both these periods, but the first does not begin until the long devotions after Prime, Morrow Mass and Chapter are over. The afternoon period, however, may have been exactly as in the Rule, save for the time taken by the drink after None.

The intellectual work—*lectio*, *meditatio*—of the Anglo-Saxon monks would have been the same as that practised by St Benedict's monks: the pondering over the Scriptures, learning the psalms by heart, the preparation of the ceremonies and readings connected with the Office and, doubtless, the study of the arts and sciences of the day. It would have been in the times allotted to *lectio* that books were written and illuminated; and the work of the so-called 'Winchester' school alone shows how flourishing was this department in an English monastery of the period.

As regards the manual side of the work we have little to go on in the Concordia. The suggestion has often been made that, in the tenth century, manual work as understood by St Benedict had become non-existent. Certainly a large portion of the work prescribed by the Concordia was merely the necessary work of the house—as indeed must have been the case in St Benedict's own monastery—for no lay brothers are mentioned in the Concordia; and we may note that, as in the Rule, so in the Concordia no-one might be excused from the work of the kitchen and bakehouse. Perhaps it was only in the early days of the movement that manual work apart from that of the house was done. Even here, however, we cannot be sure of our ground; for though on the one hand Aelfric tells us [2] that St Ethelwold and his monks assisted at the erection of the monastic buildings at Abingdon and of the church of the Old Minster at Winchester, on the other it

[1] In the Lenten horarium of the Rule there is work between Tierce and None interrupted by Sext. Here no comparison is possible, since the Concordia does not give the Lenten times for work and reading.

[2] *Vita Ethelwoldi*, pp. 259 and 264.

would seem that at Westbury-on-Trym, St Oswald's first foundation, the brethren gave themselves up wholly to exercises of devotion, leaving the entire work of the house to be done by persons of humble station—servants (*contemptibiles personae*).[1] Nevertheless, so far as we can see, St Benedict's 'work'—intellectual and manual—is still, in the Concordia, an integral part of monastic life, though its place has been very largely usurped by a number of devotional practices—a state of things consonant with the monastic ideas of the day.

In the Concordia, as in the Rule, two meals, *prandium ad sextam* (noon) and *cena*—evidently between Vespers and Compline—were allowed daily from Easter to September 14th (certain fast days excepted) and on all Sundays and feasts of twelve lessons during the rest of the year (including Lent); a single meal *ad nonam* (between None and Vespers) was the rule for the winter period from September 14th to Lent; in Lent (and on Quarter Tense days) the one meal was *ad vesperam* (after Vespers).

It may be useful to note here that *cena*, in the Concordia, is to be understood not only of the second meal, allowed on all days when the chief meal (*prandium*) was *ad sextam*, but also of the single Lenten meal *ad vesperam*: it is not used of the single meal *ad nonam*, for which the terms are *ad* or *post mensam*.

The Concordia has nothing to say of the ordinary monastic diet, merely giving the general reminder that St Benedict's instructions regarding the amount and quality of food, abstinence and fasting are to be followed.[2] Probably, then, the diet of the English monks was not far removed from St Benedict's allowance of two dishes (*cocta duo pulmentaria*) to which might be added *poma aut nascentia leguminum* or even, if the field labour was specially severe, other dishes at the abbot's discretion. The Concordia expressly forbids the use of *pinguedo*

[1] *Vita Oswaldi*, p. 424.

[2] 'Victum cum pondere, mensura et numero, uestitum, ieiunium, abstinentiam, uigiliam, taciturnitatem, oboedientiae bonum . . . totis uiribus custodientes' (Proem).

(fats) on ferias in Advent and from Septuagesima until Quinquagesima: from Quinquagesima to the end of Lent there was *abstinentia quadragesimalis*—explained by Aelfric as abstinence even from milk and eggs. This Lenten abstinence was observed also on all Quarter Tense days except when these fell in Whit week.

The eating of meat, forbidden by the Rule except in the case of the sick, is indirectly forbidden by the general resolution of the Concordia, referred to above, expressing adherence to the injunctions of the Rule on this point. It is said that St Ethelwold himself never ate meat save once, for the space of three months, at the command of St Dunstan, and again in his last illness. This, however, may have been a personal asceticism; indeed, the very fact that Ethelwold is specially praised for his abstinence suggests that he went beyond the common practice. An interesting item of evidence is afforded by a passage from Aelfric's *Colloquium*—a dialogue between a *puer* and his master—in which the boy, describing the monastic fare, says of himself: 'adhuc carnibus vescor quia puer sum.'[1] This is substantially in accordance with St Benedict's ruling that children were not bound by the Rule as regards diet. But the *Colloquium* is not a piece of authoritative legislation, and all that we can safely argue from it is that abstinence from meat was taught by Aelfric and was probably the rule for the monks of the houses of the Ethelwold tradition.

Besides the regular meals, the *mixtum* was taken by the reader and servers before carrying out their duties in the refectory. This indulgence, a measure of drink and a portion of bread, is sanctioned by the Rule. In the case of children, too, the Rule was doubtless obeyed so that they were allowed to anticipate the ordinary hours of meals. Consistently with the general observance of the day the Concordia permits certain other additions to the monastic fare: the *poculum* or drink taken on Saturdays after the *munditiae* and on certain weekdays

[1] Ed. G. N. Garmonsway (1939), p. 46

immediately before the *collatio*, the *potus* or drink after None, and the *caritas* after the Saturday Maundy.[1]

Hospitality to strangers and the care of guests and of the poor is legislated for in the Rule,[2] which specially recommends charity to the poor. The Concordia is remarkable for the way in which it has seized upon this last point: [3] throughout the whole of the tenth chapter there is not a word about any but *poor* strangers, attendance on whom is insisted on as the common duty of all from the youngest *puer* to the abbot who, in virtue of his position as *Christi uicarius*, is particularly admonished of his responsibility in this regard. A special place was to be reserved for the reception of the poor, for in them 'Christ is received and must be adored.' [4] On their arrival the Maundy was rendered to them and every kindness shown to them: on their departure they received provisions for the way. Not only were poor strangers thus succoured, but the Concordia takes it for granted that each monastery will support a number of poor men from whom three would be chosen every day to receive the Maundy ('of the poor') and to partake of food from the monks' table.

No doubt the poor were equally well cared for by the monks of other lands: certainly the daily washing of the feet of three or more poor men was, and had long been, of common observance. But the picture drawn by the Concordia of the love and reverent care lavished on the poor has not its like in any contemporary consuetudinary; and if perhaps the daily Maundy was itself taken over from Continental monasticism there is no reason to doubt that the general admonitions of the Concordia on this point, above all the advice given to the abbot, reflect the personal sanctity, the unworldliness, of one or other or all of the three chief leaders of the English movement.[5]

[1] Since none of these indulgences are in the Rule they can hardly be said to square with a strict interpretation of the passage cited above (p. xxxv *n.* 2) from the Proem. See, however, *Monastic Order*, p. 458 f.

[2] *Rule* liii (*passim*)

[3] cf. AE (p. 192): 'nam de susceptione hospitum regula docet.'

[4] *Rule* liii, 15

[5] Oswald in particular was noted for his devotion to the Maundy.

Silence, in the Concordia, is based professedly on the Rule; that is, while upholding St Benedict's principle that monks should tend to silence at all times,[1] the Concordia shows a thorough understanding of what the Rule meant by *taciturnitas* and allows conversation about necessary affairs, at the proper times, and in a low tone of voice. 'At the proper times' reminds us of St Benedict's veto on conversation at *incompetentibus horis*, which supposes that there were *horae competentes* for this. The times when silence should not be broken are given in the Concordia as the special period of absolute silence (*summum silentium*) from Vespers to the next day's Chapter and all times given up to *lectio*. Even then necessary conversation was allowed in the *auditorium*.[2]

Definite periods for community recreative conversation find no explicit mention in the Concordia; but the passage already referred to twice in connection with diet could be equally pressed in support of the view that the Concordia contemplates no relaxation of the Rule in the matter of silence. It has been argued that special times for recreative conversation were admitted as early as the ninth century,[3] but it is doubtful if there is satisfactory evidence for this until the end of the tenth century. Then indeed—witness *Trèves*, *Verdun* and the earliest Cluniac consuetudinaries (BB_1, C)—talking in the cloister was permitted at stated times, apparently as a community act. If, however, the compilers of the Concordia had in mind nothing beyond the *taciturnitas* of the Rule, we must remember that this would at times have entailed some considerable amount of talk about affairs of business at 'competent times'; but this is a different thing from assuming a regular practice of general conversation as a part of the monastic horarium. The point concerning definite periods for talking can best be summed up in the words of a competent authority: 'It is all but impossible to ascertain the exact lengths of the periods [allotted to talking in the cloister],

[1] *Rule* vi (*passim*) and xlii, 1
[2] On journeys only necessary conversation was allowed (Proem).
[3] See Morin, *Rev. Bénéd.* 1889, p. 352

and how far the conversation was intended or permitted to be merely recreative.' [1]

Here we may touch on three items which, although not recreative in the ordinary sense, nevertheless concerned the physical well-being of the monks. The first of these is the *minutio sanguinis*, or periodical blood-letting, regulations for which are met with in practically every consuetudinary except the Concordia. This omission is remarkable. Perhaps blood-letting was considered too obvious a necessity to deserve mention; perhaps, too, it was carried out with an informality and want of regimentation very different from that which we find in *Trèves*, for instance. The second item, shaving, is twice mentioned in the Concordia, where it is arranged for towards the middle of Lent and at the end. The third, the taking of baths, is mentioned only once in the Concordia, and that as taking place on Holy Saturday and, if necessary, on Good Friday, after the morning ceremonies.

The centre of the monk's spiritual life was the Divine Office, and the Psalter formed the staple of his prayer. There was probably nothing in the nature of the modern fixed period of ' mental prayer,' the *meditatio* of the Rule and the Concordia being the prayerful reading of the Scriptures. The monk's private prayer, so often mentioned in the Rule and the Concordia, would have consisted almost entirely of the psalms. So also psalms—the Psalter or the Secular Office or both—were said during work and other occupations.

Particularly marked in the Concordia is the devotion of the Anglo-Saxon monks to the Holy Eucharist. The daily Morrow and Principal Masses were of universal custom in the tenth century, but in no other contemporary document do we find specific mention of *daily* Holy Communion. Not only are the monks urged, in the Concordia, to receive the Eucharist daily but, as a preparation, sacramental Confession is prescribed weekly and indeed as often as individual consciences might require.[2]

[1] *Monastic Order*, p. 453

[2] The abbot would appear to have been the normal confessor to his community. See p. 18 *n.* 6.

The Eucharist as Viaticum is noticed, together with the Sacrament of Unction, in connection with the sick. Private Masses are mentioned but no times for them are specified.[1]

Though not in the Rule, one of the most important of the monk's spiritual exercises was the Chapter at which the Martyrology and the Rule were read and, on Sundays and feasts, a spiritual conference was given. A feature of the Chapter was the public confession of faults against discipline. Sometimes a brother accused himself, sometimes he was accused by the *circa* or by another of those in authority; but in no case was he allowed to defend himself until, having begged pardon on his knees, the abbot gave him permission to speak.

We have already spoken of the Maundy of the Poor; there was also, on Saturdays, a Maundy at which the feet of the brethren were washed by the outgoing and incoming ministers of the week. This was according to the Rule and of universal observance. It was regarded as the outward sign of the fraternal charity that should exist in a monastery, and had a twofold basis: the teaching of the Gospel of St John and the precept of the Rule.

Particular emphasis is laid, in the Concordia, on two fundamental principles of community life: no monk, not even the abbot, might possess anything of his own; everything was to be done by obedience, private enterprise (*propria adinuentio*) being utterly ruled out as opposed to St Benedict's eighth degree of humility—that a monk 'should do nothing contrary to the authority of the common rule of the monastery or the example of the seniors.'[2]

Devotion to Our Lady is evinced by the liturgical prescriptions that the Morrow Mass on Saturdays should normally be *De Sancta Maria* and that her anthem should be sung twice a day.[3]

[1] It is assumed in the Concordia (Proem) that a monk might be in the position of spiritual director to a house of nuns.

[2] *Rule* vii, 165

[3] Note also the following from the second prayer at the Veneration of the Cross on Good Friday: 'Domine Ihesu Christe . . . qui . . . dignatus es carnem *ex immaculata uirgine* sumere.'

The *pueri*, or children of the cloister, known collectively as the *schola*, were a main source of recruitment for the monasteries. As in the Rule, so in the Concordia, these future monks followed all the exercises of the monastic life.[1] Their training and upbringing were in the hands of one of the professed members of the community—the *magister scholae*, or *custos*. Under their master they kept together as a body; thus we see them in the Concordia saying the *Trina oratio* together, making the offering at Mass together by alternate choirs, washing apart from the brethren, carrying out the Maundy of the Poor on the days allotted to them. To avoid any form of favouritism, not even their master was allowed to go about alone with a single boy: at least one other being always present 'as a witness.' Abbot and monks are warned never to pet or fondle the children.[2]

We must now deal with the times of each day's duties and the regulation of those times according to the season of the year. To take the second point first: the Office was arranged on the principle of a summer and a winter period, the dividing lines of which were Easter and November 1st, the chief differences being, on ordinary days (ferias), one short lesson in summer and three lessons in winter; shorter hymns in summer at Nocturns and Matins; Nocturns followed by Matins in summer but by a considerable interval in winter since, throughout the year, Matins had to begin at early dawn.[3] The horarium for meals, work and *lectio* varied according to a threefold division of the year: Easter to September 14th (October 1st: work, *lectio*), thence to Lent, Lent to Easter. We have seen the number and the times of meals and the order for work and *lectio* within these periods; here we may note that abstinence from *pinguedo* began at Septuagesima, and the full

[1] cf. Aelfric's *Colloquium* (ed. Garmonsway, pp. 19, 44), where the *puer* describes himself as attending the round of monastic duties according to the summer timetable.

[2] This warning suggests that there were occasions when *schola* and community met together, presumably for recreative purposes.

[3] Note that the *Trina oratio* (before Prime in summer) changed to its winter position (before Tierce) on October 1st.

Lenten abstinence and fast on Ash Wednesday; and that the times for Vigils of the Dead depended to some extent on whether there were two meals or only one. In general, sleep was less and the night Office was shorter in summer than in winter, while the day's work and *lectio* were longer.

As regards the first point, we must remember that there was no such thing as a stable timetable within the periods referred to: nothing corresponding to our modern day with its duties occupying a definite length of time regardless of the seasons of the year: no regular hours of sleep regardless of the sun. All was regulated by the rising and setting of the sun, by the hours of light and darkness. In other words, as St Benedict's monks in the fifth century, so, in all probability, the Anglo-Saxon monks of the tenth century, divided the day and night each into twelve 'hours' with sunset and sunrise as the dividing lines. Thus in summer the 'hours' of the day would be longer than those of the night, in winter the reverse would be the case, while at the equinoxes the 'hours' of day and night would be of roughly equal length.[1]

The only certain indication of time in the Concordia suggests that the horarium of the Rule is being followed: the injunction that Matins should end at daybreak (54, 16; cf. 19, 15). There are, however, three other notes of time that support this view: *lectio* in winter is given as from after Matins until *hora secunda* (19, 31; cf. *Rule* xlviii, 24) and in summer as from Tierce until *mediante hora quinta* (55, 8; cf. *Rule, loc. cit.* 9: *hora quasi sexta agente*), while None was said in summer *mediante octaua hora* (55, 11; cf. *Rule, loc. cit.* 14). One further indication of time is too vague to be of much help: the reading at Compline *prout tempus permiserit:* it is uncertain whether this is a mere echo of the words of the Rule or whether it means that, as in the Rule, Compline was to be finished in the light of day. At all events early morning *lectio* until *hora secunda* and late afternoon None at *hora octaua* suggest clearly a day and, consequently, a night of twelve hours each.

[1] See *Aelfric's Homilies* (ed. Thorpe ii, 389): 'A watch has three hours; four watches complete twelve hours; so many hours has the night.'

The following tables show the monk's daily duties on Winter ferias (with the single meal) from November 1st to Lent), and on Summer ferias, when normally there were two meals a day (Easter to September 14th). The times are those given in *Monastic Order*, Appendix XVIII.

WINTER HORARIUM

c. 2.30	Rise
	Trina oratio
	Gradual Psalms
3	NOCTURNS
	Psalms, etc., for the Royal House
	Vigils Of the Dead
	Matins Of the Dead
	Matins Of All Saints
5	*Lectio*
6	MATINS of the day (at dawn)
	Miserere
	Psalms, etc., for the Royal House
	Anthems (of the Cross, B.V.M. and Patron of the House)
6.45	PRIME
	Four psalms (in all), Penitential psalms, Litany
7.30	*lectio* (*usque horam secundam*)
8	Interval (change shoes, wash, etc.)
	Trina oratio
	TIERCE
	Psalms, etc., for the Royal House
	Morrow Mass
	Chapter
	Five psalms (for the Dead)
c. 9.45	*Work*
12	SEXT
	Psalms, etc., for the Royal House
	PRINCIPAL MASS
c. 1.30	NONE
	Psalms, etc., for the Royal House
c. 2	*Cena* (the one meal *ad nonam*): see p. xxxv
c. 2.45	*Lectio* or *Work*
	VESPERS of the day
	Psalms, etc., for the Royal House
	Anthems (as after Matins)
	Vespers Of All Saints
	Vespers Of the Dead
	Change to night shoes
	Drink
6	*Collatio* (*prout tempus permiserit*)
6.15	COMPLINE
	Miserere
	Psalms, etc., for the Royal House
	Trina oratio
6.30	Retire

SUMMER HORARIUM

c. 1.30	Rise
	Trina oratio
	Gradual Psalms
2	NOCTURNS
	Psalms, etc., for the Royal House
	Short interval
3.30 or 4	MATINS of the day (ending *luce diei*)
	Miserere
	Psalms, etc., for the Royal House
	Anthems (of the Cross, B.V.M., and Patron of the House)
	Matins Of All Saints
	Matins Of the Dead
	Interval (if day: change shoes, wash, etc.; if dark: sleep for those who wish, change shoes, wash, etc.)
c. 5	*Trina oratio*
	Lectio
6	PRIME
	Four psalms (in all), Penitential psalms, Litany
	Morrow Mass
	Chapter
	Five psalms (for the Dead)
7.30	*Work*
8	TIERCE
	Psalms, etc., for the Royal House
	PRINCIPAL MASS
9.30	*Lectio*
11.30	SEXT (first signal: *mediante hora quinta*)
	Psalms, etc., for the Royal House
12	*Prandium*
c. 1.0	*Siesta*
2.30	NONE (first signal: *mediante octaua hora*)
	Psalms, etc., for the Royal House
	Drink
c. 3.0	*Work*
	VESPERS of the day
	Miserere
	Psalms, etc., for the Royal House
	Anthems (as after Matins)
	Vespers Of All Saints
	Vespers Of the Dead
	Cena
	Vigils Of the Dead
7.30	Change into night shoes
	Collatio
8	COMPLINE
	Miserere
	Psalms, etc., for the Royal House
c. 8.15	*Trina oratio*
	Retire

III

SOURCES OF THE REGVLARIS CONCORDIA

That the Regularis Concordia contains elements both of native and of alien origin appears not only from the external circumstances which gave it birth but also from the internal evidence of the document itself. For the Proem tells us openly that the leaders of reform, while retaining the good traditions of their native land, went far afield for material in their attempt to epitomise, as it were, all that was best suited to their purpose in the monastic observance of the day. Thus the Concordia is substantially a mosaic, a piece of patchwork; and some knowledge of its dependence, both on tradition and on outside influence, is necessary if it is to be rightly estimated.

Of all the material[1] which has gone to the making of the Concordia only a relatively small amount has been satisfactorily accounted for. Indeed, we can hardly hope to know the exact history of every point of Concordia practice. Many monastic customs are found so widespread in the tenth century that the time and circumstance of their introduction into this country can be a matter of conjecture only. Others, evidently primitive in origin, appear in the Concordia in a guise so altered as to obscure the manner of their derivation. Again, the great mass of material available for the study of monastic custom is frequently wanting in just such evidence as would

[1] Certain literary references, outside the scope of this section, may be briefly noticed. Thus the Rule of St Benedict is, as we would expect, taken for granted in the Concordia. Time after time its authority is invoked; often it is cited verbatim (and, so far as can be judged, from the *Textus Receptus*). No other consuetudinary of the period can compare with the Concordia in this insistence on harking back to the Rule. Then allusions—one in each case—to Aldhelm, Ven. Bede, Ps-Augustine and Isidore of Seville are worked into the text of the Concordia; but these are bits and pieces; the only clear case of quotation being a short but important passage from the *De Sacramentis* of St Ambrose (23, 22). The decisions of the Council of Winchester, embodied in the Proem, and the citations from *Ordo Romanus I* and OQ fall under the headings of traditional and borrowed material.

be most to our purpose, while many documents are of a date so late that their witness is of a roundabout and indirect nature.

Nevertheless, a beginning has been made,[1] and we shall here put down something of what is known or conjectured of the 'sources' drawn on by the compilers of the Concordia, taking first the customs native to Anglo-Saxon monasticism.

1. *Native customs.* In a document in which the note of nationality—king and country—is so uniquely stressed, we would expect to find a number of native customs. These, if not survivals of the old Anglo-Saxon monasticism of the seventh and eighth centuries, would at least go back to the days of Dunstan's early beginnings at Glastonbury, when the English monastic movement was as yet untouched by direct outside influence. One such, described as the 'usage of the people of this land,' is recorded in connection with a decision of the Synodal Council of Winchester that 'the goodly religious customs of our country be kept up' (32, 6–9); two more are put forward as traditional—if we may so interpret the expression *usu patrum*: the prayers for the Royal House (18, 1 f.) and the use of chasubles in Lent and on Quarter Tense days (34, 29 f.). To these may be added a number of practices, liturgical (e.g. the three prayers at the Veneration of the Cross: 45, 2 f.) and devotional (e.g. daily Communion: 23, 10 f.), for which there is no parallel in, or which cannot satisfactorily be assigned to, contemporary foreign monasticism.[2]

2. *Customs introduced from abroad.* These comprise practically the entire remainder of the Concordia observance. We cannot attempt to 'place' them without first considering the evidence contained in the Proem to the Concordia itself. There the English are represented as calling to mind the instructions of Pope St Gregory the Great to St Augustine of Canterbury regarding the establishment, in the young English Church, of good customs not only of the Roman

[1] See Symons, *Sources.* [I have been unable to consult the latest work on the subject: Dom K. Hallinger, *Gorze-Kluny* (Studia Anselmiana, vols. 22–23 and 24–25; Rome, Herder, 1950–51)]

[2] See also pp. 14 *n.* 6; 20 *n.* 4; 32 *n.* 4; 34 *n.* 17; 38 *n.* 13; 40 *n.* 2; 44 *n.* 2; 61 *n.* 9; 64 *n.* 4; 66 *n.* 1; 67 *nn.* 4 and 5.

Church but also of the Churches of Gaul. The Proem goes on to relate how monks were thereupon invited over from Fleury and Ghent, and how some of their customs were embodied in the Concordia.

This mention of two of the most influential of the Continental monasteries is of capital importance. For Fleury had been reformed in 930 by Odo of Cluny: thus its observance would have been substantially that of Cluny. Ghent, on the other hand, was restored *c.* 937 by Gerard of Brogne, the leader of reform in Lower Lotharingia.

It has been assumed by some writers that the observance of Fleury and Ghent must have been identical, inasmuch as the Benedictine ancestry of both houses can be traced back to the Anianian reform of the early ninth century. But Benedict of Aniane had left his mark on the whole of western monasticism, and his ideas underlay, in a general way, all the Continental reforms of more than a century later. Moreover, the English would have had no reason for selecting customs from two different houses unless each of these had its own contribution to offer.

We may then regard Fleury and Ghent as representative of the two great branches of tenth century reformed monasticism[1]: the Cluniac lying to the south-west and the Lotharingian[2] to the north-west of a line drawn, roughly, from Ghent, through Verdun and Toul, to the Alps.

Unfortunately, we possess no consuetudinary of Ghent and no early one of Fleury—the book of Fleury customs commonly assigned to the tenth century being, as it stands, no earlier than the thirteenth, though it would appear to contain a few survivals of primitive usage.[3] If we wish, then, to discover what the Concordia owes to Fleury and Ghent we can do no more than compare our English code with such monastic

[1] For these reforms see Sackur, *Die Cluniacenser*, vol. i. They are summarised in *Times of St Dunstan*, pp. 134 ff.

[2] Lotharingia, the 'Middle Kingdom,' then comprised what is now Holland and Belgium, together with parts of Rhenish Prussia, of Switzerland and of the old province of Franche Compté and the districts of Upper and Lower Lorraine (see *Encycl. Brit.* under *Lorraine*).

[3] *Sources*, p. 271 f.

documents of the tenth and eleventh centuries as are available, assigning parallels with the customs of Einsiedeln, Trèves, Verdun and other books of Lotharingian type to Ghent, and to Fleury all parallels with books of Cluniac provenance. This may serve for the moment to give an approximate idea of the extent to which monastic ideas flowed into this country through the two channels indicated in the Concordia.

Customs derived from Continental sources fall into three groups: (*a*) those consonant with early Benedictine usage, as witnessed to by documents, mostly of Cassinese origin or relationship, belonging to the period that immediately preceded the reform of Benedict of Aniane in the ninth century; (*b*) those taken over from documents of the Anianian reform; (*c*) customs, liturgical and monastic, characteristic of the elaborated and, to a certain extent, stereotyped observance known to us from the consuetudinaries of the tenth and eleventh centuries.[1]

(*a*) To the first group belong practices such as the Drink after None (30, 3), the observance of claustral enclosure (64, 7), the psalmody accompanying the manual labour (25, 9), arrangements for saying the Office when journeying on horseback (11, 4 f.) and, notably, the observance taken bodily from the tract known as *Ordo Qualiter* (OQ), the only document which we can affirm to have been extensively used in the Concordia (Ch. I *passim*). Nearly all this primitive usage, however, passed into general observance and can be found in one or other of the Cluniac and Lotharingian consuetudinaries ; thus unless it is a survival of ancient Anglo-Saxon monasticism, as may possibly be the case with the material derived from OQ,[2] it would in all likelihood have been introduced into this country under the influence of the Continental reforms of the tenth century.

[1] For the documents relative to these three groups see *Sources*, pp. 163, 166–167, 268–274.

[2] See *Times of St Dunstan*, p. 154 *n.* 2 and, for relationship between the Concordia and MSS of OQ, p. 151. Some of the major differences between the Concordia and OQ readings here should probably be put down to material ' woven ' into OQ (just as OQ itself is ' woven ' into the Concordia).

(*b*) To the second group[1] belong one short citation (8, 10) from Amalar's *Rule for Canons*, drawn up in 816 at the first of the two Aix assemblies, and two (11, 21–23; 63, 12–13) from the famous *Capitula* put forward by Benedict of Aniane at the second assembly in 817. To these may be added a parallel (4, 16 f.) with a passage from the Praefatio to the *Rule for Canons* and an allusion (5, 13) to the *Via Regia* of Smaragdus, abbot of S. Mihiel. For two possible connections with the Aix *Capitula* see pp. 17 *n.* 4; 22 *n.* 10. Several other Concordia practices such as *Trina oratio* (16, 1 f.) and the recitation of the Gradual psalms before Nocturns (17, 7) can be traced back to the observance of Benedict's model monastery of Inda (Cornelimünster); but they were widespread in the tenth century and form, as they stand in the Concordia, distinctive customs for which there is no exact parallel. As there is nothing to show that early ninth century Saxon monasticism had been influenced by the Anianian reform we may assume that the English obtained their knowledge of that movement and of its writings through direct contact with Continental monasteries in the tenth century.[2]

(*c*) To the third group belong a very large number of customs liturgical and monastic. As regards liturgical customs, it looks very much as though in some instances the English must have drawn on liturgical books newly obtained from abroad, some of them, indeed, from some monastery of the Lotharingian reform. Thus the principal services of Holy Week and Easter are based on, and some half dozen rubrical directions are cited verbally from, *Ordo Romanus Primus* (OR I), or some form of that document[3]; of two special Holy Week rites, one (37, 6 f.) is almost certainly indirectly dependent on *Verdun;* another (46, 6 f.) is closely related to a rite given in

[1] For the reform under St Benedict of Aniane see Bishop, *Liturgica Historica*, pp. 212 ff.

[2] We should not exaggerate the extent to which the Concordia depends directly on Anianian observance: in two cases at least (pp. 27 *n.* 6 ; 34 *n.* 17), the Concordia goes counter to the *Aix Capit.*; see DR, July 1947, p. 273 f.

[3] The Concordia is probably our earliest witness to the use of the Ordo Romanus in this country. See *Sources*, p. 35.

an Ordinarium of Toul; the famous Easter 'play' (51) has points of contact with a large number of versions of a custom then widespread on the Continent. Further, the practice of substituting the Secular for the Monastic Office (in Holy Week, Easter Week and at Nocturns on Whit Sunday) was almost certainly derived from Lotharingian usage as known to us from *Verdun*, *Trèves* and Hartker's Antiphonar.

Of a large number of the monastic observances of this group little can be said. Most of them appear in both Cluniac and Lotharingian consuetudinaries and, in the absence of literary connection with any given document, we must be content to put them down for the present as 'borrowed' from the observance of the day. Among such may be mentioned the recitation of the Offices Of All Saints and Of the Dead, of the Gradual and Penitential psalms in Lent (35, 11 f.), of the five Chapter psalms (25, 1), and of the Penitential psalms and Litany after Prime (19, 24–26); the Drink after None (30, 3).

There are, however, a few customs that can with fair confidence be assigned definitely to either one or the other of the great branches of Continental tradition of which we have spoken—the Cluniac and the Lotharingian. Thus the relations between master and 'pueri' (11, 16 f.), silence on feast days (24, 13), a custom connected with the reading of the Martyrology on Christmas Eve (31, 2 f.), details of the Blessing of the New Fire (41, 6) and of the Easter 'play' (51, 27–28) find parallels only in Cluniac documents [1]; while the manner of 'offering' at the Mass (20, 22–26), the arrangements for the Maundy carried out by the children (62, 12–15), the special 'confession' on Christmas Eve and Maundy Thursday (31, 25–30; 39, 7), the psalmody during the manual labour (25, 10), the recording of the name of a dead brother (68, 16) are common only to the Concordia and the consuetudinaries of Lotharingian type.[2]

[1] See also p. 15 *n.* 15.

[2] See also pp. 15 *n.* 6; 17 *n. b*; 19 *n.* 3; 21 *n. f*; 23 *n.* 2; 24 *nn. d* and *e*; 41 *n.* 2; 42 *n.* 5; 48 *n.* 18; 49 *n.* 4; 56 *nn.* 3 and 5; 58 *n.* 6; 60 *n.* 3; 65 *n.* 6; 66 *n.* 2.

We may sum up by saying that the Concordia, for all its spirit of national independence, reflects the ideas of an age when monasticism, pursuing the course into which it had been directed by Benedict of Aniane, was finally settling down to a type of observance that remained generally typical of Benedictine life until the days of St Bernard.

Yet, in spite of its comprehensiveness, the Concordia is in no sense a mere copy; it has been put together by a process of selection, adaptation, alteration and blending of the borrowed material on which it is largely based. As for this material itself, what little we know of it shows a higher proportion of agreement with Lotharingian than with Cluniac usage. In other words, it looks as though the customs of Ghent, indirectly discernible in the Concordia through Lotharingian parallels, had specially commended themselves to the English.

Here, in this Ghent connection, we may recognise the influence of Dunstan, who had had first hand experience of the observance of St Peter's some twenty years before. With this suggestion we may now turn to the question of the authorship of the Concordia.

The Concordia is an anonymous document. The Proem merely says that the 'bishops, abbots and abbesses' assembled at the Council of Winchester gathered customs from all quarters, 'edited' them and embodied them 'in this little book.' Some thirty years or so later, Aelfric, writing to the monks of Eynsham, tells them that the Concordia had been 'put together from various sources (*undique*)' and 'imposed' on all the monasteries 'by Ethelwold *and his fellow bishops and abbots*': he makes no reference to the Council. Aelfric is not clear; but his words are commonly quoted as evidence that Ethelwold was the 'author' of the Concordia.[1]

[1] Aelfric's words (p. 174 f.) are: '. . . ideoque haec pauca de libro consuetudinum quem sanctus Athelwoldus Wintoniensis episcopus *cum coepiscopis et abbatibus* tempore Eadgari felicissimi regis Anglorum undique *collegit* ac monachis *instituit observandum* scriptitando demonstro.' Aelfric was Ethelwold's disciple; and *scriptitando* goes surely with *demonstro.*

Seventy years after Aelfric penned his Letter we find St Anselm writing to Archbishop Lanfranc as follows: 'I have heard that St Dunstan drew up (*instituit*) a rule of monastic life: I should like, if it be possible, to see the Life and *Instituta* of so great a father.'[1] This suggests that in the course of a hundred years or so the Concordia had come to be looked upon as Dunstan's.

Of 'authorship,' in the strict sense, there can be no question in a work such as the Concordia; but we shall probably not be far wrong if we reconcile Aelfric's statement, vague and unsatisfactory as it is, with the later tradition by ascribing execution to Ethelwold and inspiration to Dunstan. For if it was Ethelwold who actually put together the Concordia as we know it—who even, perhaps, penned it, he can only have done so after collection and modification of material and after debate and decision—the work, partly, of the Council of Winchester and in which his fellow bishops and abbots had a share. And there can be little doubt that, behind all, it was Archbishop Dunstan who sensed the dangers of dissension, who conceived the remedy—one common norm of observance —and who took the initial steps to ensure its application.[2]

[1] Epp. i. 31 (*PL* clviii, 1104); Ep. 39 (ed. Schmitt iii, 151).

[2] See H. Logeman, *The Rule of St Benet* (E.E.T.S. 1888), p. xvi: 'If this Regularis Concordia is not Dunstan's it owes its origin at least to his mind which pervades the times in which he lived.' 'Dunstan the mind, Ethelwold the pen' (from an unpublished letter of Edmund Bishop to J. Armitage Robinson, July 10th, 1916).

IV

THE MANUSCRIPTS

Only two texts of the Regularis Concordia are extant. The older, of the late tenth century, is contained in Cotton MSS Faustina B 3, folios 159*a*–198*a* (=F) and Tiberius A 3, folio 177*a* and *b* (F_2). F has no title and begins abruptly with the first words of the Proem: *Gloriosus etenim Eadgar*, etc. The various sections of the latter portion of the Proem, from the words *Episcoporum quoque electio* onwards, appear to be displaced (*Apparat.*, p. 6); thus the passage dealing with the election of bishops is detached from that dealing with the election of abbots and abbesses; the section defining the relationship between the monasteries and the king is separated from that forbidding any form of lay control over the monasteries save only that exercised by the king and queen; the direction that only those who will edify be taken as companions on a journey is detached from further instructions dealing with journeys in general; the passage ending with the doxology, *Qui cum Patre*, etc., and forming a natural conclusion to all this introductory matter is placed towards the beginning of the latter portion of the Proem; after the section ending with the words *cum benedictione eat*, with which the F text of the Proem actually closes, comes the note *hic inserenda sunt capitula*, but no list of chapters is given (*Apparat.*, pp. 8 and 10). In Ch. XI there is a transposition of two sentences.

The Proem is followed by eleven complete chapters. Then, in the course of Ch. XII, the MS breaks off at the bottom of folio 198*a* with the words *quibus fuerit unitus* (*Apparat.*, p. 66). To these words have been added partly in the margin and, seemingly, in another hand, the completion of the sentence: *in ordinis communione uat*. On the reverse of the folio is a variant form of the letter to be sent round the monasteries on the death of a monk (*Apparat.*, p. 66). This variant is of the tenth century but by another hand.

F_2 is by the same hand as F, and is almost certainly the missing folio of that text. Beginning at the top of folio 177*a* with the words *in ordinis communione* (without *uat.*), and continuing *Quod si ex alio monasterio noto ac familiari quis nuntiatus fuerit defunctus*, etc., it completes the Concordia text down to the end of Ch. XII. There is no Epilogue. In the margin of folio 177*a* is a neumed antiphon: *Hodie in pace fiat locus eius et in Sion habitatio eius. Hodie beatae Mariae uirginis tueatur praesidiis. Hodie sanctissimi monachorum patris Benedicti muniatur auxiliis. Domine miserere.* This is by another hand, and is in parts almost illegible. On folio 177*b* are two further variant forms of the letter announcing the death of a monk (*Apparat.*, p. 68). Both of these are by the same hand [1] as the variant form in F and the words added to the F text at the bottom of folio 198*a* (*in ordinis communione uat.*).

Both F and F_2 must have been written for, or at least adapted to, the use of Christ Church Canterbury; for in the F text of the letter already referred to, the words *abbas monasterii illius* have added above them the note *uel episcopus ecclesiae Christi*, while the three variant forms of the letter begin respectively *Gratia Dei archiepiscopus ille humilisque Christi ecclesiae monachorum coetus* (F); *Gratia miserationis Dei archiepiscopus ille omnisque⟨congregatio ecclesiae Christi⟩* (F_2); and *Gratia miserationis Dei archiepiscopus ille omnisque congregatio ecclesiae Christi* (F_2).

F abounds in erasures and corrections made apparently by the scribe himself; chapter headings and, in many cases, capitals are rubricated; there are the usual contractions. The scribe has peculiarities of his own: for *largiente* he writes *lariente, larigente, largente*; he constantly inserts or omits vowels and consonants, thus: *sii, quiibus, catholiceis, soleet, peroreet, ausilis, tempre, bendictus, oportuno, intermisione, necesaria, praefattio, respontdentibus, penstecosten;* he writes *unianimes* (twice) and

[1] Yet another hand, it would seem, wrote the ' notes ' (in the *episticula*, its variants and the *Satisfaciat*: *Apparat.*, pp. 66–67) in F and F_2. For judgments expressed here and elsewhere on the date, identity and difference of hands in text and variants of F and F_2 I am indebted to the late Mr J. P. Gilson and to Mr J. A. Herbert, late of the British Museum MS Department.

unianimiter; he omits syllables: *des⟨is⟩tat, muni⟨mi⟩nis, inmin-⟨en⟩te, in⟨it⟩ietur princi⟨pi⟩um, ca⟨ni⟩mus*, etc. Occasionally he leaves out a whole line or more of the text, and at times he is unintelligible as in the forms *nonceptorum*, *pappate* and *babbate* (=*ab abbate*), *ati* and *atit* (=*ait*). A similar characteristic may be remarked in F_2 (*ad caticuminum istum*=*at ex ignoto tantum*) and T (*fremen*=*fratrem*).

The later text of the Regularis Concordia, contained in Cotton MS Tiberius A 3, folios 3*a*–27*b* (=T), is of the second half of the eleventh century.[1] Special interest attaches to it on account of its interlinear Anglo-Saxon glosses.[2]

While omitting nothing that is found in F and F_2, T re-arranges those portions of the Proem and of Ch. XI which are displaced in F, giving in addition a title, list of chapters and Epilogue. In Ch. I, instead of the collect *Rege quaesumus* being repeated in full, as in F, only the incipit is given, with the note *Require in praecedenti folio.* Before the last sentence of Ch. XII are the words *Explicuit liber:* the last sentence and the Epilogue follow.

On folio 2*b* is a full page illustration depicting three figures seated under a canopy of triple arcading: in the centre, a king; on the right, an archbishop with pallium; on the left, a bishop. Both archbishop and bishop are represented with the nimbus. The three figures together hold a long scroll. Below is a monk, apparently in the act of genuflecting: he is looking upwards and holds a scroll, part of which is behind his back, as though binding or girding himself with it.[3]

[1] I am indebted to Dr F. Wormald for the information that T cannot be dated earlier than 1050, and may be as late as 1100.

[2] Apart from their interest to students of Anglo-Saxon, these glosses are very helpful in the several cases where the Latin of T gives an uncertain reading.

[3] See plate facing p. ix. Evidently the king is Edgar and the figures on either side are St Dunstan and St Ethelwold. The scroll which they are holding would be the Regularis Concordia put forward at the Council of Winchester. The kneeling figure below represents the monks who, at the Council, bound themselves by vow to obey the Concordia which is, again, typified by the scroll with which the monk is binding or girding himself. For an adaptation of this miniature as a frontispiece to Aelfric's *Grammar* see F. Wormald, *Two Anglo-Saxon Miniatures Compared* (Brit. Mus. Quarterly, vol. ix, 1934–1935, pp. 113 ff.).

T, like F, is full of textual errors. On the other hand, T frequently 'corrects' F: e.g., sixteen times the subjunctive is substituted for the indicative; seven times the order of words found in F is reversed. Where F usually has *sollemnitas, antifona, ebdomada,* T as a rule gives *sollempnitas, antiphona, epdomada.*

Nothing is known of the origin of T except that the volume of which it forms part is intimately connected with a book mentioned in the Christ Church Canterbury Catalogue of the early fourteenth century (see below).

That relationship between F and T is close appears from their agreement in incorrect or unusual readings such as *intra infraue* (10, 13); *finitis cum* (17, 10); *adiutor⟨ium⟩* (25, 16); *cacumenae* (F) *ca⟨c⟩umene* (T) (29, 6); *sola* (35, 11); *reli⟨gi⟩osorum* (37, 3); *uniuersum mundum* (37, 24). But T is not a copy of F: witness the different arrangement of portions of the Proem and of Ch. XI in the two MSS; the additional matter found in T; the notes *hic inserenda sunt capitula* (F) and *explicuit liber* (T). Both MSS are of the same family, copies perhaps of sister MSS or of one exemplar of which the original form is given by F and a revised and amplified form by T.

Besides our two texts, F, F_2 and T, we have an abridgment of the Concordia in Aelfric's *Letter to the monks of Eynsham* of about the year 1005 (= AE). This is preserved in one MS only: CCCC 265, folios 237 ff., of the beginning of the eleventh century. Although AE is not divided into chapters, the greater part of the Concordia can be recognised in it with the exception of the Proem, Chs. VII and XI, the last sentence of Ch. XII and the Epilogue. AE's references to the Concordia close with the words *Finiunt consuetudines.* The value of the *Letter* as a check on the text of the Concordia is evident from the fact that it frequently cites that document verbally. Of special interest are AE's divergencies from Concordia practice; e.g., although the first of the two special Holy Week customs of the Concordia is treated fully, no reference is made to the other or to the Easter 'play.'

The Glastonbury Library Catalogue of 1247 mentions two books of customs: *Libri de consuetudinibus duo, unus editus sub Edgaro de racionabili obseruantia—legibilis* [*alius de Cadomo*].[1] The book connected with the name of Edgar can only be our Concordia. Another lost MS of the Concordia would seem to be the tract described in the fourteenth century Catalogue of Christ Church Canterbury as *Consuetudines de faciendo seruitio diuino per annum glosate Anglice*.[2] When we recall the interlinear Anglo-Saxon glosses of T and the fact that the Concordia is referred to in the Proem as *morum consuetudines* and in AE as *consuetudines* the identity of this tract hardly appears in doubt. It is found in the second of two companion volumes written by Aelfric Batta, the combined contents of which closely resemble those of the codex in which T is preserved. So evident is the connection between the two Canterbury books and the Tiberius codex that Dr James himself has not hesitated to identify Batta's first volume with Tib. A 3.[3] But the difference between these two volumes and the Tiberius codex both in arrangement and in actual content seems too great to justify such a conclusion: Batta's volumes and Tib. A 3 are probably sister codices.[4]

Portions of the text of the Concordia are found in MS CCCC 190, of the eleventh century, one of the books given to Exeter by Bishop Leofric. This MS reproduces verbatim the greater part of sections 31-34, 36, 37, 39-44, 47-50, 52, 53, 58 and 59. Some of the more interesting points of contact with Concordia practice are given in the textual notes. The Missal of Robert of Jumièges (pp. 30 *n.* 7; 57 *nn.* 1 and 10), the Canterbury Benedictional (pp. 30 *n.* 7; 35 *n.* 2), the Wulfstan Collectar (pp. 38 *n.* 17; 39 *n.* 11), the Leofric Collectar (p. 48 *n.* 16), and the *Liber Vitae* (pp. 5 *n.* 2; 36 *n.* 1), each contains a small amount of material derived from or in some way

[1] *John of Glastonbury* (Hearne), ii, p. 435.

[2] M. R. James, *Ancient Libraries of Canterbury and Dover*, p. 50.

[3] *Loc. cit.*, p. 508.

[4] See W. S. Logeman, *Anglia* xv Neue Folge iii, p. 25. N. R. Ker (*Mediaeval Libraries of Great Britain*, London, 1941, p. 22) accepts Tib. A 3 as a Christ Church Canterbury book.

connected with the Concordia. A passage in Wulfstan's *Life of Ethelwold* (p. 26 *n.* 3) and one in the *De Obedientiariis Abendoniae* (Chron. Abingd. ii, p. 352) show that the authors of these works were acquainted with the Concordia. Lastly, in certain spurious or doubtful charters connected with Abingdon, Winchester, Thorney, Worcester and other monasteries we meet with passages taken from the Concordia.

For fragments of an Anglo-Saxon translation of the Concordia in Tib. A 3 (ff. 174*a*–176*b*) and CCCC 201 see Bateson, *Rules for Monks and Canons*, EHR ix, p. 707 and Breck, *Translation of Aethelwold's De consuetudine monachorum* (Leipsic, 1887).

The first to edit the Regularis Concordia in its entirety was Dom Clement Reyner,[1] who printed the Latin text of T in his *Apostolatus Benedictinorum in Anglia* (Douai, 1626). John Selden had already edited the Proem and the greater part of the Epilogue in the Notes to his *Eadmeri Monachi Cantuariensis Historia Novorum* (London, 1623): a very beautiful piece of work in which both the Latin text and the Anglo-Saxon glosses of T are most faithfully reproduced. Reyner's text has been reprinted in the first volume of Dugdale's *Monasticon* (pp. xxvii–xlv) and in Migne (*PL* cxxxvii, 475–502). There is a complete critical edition of T by W. S. Logeman in *Anglia* (XIII Neue Folge I, pp. 365–448). There T is printed exactly as it stands in the MS, with the Anglo-Saxon glosses above the Latin text. For two other prints of portions of the T text of the Concordia, see Birch, *Cartularium Saxonicum* 1168 (Proem and Epilogue), and Breck, *Trans. of Aethelwold's De consuet. monach.* (Leipsic, 1887).

The older text (F, F_2), noticed incidentally by writers on the period, has never yet been edited independently and is here made use of for the first time.

In the present edition T has been taken as the basis of the text; thus Title, Epilogue and a satisfactory arrangement of displaced passages are retained and the few *lacunae* occurring

[1] For a more accurate attribution of responsibility for the documentary material as printed in the *Apostolatus* see Knowles, *Lanfranc's Monastic Constitutions* (Mediaeval Classics), Introd., pp. xxvi ff.

in F are supplied. On the other hand, not only has F been used to correct mistakes in T, but in many cases the readings of F have been preferred.[1] The *Apparatus* has been reduced to the smallest possible proportions: readings which affect the text are given, but obvious copyist's mistakes are omitted except where they are of interest. The spelling of the manuscripts has been for the most part normalised in the body of the text but preserved in the *Apparatus*. The 'punctuation' of the MSS has been necessarily ignored.

[1] Unless otherwise stated the readings in the text are always those of either T or F, F_2.

LATIN TEXT

and

ENGLISH TRANSLATION

REGVLARIS CONCORDIA

[PROOEMIVM REGVLARIS CONCORDIAE[1] ANGLICAE NATIONIS MONACHORVM SANCTIMONIALIVMQVE ORDITVR][a]

1. Gloriosus etenim Eadgar, Christi opitulante gratia Anglorum ceterarumque gentium intra ambitum Britannicae insulae degentium rex egregius,[2] ab ineunte suae pueritiae aetate licet, uti ipsa solet aetas, diuersis uteretur moribus, attamen respectu diuino attactus, abbate quodam [3] assiduo monente ac regiam catholicae fidei uiam [4] demonstrante, coepit magnopere Deum timere, diligere ac uenerari. Radiante paulatim fidei scintilla, ne otiositatis torpore [b] explosa delitesceret, quibus sanctorum operum meritis in feruidum perfectionis ardorem accendi ualeret, studiose percunctari sollicitus coepit.

2. Comperto etenim quod sacra coenobia diuersis sui regiminis locis diruta ac paene Domini nostri Ihesu Christi seruitio destituta neglegenter tabescerent, Domini

[a] [ ] *om.* F   [b] corpore F

[1] An echo, possibly, of the title of Benedict of Aniane's collection of monastic rules: *Concordia Regularum.*

[2] cf. regnal titles in BCS 295, 959, 1158. See also W. H. Stevenson, *Asser*, p. 148.

[3] Either Dunstan or Ethelwold. From, say, 949 to 955–956, i.e., from Edgar's sixth to his twelfth or thirteenth year, Abbot Dunstan was the most likely person to have had charge of the young prince's education. From 954–955, when he became abbot, Ethelwold may have been Edgar's instructor, as he must certainly have been from 955–956 (when Dunstan went into exile under Eadwig) to 957, when, at the age of fourteen, Edgar was chosen as king by the Mercians. The anonymous terms of the

THE MONASTIC AGREEMENT

HERE BEGINS THE FOREWORD TO THE MONASTIC AGREEMENT[1] OF THE MONKS AND NUNS OF THE ENGLISH NATION

1. Edgar the glorious, by the grace of Christ illustrious[2] King of the English and of the other peoples dwelling within the bounds of the island of Britain, from his earliest years began to fear, love and worship God with all his heart. For while he engaged in the various pursuits that befit boyhood, he was nevertheless touched by the divine regard, being diligently admonished by a certain abbot[3] who explained to him the royal way[4] of the Catholic faith. Wherefore, lest the spark of faith, which was beginning gradually to brighten, should be extinguished by sloth and idleness, he began carefully and earnestly to consider by what holy and deserving works it could be made to burn with the brilliance and ardour of perfection.

2. When therefore he learned that the holy monasteries in all quarters of his kingdom, brought low, and almost wholly lacking in the service of our Lord Jesus Christ, were wasting away and neglected, moved by

---

reference ('a certain abbot') suggest Ethelwold; but the considered opinion of the late Edmund Bishop—that Abbot Dunstan is referred to here—deserves to be set on record. The story in Cockayne, *Leechdoms* (RS iii. 433 ff.) is irrelevant: see *Times of St Dunstan*, pp. 159 ff.

[4] For *regiam uiam* see p. 4 *n.* 1.

compunctus gratia, cum magna animi alacritate festinando ubicumque locorum decentissime restaurauit[1]; eiectisque neglegentium clericorum spurcitiis[2] non solum monachos uerum etiam sanctimoniales, patribus matribusque constitutis, ad Dei famulatum ubique per tantam sui regni amplitudinem deuotissime constituit, bonisque omnibus locupletans gratulabundus ditauit.

3. Regali utique functus officio ueluti Pastorum Pastor[a] sollicitus a rabidis perfidorum rictibus, uti hiantibus luporum faucibus, oues quas Domini largiente gratia studiosus collegerat muniendo eripuit; coniugique suae Ælfthrithae[b][3] sanctimonialium mandras ut impauidi more custodis defenderet cautissime praecepit; ut uidelicet mas maribus, femina feminis, sine ullo suspicionis scrupulo subueniret.

4. Regulari itaque sancti patris Benedicti norma honestissime suscepta, tam abbates perplurimi quam abbatissae, cum sibi subiectis fratrum sororumque collegiis, sanctorum sequi uestigia una fide, non tamen uno consuetudinis usu, certatim cum magna studuerunt hilaritate. Tali igitur ac tanto studio praefatus rex magnopere delectatus, arcana quaeque diligenti cura examinans, synodale concilium Wintoniae[4] fieri decreuit; illucque uerba exhortatoria ac pacifica pitacio luculentissime caraxata humillimus destinauit, cunctosque Christi compunctus gratia monuit ut concordes

[a] For this expression as applied to Christ, see Amort, *Vet. Discipl. Canon.*, p. 221; Bede's *Letter to Egbert* (*Opp. Hist.*, i. 409); *Vita Folcuini* (*PL* cxxxvii. 541).

[b] aelꝼþꞃiðe F; aelꝼþꞃyþę T

[1] In a work of national importance the first place is naturally given to the head of the realm. The Glastonbury-Abingdon phase of the movement is here ignored; but about thirty years later, Edgar's part in the reform appears as *consentiente rege*, and the reform is more accurately dealt with (*Vita Ethelwoldi*, p. 262).

[2] cf. Bede, H. E., ii. 4 (*Opp. Hist.*, i. 88: 'eliminata omni spurcitia'; cf. *ibid.*, p. clxvi.). For the expulsion of clerks see Introd., p. xxii.

the grace of the Lord he most gladly set himself to restore them everywhere to their former good estate.[1] Wherefore he drove out the negligent clerks with their abominations,[2] placing in their stead for the service of God, throughout the length and breadth of his dominions, not only monks but also nuns, under abbots and abbesses; and these, out of gratitude to God, he enriched with all good things.

3. Thus, in fulfilment of his royal office, even as the Good Shepherd, he carefully rescued and defended from the savage open mouths of the wicked—as it were the gaping jaws of wolves—those sheep which by God's grace he had diligently gathered together. And he saw to it wisely that his Queen, Aelfthrith,[3] should be the protectress and fearless guardian of the communities of nuns; so that he himself helping the men and his consort helping the women there should be no cause for any breath of scandal.

4. When therefore the Rule of the holy Father Benedict had been accepted with the greatest goodwill, very many of the abbots and abbesses with their communities of monks and nuns vied with one another in following in the footsteps of the saints; for they were united in one faith, though not in one manner of monastic usage. Exceedingly delighted with such great zeal the aforesaid king, after deep and careful study of the matter, commanded a Synodal Council to be held at Winchester.[4] To this assembly he most humbly sent a letter, set forth magnificently on parchment and couched in encouraging and peaceable terms, in which, moved by the grace of Christ, he urged all to be of one

---

[3] See Chron. (D) *s.a.* 965: 'Her on þissum geare Eadgar cyning genam Aelf[ðr]yðe him to cwene.' [4] See Introd., p. xxiv.

aequali consuetudinis usu, sanctos probatosque imitando patres, regularia praecepta tenaci mentis ancora seruantes nullo modo dissentiendo discordarent; ne impar ac uarius unius regulae ac unius patriae usus probrose uituperium sanctae conuersationi irrogaret. Huius[1] praecellentissimi regis sagaci monitu spiritualiter compuncti non tantum episcopi, uerum etiam abbates ac abbatissae, quod *talem ac tantum meruerunt habere*[a] doctorem *erectis ad aethera palmis immensas* celsithrono *grates*[b] uoti compotes referre non distulerunt.

5. Nam ilico eius imperiis toto mentis conamine alacriter obtemperantes, sanctique patroni nostri Gregorii documenta, quibus beatum Augustinum monere studuit ut non solum Romanae uerum etiam Galliarum honestos ecclesiarum usus ⟨in⟩ rudi Anglorum ecclesia decorando constitueret,[c] recolentes; accitis Florensis beati Benedicti[2] necnon praecipui coenobii quod celebri Gent[3] nuncupatur uocabulo monachis, quaeque ex dignis eorum moribus honesta colligentes, uti apes fauum nectaris diuersis pratorum floribus in uno alueario,[4] ita has morum consuetudines ad uitae honestatem et regularis obseruantiae dulcedinem, ut ab

[a] Blessing of the Paschal Candle (*Greg*, p. 152): 'O felix culpa quae *talem ac tantum meruit habere* Redemptorem'

[b] Aldhelm, *De Virg.* (M.G. Auct. Antiquiss. xv. 229): '*Erectis ad aethera palmis immensas* Christo pro sospitate vestra gratulabundus impendere *grates* curavi'

[c] Bede, H. E., i. 27 (*Opp. Hist.*, i. p. 49): . . . mihi placet ut, sive in Romana, sive in Galliarum, seu in qualibet ecclesia aliquid invenisti . . . sollicite eligas et in Anglorum ecclesia . . . infundas.'

[1] For this sentence cf. *Regula Canonicorum* (Praefatio), *PL* cv. 817: 'Ad quam etiam admonitionem sacer conventus, intimo gaudio repletus, expansis in coelum manibus, creatori omnium gratias agens benedixit. Quippe qui talem tam pium tamque benignum ecclesiae suae sanctae principem cunctisque eius necessitatibus sapientissimum ac devotissimum praetulerit procuratorem' . . . See *Sources*, p. 168.

mind as regards monastic usage, to follow the holy and approved fathers and so, with their minds anchored firmly on the ordinances of the Rule, to avoid all dissension, lest differing ways of observing the customs of one Rule and one country should bring their holy conversation into disrepute. Deeply moved by the wise advice of this excellent King,[1] the bishops, abbots and abbesses were not slow in raising their hands to heaven in hearty thanksgiving to the throne above for that they were thought worthy to have so good and so great a teacher.

5. Straightway, then, they obeyed his commands with the utmost gladness; and calling to mind the letters in which our holy patron Gregory instructed the blessed Augustine that, for the advancement of the rude English Church, he should establish therein the seemly customs of the Gallic Churches as well as those of Rome, they summoned monks from St Benedict's monastery[2] at Fleury and from that eminent monastery which is known by the renowned name of Ghent,[3] gathered from their praiseworthy customs much that was good and thus, even as honey is gathered by bees from all manner of wild flowers and collected into one hive,[4] so also the said monastic customs, tempered by great and subtle judgment of reason were, by the grace of Christ the Saviour of the world, embodied in this small book. Now the said customs are such as will tend to uprightness of life and sweetness of regular observance; they

---

[2] The Abbey of Fleury-sur-Loire, reformed in 930 by St Odo of Cluny

[3] The Abbey of St Peter (Blandinium) at Ghent, reformed by Gerard of Brogne, *c.* 937

[4] A literary commonplace: cf. e.g. Sedulius, *Lib. de Rect. Christ.* (*PL* ciii. 330); *Reg. Can.* (*PL* cv. 818). See Bishop, *Lit. Hist.*, p. 346 *n.*, and Stevenson, *Asser*, p. 302 f.

his qui uiam regiam mandatorum Domini[1] absque iactantiae uitio lactei adhuc humiliter incedunt, depulso nausiae taedio, sine querela legitime haustu degustari libentissimo[a] ac auidi amabili possent impleri deuotione, temperate cum magna ac subtili rationis discretione, Christi mundi Saluatoris opitulante gratia, hoc exiguo apposuerunt codicello.

6. Ne igitur singuli, si suam, quod absit, adinuentionem[2] suapte praesumptuosi eligerent, excellentissimum sanctae oboedientiae fructum, alicuius arrogantiae fastu[3] inopinate seducti, miserabiliter amitterent, ac Sarabaitae[b] uel ferae potius quam monachi aut homines uiderentur legitimi, uotum Domino nostro Ihesu Christo unanimes[c] uouerunt pactoque spirituali confirmauerunt se uita comite iugo regulae deditos has annotatas morum consuetudines[4] communi palam custodire conuersatione. Ceterum unusquisque secretis oratorii locis,[5] in quantum Sancti Spiritus gratia clementer instigauerit, *peculiaribus* teste Deo cum bonorum operum uigilantia consulte utatur *orationibus*.[d]

7. Hoc etenim Dunstanus, egregius huius patriae archiepiscopus, praesago afflatus spiritu, ad corroborandum praefati synodalis conuentus conciliabulum, prouide ac sapienter addidit : ut uidelicet nullus monachorum, uel alicuius altioris gradus uir uel inferioris, secreta sanctimonialium audax ingredi lustrando praesumeret; et hi qui spiritualis imperii prioratum ad disciplinae utilitatem non ad saecularis tyrannidem potentatus super eas

[a] libentissime F   [b] *Rule* i. 14   [c] unianimes F
[d] cf. *Rule* xlix. 12: '*orationes peculiares*,' and lii. 5: 'frater qui forte sibi peculiariter vult orare.'

[1] cf. the title of the second chapter of the *Via Regia* of Smaragdus, abbot of S. Mihiel (*c.* 819): *De observatione mandatorum Domini* (*PL* cii. 925). *Via regia*, already used above (1, 6–7) in a general religious sense, is here applied to the monastic life. The expression is a common one, and is found in Alcuin. Both Smaragdus and Alcuin quote *Num.* xxi, 22.

may be tasted rightfully and with the fullest enjoyment and eagerness, and may be fulfilled with affectionate devotion by those who would walk humbly and like little ones in the royal way of the Lord's commandments,[1] putting away all wickedness of boasting, weariness or grumbling.

6. Lest therefore they should all, which God forbid, prefer to act according to their own devices [2] and thus wretchedly lose the most excellent fruit of holy obedience, helplessly seduced by the pride of arrogance,[3] as Sarabaites or wild beasts rather than as monks and rational beings, the assembly as one man made a solemn vow to our Lord Jesus Christ, confirming their oath with a spiritual pact, that, living all their life under the yoke of the Rule, they would carry out these selfsame monastic customs [4] openly and with one uniform observance. For the rest, all shall be free to give themselves voluntarily to private prayer in the secret places of the oratory,[5] with God as their witness, and to be watchful in good works according as the grace of the Holy Ghost in His mercy shall inspire them.

7. Now in order to confirm the deliberations of the aforesaid Synodal Council, Dunstan, the noble archbishop of our country, moved by the spirit of prophecy, providently and wisely added these further instructions : that no monk, nor indeed any man whatever his rank, should dare to enter and frequent the places set apart for nuns; and that those who have spiritual authority over nuns should use their powers not as worldly tyrants but in the interests of good discipline.

---

[2] See 64, 4–6 below: 'Nullus, . . . quasi propria *adinuentione* . . . agere praesumat.'

[3] *Fastu arrogantiae* is found in Alcuin's Preface to the Supplement of *Greg*, p. 145. See again 8, 15.

[4] i.e., the Regularis Concordia.

[5] See 67, 13.

exercent, ita suum, ut beatus hortatur Isidorus, secretorum temperate praeuideant accessum, ut earum regulari obseruantiae minime contradicant.[1]

8. Id solummodo catholicis regulari iugo deditis attendendum censuimus, ne ea quae usu patrum pro rege ac benefactoribus, quorum beneficiis Christo largiente pascimur,[2] intercessionis oramine consuete canimus, nimia uelocitate psallendo Deum potius ad iracundiam inconsiderate, quod absit, prouocent quam prouide ad peccaminum ueniam inuitent. Ita igitur hortante patre nostro Benedicto, omnia distincte psallendo modificentur *ut mens nostra concordet uoci nostrae*[a] et *impleatur illud apostolicum, Psallam spiritu, psallam et mente.*[3] Si autem pro qualibet necessitate quid extra communem regularis consuetudinis usum addendum fuerit, tamdiu agatur quoadusque negotium pro quo agitur Christi opitulante gratia melioretur; et ut, contempto arrogantiae fastu,[4] gratissimus oboedientiae acquiratur fructus, et gradus ille regularis in quo praecipitur ut *nihil agat monachus nisi quod communis monasterii regula vel maiorum cohortantur exempla*[5] diligentissime custodiatur, nequaquam ulterius praesumptuose usu[b] teneatur temerario, nisi concilio synodali electum traditumque cum *discretione uirtutum* omnium *matre*[c] ab uniuersis fuerit catholicis.

[a] *Rule* xix. 12. [b] for *ausu*, perhaps; cf. 11, 25.
[c] *Rule* lxiv. 48: '. . . testimonia *discretionis matris virtutum* sumens.'

[1] cf. the Second Council of Seville, presided over by St Isidore in 698, where the *patres spirituales* of the houses of nuns are warned 'ut remoti ab earum peculiaritate, nec usque ad vestibulum habeant accedendi familiare permissum . . . ita ut rara sit accessio . . . ut Christi famulae . . . solis divinis cultibus vivant' (*PL* lxxxiv. 598).

[2] cf. the reference to benefactors in *Liber Vitae*, p. 12: '*Quorum beneficiis* elemosinarum cotidie haec ipsa familia *Christo largiente* pascitur.'

[3] 1 Cor. xiv. 15. For the entire passage cf. *Reg. Can.*, I. cxxxii (*PL* cv. 925): 'Psallentium in ecclesia Domino mens concordare debet cum voce ut *impleatur illud apostoli: Psallam spiritu, psallam et mente.*'

Wherefore, as the blessed Isidore exhorts, let the brethren take care so to arrange their going into the dwelling places of nuns that they in no way hinder their regular observance.[1]

8. And this one thing we have thought ought to be looked to by the faithful who live under the yoke of the Rule, namely, that those prayers of intercession which, following the usage of our fathers before us, we are accustomed to say for the King and benefactors by whose bounty, under Christ, we are maintained,[2] shall not be chanted at excessive speed lest rashly we provoke God to anger, which God forbid, instead of wisely beseeching Him to forgive us our sins. Therefore, as our Father Benedict exhorts, let all these prayers be chanted distinctly so that mind and voice agree and that we may thus fulfil the words of the apostle: *I will sing with the spirit, I will sing also with the mind.*[3] And if, in case of need, any practice be added over and above the common monastic use and custom, let it be continued only until, by the help of Christ's grace, the matter for which it was undertaken be settled. Moreover, in order that the most acceptable fruit of obedience be acquired and the pride of arrogance[4] be brought low and that degree of humility, set forth in the Rule, which ordains *that a monk should do nothing beyond that which the common rule of the monastery and the example of the elders exhort,*[5] be most carefully fulfilled, let none henceforth dare rashly to hold any custom that has not been sanctioned by this Synodal Council and handed down with discretion, the mother of all virtues, by all Catholic men.

---

[4] See 6, 3.
[5] St Benedict's eighth degree of humility: *Rule* vii. 165.

9. Praefato equidem synodali conciliabulo hoc attendendum magnopere cuncti decreuerunt, ut abbatum ac abbatissarum electio[1] cum regis consensu et consilio sanctae regulae ageretur documento.[a] Episcoporum quoque electio uti abbatum, ubicumque in sede episcopali monachi regulares conuersantur,[2] si Domini largiente gratia tanti profectus inibi monachus reperiri potuerit, eodem modo agatur; nec alio quolibet modo dum eiusdem sunt conuersationis a quoquam praesumatur. Si autem, imperitia impediente uel peccatis promerentibus, talis qui tanti gradus honore dignus sit in eadem congregatione reperiri non potuerit, ex *alio noto*[3] *monachorum monasterio*, concordi regis et fratrum quibus dedicari debet consilio eligatur.[4] Qui ordinatus uidelicet episcopus in omnibus eundem morem regularem cum monachis suis quem abbas tenet regularis, diligenti cura et magnopere[b] excellenti iugiter sine intermissione custodiat; nec episcopatus occasione[5] regulae praecepta tumidus uel obliuiosus temere intermittat, sed quantum ⟨excellit honore tantum⟩[6] [cu⟨m⟩ grege sibi subiecto sancto][c] excellat et opere.

[a] After the word *documento* F arranges the remainder of the Proem as follows: 1. *Saecularium uero . . . iusserunt* (10, 1–7); 2. *Victum cum pondere . . . saeculorum Amen.* (12, 1–19); 3. *Episcoporum quoque . . . excellat et opere* (9, 4–21); 4. *Ad regis uero . . . compunctione compleant* (10, 7–11, 7); 5. *Villarum autem . . . adire praesumant* (11, 21–26); 6. *Iterantes . . . benedictione eat* (11, 7–21).

[b] manoopere F   [c] [ ] *om.* T

[1] For the election of an abbot see *Rule* lxiv. *passim.*

[2] At the time when the Concordia was written it would seem that only Winchester and, possibly, Worcester were monastic sees. For Canterbury see Introd., p. xxi.

[3] The meaning of *notus* appears from the Rule (lxi. 31 f.), where St Benedict warns the abbot against the acceptance, as a subject, of a monk 'de *alio noto monasterio monachorum*' without the consent of that monk's own abbot or letters of recommendation.

9. It was further decided by the whole assembly at this Synodal Council that another very important matter should receive attention; namely, that the election of abbots and abbesses[1] should be carried out with the consent and advice of the King and according to the teaching of the Holy Rule. Thus wherever monks live the monastic life in a bishop's see,[2] the election of the bishop shall be carried out in the same way as that of an abbot if, by the Lord's grace, a monk of sufficient worth be found in that see; nor shall anyone presume to act in any way contrary to this so long as such a manner of life is led in that place. But if, owing to their ignorance or sinfulness, there shall not be found in that community one worthy of so high a dignity, let a monk be chosen from another monastery that is well-known,[3] with the consent of the King and the counsel of the brethren to whom he is to be presented.[4] As for him who is chosen to be bishop, he shall live with his monks, unceasingly and with exceeding diligence and care keeping to the monastic life in everything, as would the abbot of a monastery. Nor shall he, by reason of his episcopal office,[5] proudly or forgetfully dare to neglect the ordinances of the Rule but, as he excels in honour,[6] so let him, together with the flock subject to him, excel also in holy deeds.

---

[4] cf. the ruling on the election of abbots and abbesses given in 787 by the legates George and Theophilact (Haddan and Stubbs, *Councils and Eccl. Documents* iii. 450, *c.* 5), and a passage in Bede's *Letter to Egbert* (*Opp. Hist.*, i. 413).

[5] cf. *Rule* lxii. 7: 'nec occasione sacerdotii obliviscatur regulae oboedientiam.'

[6] I owe this conjecture to the late J. Armitage Robinson. For a parallel cf. Bede, *De Templo Salomonis* c. xv. (viii. 308, ed. Giles): 'quantum gradu praeeminent caeteris tantum et merito praecellant bonae actionis.'

10. Saecularium uero prioratum,[1] ne ad magni ruinam detrimenti uti olim acciderat miserabiliter deueniret, magna animaduersione atque anathemate suscipi coenobiis sacris sapienter prohibentes, regis tantummodo ac reginae dominium ad sacri loci munimen et ad ecclesiasticae possessionis augmentum uoto semper efflagitare[a] optabili prudentissime iusserunt. Ad regis uero obsequium et reginae patres monasteriorum matresque, quotiens expedierit ad sacri coenobii cui praesunt utilitatem, cum Dei timore et regulae obseruantia humiliter accedant; potentibus uero, non causa conuiuandi[b] sed pro monasterii utilitate atque defensione quotiens expedierit, obuiandi[c] intra infraue[d] monasterium licentiam habeant.

11. Equitando autem uel pedites iter agendo non otiosis fabulis uacent, sed uel psalmodiis inseruiant uel de re necessaria opportuno tempore loquantur; hoc considerantes ut horas regulares non equitando sed de equis desiliendo, genuflectentes nisi dies festiua fuerit, conuenienter uti potuerint cum diuina compunctione compleant.[e] Iterantes uero non iuuenculos sed adultos quorum admonitione meliorentur secum in comitatu ducant; domi uero degentes, non solum fratres sed etiam abbates, adolescentes uel puerulos[2] non brachiis

[a] for *efflagitari*, perhaps.

[b] cf. AE, p. 192: 'nec quispiam secularium in refectorio manducat aut bibat excepto rege et filiis eius.'

[c] + ex F

[d] oþþe ƿiþutan T (gloss). Possible corrections of the text here would be *extra infraue* (based on the reading of F: *ex intra infraue*) or *intra extraue* (based on T (gloss): 'ƿiþinnan oþþe ƿiþutan'). I have preferred to ignore the *ex* of F as of no practical moment, and to treat *infra*, in spite of its late meaning of 'within,' as equivalent to *sub* (*infraue monasterium* = *sub monasterio*).

[e] cf. *Rule* l, 5–8: 'qui in itinere directi sunt, non eos praetereant horae constitutae : sed ut possunt agant sibi'; *Warnfrid*, p. 407 : 'si equitant, in terram descendant ut non praetereant horas constitutas'; and *Farfa*, p. 144: 'Fratres in itinere directi cum viderint horae tempus

10. The assembly wisely, and under severe censure and anathema, forbade the holy monasteries to acknowledge the overlordship [1] of secular persons, a thing which might lead to utter loss and ruin as it did in past times. On the other hand, they commanded that the sovereign power of the King and Queen—and that only—should ever be besought with confident petition, both for the safeguarding of holy places and for the increase of the goods of the Church. As often therefore as it shall be to their advantage the fathers and mothers of each house shall have humble access to the King and Queen in the fear of God and observance of the Rule. They shall not, however, be allowed to meet persons of importance, either within or just outside the monastery, for the purpose of feasting together, but only according as the well-being and defence of the monastery demand.

11. When the brethren are on a journey, whether riding or walking, they shall not waste time in idle talk but shall either busy themselves with psalms or, at the proper time, speak on necessary matters. Let them remember to celebrate the regular hours with holy compunction, not on horseback but dismounted: indeed it will be fitting to do so on their knees if this is possible and it is not a feast day. Again, let the brethren take with them as companions on a journey not youths but grown-up persons from whose conversation they may take profit. In the monastery moreover let neither monks nor abbots embrace or kiss, as it were, youths or children [2]; let their affection for them be spiritual, let

. . . flectant genua descendentes de equis.' For two instances of the recitation of the Office outside choir see *Memorials*, pp. 15 and 39.

[1] This word is used above (7, 7) of spiritual authority. Here it means lay dominion over monasteries. In both cases T(gloss) has 'ealdoþscype.'

[2] These youths and young boys were the children of the cloister who were being trained for the monastic life.

amplexando uel labris leuiter deosculando, sed caritatiuo animi affectu sine uerbis adulatoriis reuerenter cum magna cautela diligant.[a] Nec ad obsequium priuatum quempiam illorum nec saltem sub spiritualis rei obtentu solum deducere praesumant, sed uti regula praecipit[b] sub sui custodis[1] uigilantia iugiter maneat; nec ipse custos cum singulo aliquo puerulo sine tertio qui testis assistat migrandi licentiam habeat, sed solito[c] cum tota schola,[2] si res rationabilis[d] exigerit, quo necesse est sub silentio uel psalmodiis inseruiendo cum benedictione[3] eat.[e] Villarum autem circuitus, nisi necessitas magna compulerit et necessariae rationis discretio hoc dictauerit, uagando nequaquam frequentent.[f] Saecularium uero conuiuia, ni forsan itineris hospitalitas inopinate superuenerit, nullo modo ausu temerario nec praelati nec subiecti adire praesumant.

12. Victum cum pondere, mensura et numero, uestitum, ieiunium, abstinentiam, uigiliam, taciturnitatem, *oboedientiae bonum*[g] et cetera quaeque, quae patroni nostri beati Benedicti traditione uoluntarie suscepimus, Domini nostri Ihesu Christi annuente gratia totis uiribus custodientes, de consuetis sanctae regulae moribus, tam a praedicto patre Benedicto quam

[a] For this and the following sentence see the *Vita Odonis, PL* cxxxiii. 56: ‘ Mos enim eiusdem loci fuerat ut magister scholae solus cum solo puero nec quoquam iret saltem nec ad naturae digestionem, sed nec solus puer secretius illi loqui praesumeret; sed et propter bonum testimonium alium e pueris aut unum ex fratribus in comitatu vel locutione semper assumeret.’

[b] *Rule* lxiii. 39–44: ‘ Pueri parvi vel adulescentes in oratorio vel ad mensas cum disciplina ordines suos consequantur. Foris autem vel ubiubi . . . habeant et disciplinam ’; cf. *ibid.*, 21–2.

[c] For *solito* as an adverb see Stevenson, *Asser* §§ 96, 97 (where, however, the editor has given ⟨*more*⟩ *solito*). Elsewhere in the Concordia *more solito* is the rule.

[d] + ita T

[e] + hic inserenda sunt capitula F

[f] *Aix Capit.*, p. 122: ‘ Ut villas frequenter, nisi necessitas cogerit, non circumeant ’; cf. *Statuta Murbacensia, C.M.* iii. 85.

[g] *Rule* lxxi. 1

them keep from words of flattery, and let them love the children reverently and with the greatest circumspection. Not even on the excuse of some spiritual matter shall any monk presume to take with him a young boy alone for any private purpose but, as the Rule commands, let the children always remain under the care of their master.[1] Nor shall the master himself be allowed to be in company with a boy without a third person as witness; but let master and *schola*[2] go together in the accustomed manner wherever reason and necessity demand, reciting the psalms in silence and having received a blessing.[3] The brethren shall not gad about visiting the properties of the monastery unless either great necessity or reasonable discretion require it. Neither prelates nor subjects should ever think of presuming to be present at worldly feastings, unless perchance in case of unexpected hospitality when travelling.

12. By the grace of our Lord Jesus Christ we purpose to uphold by every means in our power those things which have been handed down to us from our Father Benedict, and which we have freely taken upon ourselves: victuals according to weight, measure and number; clothing, fasting, abstinence, watchings, silence, the virtue of obedience. Now, then, in fulfilment of our promise, solicitously and according to our ability and as the grace of the Holy Ghost shall dictate, we shall set forth plainly in writing those customs of the Holy Rule which have been constantly and everywhere observed both by the aforesaid Benedict and by his

---

[1] The *custos* (or *magister*, 20, 7) had charge of the children. Two *custodes* are found below (62, 13–15). The *magister scholae* mentioned below (48, 28) is probably the cantor. See p. 48 *n*. 4.

[2] The children of the cloister as a body; see 20, 7 and 22, 8. The *schola* mentioned below (44, 6 f.; 48, 22; 58, 13) would be the *schola cantorum* or body of official singers. See p. 48 *n*. 2.

[3] See p. 11 *n*. 4.

a sanctis sequacibus et imitatoribus suis partim cum magna examinis discussione iugi custoditis usu, praedicti regis monitu freti ac patrum imperiis confisi, sollicite, uti polliciti sumus, in quantum uires suppetent[a] et Spiritus Sancti gratia instinxerit, ad caritatiuam fraternae unitatis custodiam scribendo dilucidemus; ut ab ipso aeternae uitae remunerationem cuncti concorditer et gratulabunde conseruantes recipiant, *qui facit unanimes*, id est *unius moris*, *habitare in domo*,[1] ubi est rex Deus, Dei et uirginis filius,[2] qui cum Patre et Spiritu Sancto uiuit et regnat Deus in saecula saeculorum. Amen.

[a] suppetunt F

[1] Ps. lxvii. 7. *unanimes* is the reading of the Old Latin and Roman Psalters: *unius moris* of the Gallican.

[2] cf. *Vita Isidori*, *PL* lxxxii. 40: '. . . detestantes eos qui *Dei et virginis Filium* Dominum nostrum Iesum Christum . . . esse verum, cum Patre et Spiritu Sancto permanentem in aeternum negarent. . . .'

holy followers and imitators after deep consideration and examination. This we shall do in loving care for brotherly unity, relying on the advice of our King aforesaid and trusting in the commandments of our fathers; and we pray that all who observe these customs in peace and thanksgiving may receive the reward of eternal life from Him *Who maketh those of one mind*, that is, *of one way of life, to dwell in that house*[1] where God is King, even the Son of God, born of a Virgin,[2] Who with the Father and the Holy Ghost liveth and reigneth God for ever and ever. Amen.

13. [INCIPIVNT CAPITVLA

EXPLICVIT[b] CAPITVLA.][c]

[a] fremen T [b] *sic* [c] [ ] *om.* F

13. HERE THE CHAPTERS BEGIN

i OF THE MANNER IN WHICH THE CUSTOMS OF THE REGULAR LIFE OUGHT TO BE OBSERVED BY MONKS DAY AND NIGHT THROUGHOUT THE YEAR.

ii OF THE ORDER OF THE HYMNS IN WINTER; AND OF THE MANNER IN WHICH CERTAIN OTHER MONASTIC DUTIES SHALL BE FULFILLED.

iii OF THE MANNER IN WHICH THE VIGIL OF CHRISTMAS SHALL FITTINGLY BE KEPT; AND OF THE PERIOD FROM THAT SOLEMNITY UNTIL SEPTUAGESIMA.

iv OF THE ORDER OF THE REGULAR LIFE FROM SEPTUAGESIMA TO THE END OF LENT.

v OF THE MANNER IN WHICH THE DAY AND NIGHT OFFICE SHALL BE CARRIED OUT ON THE FEAST OF EASTER.

vi OF THE MANNER IN WHICH SATURDAY, THE OCTAVE OF EASTER, AND THE WHOLE OF SUMMER TIME SHALL BE KEPT.

vii OF THE MANNER IN WHICH THE BROTHER WHO IS CALLED *CIRCA* SHALL FULFIL HIS OFFICE.

viii OF THE MANNER IN WHICH THE DAY AND NIGHT OFFICE SHALL BE CARRIED OUT IN WHIT WEEK.

ix OF THE MANNER IN WHICH THE QUARTER TENSE DAYS SHALL BE KEPT.

x OF THE ORDER IN WHICH THE DAILY MAUNDY SHALL BE OFFERED TO THE POOR BY THE BRETHREN; AND IN WHAT MANNER THE ABBOT SHALL ENTERTAIN STRANGERS.

xi OF THE ORDER IN WHICH THE BRETHREN SHALL CARRY OUT THE *MUNDITIAE* ON SATURDAY; AND OF CERTAIN DUTIES WHICH THEY SHALL PERFORM FOR THE GOOD OF THEIR SOULS.

xii OF THE CARE OF A SICK BROTHER; AND OF THE MANNER IN WHICH THE DEAD SHALL BE COMMITTED TO THE EARTH.

HERE THE CHAPTERS END

CAPVT I

INCIPIT ORDO QVALITER[1] DIVRNIS SIVE NOCTVRNIS HORIS REGVLARIS MOS A MONACHIS PER ANNI CIRCVLVM[2] OBSERVARI CONVENIAT

14. A Kalendis enim Octobris [3] religiosorum morum Domini opitulante gratia exordium sumendo, omnia quae usu regulari et sanctorum patrum imitatione, spiritualia siue corporalia, humili ac necessario agenda sunt officio cum benedictione [4] incohentur. Hic igitur maximi muniminis mos pernecessarius, tam in modicis rebus quam magnis,[5] legitime a cunctis iugo regulae deditis iugi teneatur custodia, etiam si singuli quippiam incohaverint minime intermittatur: nihil proculdubio firmum ualidumue permanebit quod cuncticreantis [a] ac iusto moderamine creata gubernantis Christi benedictione carebit.

15. Ideoque [6] omni tempore *nocturnis horis cum ad opus diuinum* [*de lectulo*] [b] *surrexerit frater, primum sibi signum sanctae crucis imprimat per sanctae Trinitatis inuocationem. Deinde dicat uersum Domine labia mea aperies* [7]*:* dehinc *psalmum Deus in adiutorium meum intende* [8] *totum cum*

[a] cf. *cunctipotentis, omnicreatoris, omnipotentis*

[b] [ ] dilectulo T; oF bedde T (gloss)

[1] Doubtless suggested by the title of the famous eighth century tract, *Ordo Qualiter* (OQ).

[2] cf. *Lib. Antiph.*, *PL* lxxviii. 641: 'ordinatus *per circulum anni,*' and the second line of the fourth verse of the hymn *Christe Redemptor*: 'currens *per anni circulum.*'

[3] The period from October 1 to November 1 was regulated partly according to St Benedict's summer and partly according to his winter horarium.

[4] cf. *Rule*, Prologue 10–12: 'ut quidquid agendum inchoas bonum, ab eo perfici instantissima oratione deposcas,' and OQ, p. 38: 'nullum opus . . . sine permissione vel benedictione agere praesumant.' What this 'blessing' was we learn from *Warnfrid*, p. 335: 'Consuetudo fuit et est monachorum ut in omnibus operibus, tam spiritualibus quam temporalibus, cum aliquid incipiunt, terna vice hunc versiculum dicere [*Deus in*

CHAPTER I

HERE BEGINS THE ORDER[1] IN WHICH THE CUSTOMS OF THE REGULAR LIFE OUGHT TO BE OBSERVED BY MONKS DAY AND NIGHT THROUGHOUT THE YEAR[2]

14. Taking the Kalends of October[3] as a starting point, by the Lord's grace we begin this treatise on the observance of the monastic way of life with the reminder that every action, spiritual or temporal, to which, in the humble performance of our duty, we are bound by monastic custom and the imitation of the fathers, should be begun with a blessing.[4] This is a most necessary custom and a very great safeguard in small things as in great[5]; wherefore it should ever be kept as law by all those who live under the yoke of the Rule; nor may it ever be omitted even though perchance some work has already been begun. For it is beyond doubt that nothing can stand firm and strong which lacks the blessing of Christ Who created all things and Who rules justly that which he has created.

15. Therefore[6] at all times when a brother arises from bed in the night hours for the work of God, he shall first of all sign himself with the sign of the Holy Cross, invoking the Holy Trinity. Next, he shall say the verse, *Domine labia mea aperies*,[7] and then the whole of the psalm *Deus in adiutorium meum intende*[8] with the *Gloria*. After this, having provided for the necessity of nature,

---

adiutorium meum intende].' See 25, 7, where the Concordia is dealing specifically with the manual labour.

[5] 'Tam in modicis rebus quam magnis' occurs in Anglo-Saxon charters of the period.

[6] This section, from *nocturnis horis* down to the words *illius vox* is taken from OQ, pp. 26–7. See Introd., p. xlviii *n.* 2. [7] Ps. l. 17 [8] Ps. lxix

Gloria. Tunc prouideat sibi corpoream naturae necessitatem si ipsa hora indiguerit, *et sic ad oratorium festinando psallat psalmum Ad te Domine leuaui animam meam,*[1] *cum summa reuerentia et cautela intrans ut alios orantes non impediat: at tunc* flexis genibus *in loco congruo* et consueto, *in Domini conspectu effundat preces corde magis quam ore, ita ut illius uox,* per magnam animi compunctionem [et peccaminum suorum recordationem],[a] aures misericordis Domini efficaciter penetret ac scelerum omnium, Christi annuente gratia, ueniam obtineat.

16. In prima itaque oratione[2] decantet tres primos paenitentiae psalmos,[3] cum oratione dominica uti in sequentibus, pro seipso primum intercedendo; post hos orationem istam: *Gratias*[4] *tibi ago omnipotens Pater, qui me dignatus es in hac nocte custodire; deprecor clementiam tuam, misericors Domine, ut concedas mihi diem uenturum sic in tuo sancto seruitio peragere cum humilitate et discretione, ut tibi complaceat seruitus nostra. Per Dominum.* Inde ueniat ad secundam orationem ubi sequentes duos dicat psalmos[5] pro rege[6] et regina atque familiaribus,[7] cum oratione[8] *Deus qui caritatis dona per gratiam Sancti Spiritus tuorum cordibus fidelium infudisti; da famulis et famulabus tuis, pro quibus tuam deprecamur clementiam, salutem mentis et corporis ut te tota uirtute diligant et quae tibi placita sunt tota dilectione perficiant. Per Dominum.* Inde ad tertiam orationem ueniens, duos posteriores psalmos[9] pro

[a] [ ] *om.* F

[1] Ps. xxiv

[2] The psalms and collects given here went by the name of *Trina oratio*, a form of threefold prayer (in honour of the Blessed Trinity: 27, 12). It was performed three times daily: before Nocturns (as here), before Tierce (winter 20, 16), or Prime (summer: 54, 18), and after Compline (27, 14 f.); cf. AE, p. 175: 'Omni die ter faciendae sunt orationes tres in oratorio: tres in nocte audito primo signo, tres ante Primam tota aestate et in hieme ante Tertiam, tres post Completorium.' See DR, April 1948, pp. 191 ff.

[3] Pss. vi, xxxi, xxxvii

[4] This prayer is from OQ, p. 27

[5] Pss. l, ci

[6] For prayers for the Royal House see p. 14 *n.* 3

if at that time he must, he shall hasten to the oratory saying the psalm *Ad te Domine levavi animam meam*,[1] entering with the most profound reverence and taking the greatest care lest he disturb others at their prayers. Then, kneeling down in his proper and accustomed place, he shall pour forth in the Lord's sight prayer from the heart rather than from the lips, so that his voice, through deep compunction of heart and recollection of his misdeeds, may efficaciously reach the ears of the merciful Lord and, by the grace of Christ, obtain the pardon of all his sins.

16. For his first prayer,[2] then, he shall recite the first three Penitential psalms[3] with the *Pater noster*—which shall be repeated in the following prayers—for his own intentions. He shall then say this collect[4]: *I give thanks to Thee, Almighty Father, Who hast deigned to protect me this night: I beseech Thy clemency, merciful Lord, to grant me this day so to bear myself with humility and discretion in Thy holy service that our worship may please Thee. Through our Lord.* He shall now go on to the second prayer in which he shall recite the next two Penitential psalms[5] for the King,[6] Queen and benefactors[7] with this collect[8]: *O God Who hast poured forth the gifts of love into the hearts of thy faithful through the grace of the Holy Ghost, grant to Thy servants, for whom we beseech Thy clemency, health of mind and body that they may love Thee with all their strength, and with all their love do those things which are pleasing to Thee. Through our Lord.* Passing thence to the third prayer he shall say the last two Penitential psalms,[9] for the faithful

[7] The MSS of the Concordia draw no consistent distinction between *familiares* and *benefactores*. See 18, 14 and 27, 11. For *familiares* see Bishop, *Lit. Hist.*, p. 352, and *n.* 1 *ibid.*

[8] See collect from the 'Missa pro familiaribus' in *Greg* (Suppl.). It is found, as modified in the Concordia, also in *Jumièges* and *Leofr* (C). See again 18, 14.

[9] Pss. cxxix, cxlii

fidelibus defunctis decantet cum oratione[1] *Inueniant quaesumus Domine animae famulorum famularumque tuarum lucis aeternae consortium, qui in hac luce*[2] *positi tuum consecuti sunt sacramentum.*[a] *Per Dominum.*

17. Et donec quidem pueri introeunt[b] ecclesiam unum continuatim pulsetur tintinnabulum[3]; ipsi quoque pueri ingressi, ut Trinitatis reuerentia ab omnibus legitime teneatur, trina utantur oratione.[4] Finitis uero tribus orationibus a pueris, sonetur secundum signum,[5] residentibus cunctis in sedilibus[c] suis ordinatim atque canentibus quindecim psalmos graduum[6] singillatim,[d] trina partitione uti superiores septem, flectentes genua post quinque psalmos, facto signo a priore. Interim[e] autem pulsatis reliquis signis[7] atque finitis[f] eisdem psalmis, incipiant Nocturnam.

18. Peractis Nocturnis dicant duos psalmos, *Domine ne in furore tuo* (*i*)[8] et *Exaudiat te Dominus,*[9] [g] unum uidelicet pro rege specialiter, alterum uero pro rege et regina ac familiaribus, cum his collectis: [pro rege],[h] *Quaesumus*[10] *omnipotens Deus ut famulus tuus rex noster ille, qui tua miseratione suscepit regni gubernacula, uirtutum etiam omnium percipiat incrementa; quibus decenter ornatus, et*

[a] T (gloss) has 'halignesse.' [b] introeant T
[c] sedibus T [d] *om.* F [e] Iterim T
[f] + cum FT [g] ds̄ T [h] [ ] *om.* T

[1] See postcommunion of the 'Missa in agenda mortuorum plurimorum' in *Gelas, Greg* (Suppl.) and *Leofr* (A), all of which add to 'famulorum famularumque tuorum' the words 'omnium in Christo quiescentium.'

[2] cf. *Rule,* Prol. 113: '. . . et haec omnia per hanc *lucis vitam* vacat implere.'

[3] The small bell, used here to give the first signal for Nocturns. Three signals for this Office was probably the established rule: they are mentioned in *Warnfrid* (p. 261) and formed part of the Inda observance (C.M. iii., 154). The *tintinnabulum, secundum signum* and *interim autem pulsatis reliquis signis* of the Concordia correspond to the *minimum signum, sequens signum* and *interim alia signa pulsantur* of *Eins* (pp. 74 and 106).

[4] See 16, 1 above [5] The second signal for Nocturns

[6] Pss. cxix–cxxxiii. This devotion, like that of *Trina oratio,* goes back to Benedict of Aniane, whose monks, Ardo tells us (C.M. iii. p. 154), on

departed, with this collect[1]: *We beseech Thee O Lord that the souls of Thy servants may attain to the fellowship of eternal light who in the light of this life[2] have followed after holiness. Through our Lord.*

17. The little bell[3] shall be rung continuously until the children enter the church; and when they have all come in they too shall say the *Trina oratio*,[4] so that reverence to the Trinity shall be duly observed by all. When they have finished the *Trina oratio* the second bell[5] shall be rung and all, ranged in order in the stalls, shall recite the fifteen Gradual psalms,[6] one by one, in threefold division as the Penitential psalms were said, genuflecting at a sign from the prior after each set of five psalms. Meanwhile the remaining bells[7] shall be rung and, when the psalms have been ended, Nocturns shall be begun.

18. After Nocturns they shall say two psalms, *Domine ne in furore tuo* (*i*)[8] and *Exaudiat te Dominus*,[9] the first specially for the King, the other for the King, Queen and benefactors, with these collects: for the King: *We beseech*[10] *Thee, Almighty God, that Thy servant our King, N, who has received of Thy mercy the government of this realm, may obtain also an increase of all virtues, wherewith being fittingly adorned he may be able to avoid the evils of wickedness, to overcome his enemies and to attain to Thee Who art the*

---

entering the choir after the prayers before the altars (*Trina oratio*), used to say fifteen psalms in groups of five, before Nocturns. In the tenth century the custom was general; but an additional fifteen psalms (i.e., to the end of the Psalter, the last three counting as one), were said in winter, the Concordia and *Trèves* being the only important consuetudinaries to omit mention of the extra winter psalms. See DR, April 1948, pp. 194 ff.

[7] The third signal for Nocturns [8] Ps. vi [9] Ps. xix

[10] See collect of the ' Missa cotidiana pro rege ' in *Gelas* and *Leofr* (A). The Concordia form contains what would seem to be the earliest known example of the clause ' et hostem superare.' *Jumièges* agrees exactly with the Concordia.

uitiorum monstra deuitare et hostem superare et ad te qui uia ueritas et uita es gratiosus ualeat peruenire. Per Dominum nostrum. [Pro regina],[a] *Rege*[1] *quaesumus Domine famulam tuam illam et gratiae tuae in ea dona multiplica, ut ab omnibus libera offensis, et temporalibus non destituatur auxiliis et sempiternis gaudeat institutis. Per Dominum nostrum.* Pro rege et regina ac familiaribus,[b] *Deus*[2] *qui caritatis*[c] [*dona per gratiam Sancti Spiritus tuorum cordibus fidelium infudisti, da famulis et famulabus tuis pro quibus tuam deprecamur clementiam salutem mentis et corporis ut te tota uirtute diligant et quae tibi placita sunt tota dilectione perficiant. Per*].[d] Et sic finitis omnibus regularibus horis semper agatur.[3]

19. Post hos psalmos *paruissimum*, uti regula praecipit[4e] et tota aestate conuenit, fiat *interuallum*. Egressa schola cum magistro ad necessitudinis usum, ceteri, nisi qui indigent, in ecclesia orationibus dediti resideant. Post hoc sequantur diei Laudes[5]: post *Miserere mei Deus*[6] addant duos psalmos pro rege reginaque et familiaribus, *Beati quorum*[7] et *Inclina Domine* [*aurem tuam*],[8f] quibus finitis cantent antiphonam[9] de cruce, inde antiphonam de sancta Maria et de sancto cuius ueneratio in praesenti colitur ecclesia aut, si minus fuerit, de ipsius loci consecratione. Post quas eundum est ad

[a] [ ] *om.* T [b] benefactoribus T
[c] + req. in preced. folio T [d] [ ] *om.* T
[e] praecepit F [f] [ ] *om.* T

[1] See the 'Oratio super populum' for Sexagesima Sunday in *Gelas* and *Leofr* (A). *Leofr* (C) has the Concordia form as the postcommunion of the 'Missa pro regina.'

[2] See p. 12 *n.* 8.

[3] That is, two psalms, differing on each occasion, with the three collects mentioned above, were said for the King, Queen and benefactors after Nocturns, Matins, Tierce, Sext, None, Vespers, Compline but not, apparently, after Prime (see 19, 20). To these we must add the two psalms and one collect of *Trina oratio* said for the King, Queen and benefactors, the two psalms, *preces* and collect said for the King and Queen after the principal Mass (24, 9 f.) and the Morrow Mass usually said for the King (20, 27 f.). There is nothing like this in any other consuetudinary. See *Sources*, pp. 147–49.

Way the Truth and the Life. Through our Lord. For the Queen: *Direct,*[1] *we beseech Thee O Lord thy servant, N, and multiply in her Thy gifts that free from all offences she may never want for temporal help and may rejoice in everlasting ordinances. Through our Lord.* For the King, Queen and benefactors: *O God*[2] *Who hast poured forth the gifts of love into the hearts of Thy faithful through the grace of the Holy Ghost, grant to Thy servants, for whom we beseech Thy clemency, health of mind and body that they may love Thee with all their strength, and with all their love do those things that are pleasing to Thee. Through our Lord.* And they shall always do in like manner after each of the regular hours.[3]

19. After these psalms there shall be the very short interval which is laid down in the Rule[4] and is customary throughout the summer period. When the *schola*, with their master, leave the church for the necessity of nature, the rest, with the exception of those who may also be under the same necessity, shall remain in the church occupied with their prayers. Lauds[5] of the day follow, after which, in addition to the *Miserere*,[6] they shall say two psalms for the King, Queen and benefactors: *Beati quorum*[7] and *Inclina Domine aurem tuam*[8]; and when these are finished they shall sing the antiphons[9] of the Cross, of St Mary and of the saint whose name is honoured in that church or, if there be none such, of the dedication of that church. After these they shall

---

[4] *Rule* viii. 10–13. This summer interval was in force from Easter to November; cf. 54, 14. For the long winter interval see p. 26 *n.* 6.

[5] An early example of the use of this word instead of the more usual *matutinae* or *Laudes matutinales*. See again 19, 14; 29, 18; 31, 19.

[6] Ps. l. The use of this psalm after Matins, Vespers (25, 40) and Compline (27, 9) would seem to be peculiar to the Concordia.

[7] Ps. xxxi [8] Ps. lxxxv

[9] For these antiphons see also after Vespers (25, 42). They were omitted in Advent (29, 26).

Matutinales Laudes De Omnibus Sanctis,[1] decantando antiphonam ad uenerationem sancti cui porticus [2] ad quam itur dedicata est; post quas Laudes [3] Pro Defunctis. Quod si luce diei ut oportet finitum fuerit incipiant Primam absque tintinnabuli signo; sin autem, expectent lucem et pulsato signo congregentur ad Primam. Deinde finita Prima duos psalmos, *Domine ne in furore tuo* [a] *(ii)* [4] et *Miserere mei Deus* (*i*),[5] canant: primum pro carnis tentatione [6] cum precibus, *Proba nos Domine* [7] et *Non ueniat nobis pes superbiae*,[8] et collecta *Vre igne* [9]; sequentem uero pro defunctis fratribus cum collecta, *Inueniant quaesumus Domine*,[10] et prece *Animae fratrum nostrorum*.[b] Et sic, more solito, paenitentiae psalmos percurrant deuote interposito psalmo *Inclina Domine*.[11] His uero finitis subsequatur letania [12] quam uniuersi, more solito prostrati humiliter nullo excepto, signo pulsato compleant. Qua expleta, post orationem dominicam intercanitur psalmus *In te Domine speraui* (*ii*),[13] consequentibus precibus et orationibus; quibus finitis *uacent* fratres *lectioni usque* ad *horam secundam*,[14] secundum regulae praeceptum.

20. Tunc facto signo eant et se diurnalibus induant calceamentis; nullus [15] enim hoc debet praesumere

[a] *om.* F [b] *om.* F

[1] For the Offices Of All Saints and Of the Dead see Introd., p. xxxii.
[2] i.e., what would now be called a 'side chapel.'
[3] See 19, 5 [4] Ps. xxxvii [5] Ps. l
[6] The intentions prescribed here show that these cannot be the devotions for the Royal House, ordered to be said 'finitis omnibus regularibus horis' (18, 19). For the total of four psalms, the Penitential psalms, the Litany, and other devotions which follow Prime, cf. *Trèves*, p. 9: 'Post Primam pro defunctis abbatibus et temtacione tres psalmi quorum non estis ignari; hos itaque secuntur septem psalmi cum letania quae cantatur terraneus congregacione prostrata preter *In Te Domine speravi* adiungentes ceteras quoque oraciones multiplices.' No other consuetudinary agrees with the Concordia as regards the *four* psalms at this point.
[7] Ps. xxv 2 [8] Ps. xxxv 12
[9] See oratio of the 'Missa contra tentationem carnis' in Alcuin, *Lib. Sacr.*, *PL*, ci. 453. cf. *Jumièges* and *Leofr* (A).

go to Matins Of All Saints [1] singing an antiphon in honour of the saint to whom the chapel [2] to which they are bound is dedicated: there follow Lauds [3] Of the Dead. If this Office end at daybreak, as it should, they shall begin Prime without the little bell being rung: if not, they shall wait until dawn and then, at the sound of the bell, come together for Prime. When Prime is over they shall sing two psalms: *Domine ne in furore tuo* [4] (*ii*) and *Miserere mei Deus* (*i*),[5] the first against fleshly temptation [6] with the *preces*, *Proba nos Domine* [7] and *Non veniat nobis pes superbiae*,[8] and the collect *Ure igne* [9]; the second for departed brethren with the collect *Inveniant quaesumus Domine* [10] and the *Animae fratrum nostrorum*. Next they shall go through the Penitential psalms in the usual way, inserting, for the sake of devotion, the psalm *Inclina Domine*.[11] Then the bell shall ring for the Litany [12] at which all without exception shall humbly prostrate themselves as is the custom. After the *Pater noster*, the psalm *In te Domine speravi* (*ii*) [13] shall be sung together with the *preces* and collects. When all these are finished the brethren shall give themselves to reading until the second hour [14] according to the ordinance of the Rule.

20. When the bell is rung the brethren shall go and put on their day shoes: none[15] but the ministers should

---

[10] See p. 13 *n.* 1 [11] Ps. lxxxv

[12] See *Liber Vitae* (pp. 261 ff.) for a litany taken from an English MS of the middle of the eleventh century.

[13] Ps. lxx. This, the last of the four psalms said after Prime (see p. 15 *n.* 6.), is found after the litany (referred to in the previous note) between the *Pater* and the *preces* and prayers which follow.

[14] *Rule* xlviii. 23–25: 'A Kalendis autem Octobribus usque caput Quadragesimae, *usque* in *horam secundam* plenam *lectioni vacent*.' See Introd., p. xxxiii.

[15] cf. BB_1, C.M. ii. 2 (cf. *ibid.*, pp. 31 and 65): 'Post Primam namque nullus fratrum debet se calciare diurnalibus, nisi illi fratres quibus iniuncta est cura obedientiae.' For day and night shoes see also 27, 1 and 54, 17.

antequam illud audiatur signum, exceptis ministris, neque tunc ab aliquo intermittatur sine licentia ne praesumptione temeraria oboedientiae meritum lugubriter obnubilent. Dehinc psalmodiis dediti facies suas, uti mos est, lauent schola [1] uniuersa cum magistro et abbate; seniores uero unusquisque semotim, prout Deus in corda eorum diuino immiserit instinctu, silenter ac tota mentis intentione opus suum in his obsequiis, sicut in omnibus conuenit, sanctis orationibus decorando celebrent, horas canonicas [2] uel septem paenitentiae psalmos uel aliud quippiam spirituale ad tentationem diabolicam deuincendam psallendo [a]; sicque loti ueniant ad ecclesiam. Infantibus autem ecclesiam intrantibus, aedituus [3] primum sonet signum; peractis tribus a pueris oraminibus,[4] [b] uti prius a senioribus gestum fuerat, dispositi singuli in locis suis campana pulsata incipiant horam Tertiam, post cuius terminum dicant pro rege atque regina et benefactoribus suis psalmos *Vsquequo Domine* [5] et *Miserere mei Deus, miserere mei*,[6] subsequentibus praescriptis collectis. Inde Missam matutinalem celebrent ad quam secunda feria dexter offerat chorus, sinister ad principalem Missam: tertia rursum feria sinister offerat ad matutinalem, dexter ad principalem, sicque alternatim [c] in eo hebdomadam percurrant.[d] Eadem uero matutinalis Missa pro rege uel quacumque imminente necessitate celebretur.

[a] psallendum F [b] orationibus T [c] alternati T

[d] See *Eins*, p. 84 (cf. *Trèves*, pp. 47 and 53): 'Ad generalem vero missam secunda feria sinister chorus, tercia dexter, et suis vicibus sibi succedant usque ad Sabbatum.'

[1] See p. 8 *n.* 2.

[2] Used in the Rule (lxvii. 6) of the Office. Here it would probably mean the Roman or Secular, not the Benedictine Office. See p. 21 *n.* 2.

[3] Literally, keeper or overseer of the temple. This officer is met with also in *Trèves*. The Cluniac equivalent was *custos ecclesiae*. Both terms are found in *Eins*. For *aeditui* see p. 49 *n.* 4.

presume to do this before the bell is heard, nor fail to do so then without permission, lest the merit of obedience be sadly dimmed by his rashness and presumption. Next, the entire *schola*[1] with their master and the abbot shall wash their faces as is customary, intent on the psalms as they do so. As for the seniors, let each one separately, according as God suggests to his heart by His divine inspiration, silently and with the whole bent of his mind apply himself to his duty, sanctifying his acts of obedience, as he should everything, with holy prayers, chanting the canonical hours[2] or the seven Penitential psalms or any other spiritual prayer apt for driving away the temptation of the devil; and so, having washed, let them proceed to the church. As the children enter the church the sacrist[3] shall ring the first bell; and when they have said the *Trina oratio*[4] in the same way as the seniors have done, all shall take their places and the bell shall be rung for them to begin Tierce. After Tierce the brethren shall say for the King, Queen and benefactors the psalms *Usquequo Domine*[5] and *Miserere mei Deus, miserere mei*[6] with the appointed collects. They shall then celebrate the Morrow Mass, at which on Mondays the right hand choir shall make the offering, the left-hand choir offering at the principal Mass; while on Tuesdays the left-hand choir shall make the offering at the Morrow Mass, the right-hand choir doing so at the principal Mass. Thus the offering shall be made by alternate choirs throughout the week. The Morrow Mass itself shall be said for the King or for any pressing need.

---

[4] *Trina oratio.* See p. 12 *n.* 2.
[5] Ps. xii [6] Ps. lvi

21. *Hoc expleto,*[a] facto signo a priore,[1] *conuenientes ad Capitulum*[2] ipso praecedente, *uersa facie ad orientem salutent crucem et ceteris undique fratribus se* uultu inclinato *humilient;* cuius humiliationis ratio et *in omni conuentu* custodienda est. Tunc residentibus cunctis legatur martyrologium, quo dicto *surgentes* omnes *dicant uersum Pretiosa in conspectu Domini* cum oratione ac uersu *Deus in adiutorium meum intende,*[3] qui uersus tertio repetatur ab omnibus, *priore incipiente,* subiungentes *Gloria* et *flectentes genua* si tempus ita dictauerit. Dicente uero priore *Et ne nos inducas* surgant omnes erectoque uultu *dicant uersum Respice in seruos, subiungentes Gloria* humiliato capite. *Sequitur oratio Dirigere et sanctificare* et *Adiutorium nostrum in nomine Domini: qui fecit caelum et terram.* Iterum autem residentibus legatur regula uel, si dies festus fuerit, euangelium ipsius diei, de qua lectione a priore prout Dominus dederit dicatur.[b] Post hoc quicumque se reum alicuius culpae agnoscit, *ueniam* humiliter postulans *petat* indulgentiam. Omnis autem frater, pro quacumque causa increpatus[4] ab abbate uel a quolibet priore, antequam uerbum aliquod proferat ueniam petat. Et dum a priore interrogatus fuerit quae sit causa pro qua ueniam poscit, *respondeat* atque suam profiteatur culpam dicens *Mea culpa, domine;* dehinc iussus erigat se; nam si aliter egerit *culpabilis iudicabitur.* Quicumque enim increpatus a quolibet priore fuerit pro

[a] Most of this section (down to the words 'tribunal Christi statuant') is based on OQ (pp. 29 ff.).

[b] See *Eins,* p. 107 (cf. *Trèves,* p. 16): 'Itemque residentibus legitur regula vel in festis diebus omelia . . . et prior . . . faciat sermonem de presenti lectione.'

[1] In the Rule and in early monastic documents the word *prior* is frequently used for *abbas.*

[2] For the Chapter, or monastic parliament, see *Monastic Order,* 411 ff.

[3] Ps. lxix. 2

21. After the Morrow Mass, at a sign from the prior,[1] all shall come together for the Chapter,[2] the prior leading. Turning to the east they shall salute the Cross and with bared heads abase themselves before one another: this act of humility is to be observed whenever the brethren are assembled together. When the brethren are seated, the Martyrology shall be read; all shall then rise and say the verse *Pretiosa in conspectu Domini* with the collect and the verse *Deus in adiutorium meum intende*,[3] this verse being given out by the prior and said thrice, with the *Gloria* at the end, the brethren making a genuflection if the season of the year demands it. When the prior says *Et ne nos inducas* all shall rise, and, with unbowed heads, say the verse *Respice in servos*, adding the *Gloria* and bowing their heads. There follow the collect *Dirigere et sanctificare* and the *Adiutorium nostrum in nomine Domini: Qui fecit coelum et terram.* Then, all being seated again, the Rule or, on feast days, the Gospel of the day, shall be read and the prior shall explain what has been read according as the Lord shall inspire him. After this, any brother who is conscious of having committed some fault shall humbly ask forgiveness and indulgence. But a brother that is accused,[4] no matter for what reason, by the abbot or by one of the senior officials, shall prostrate himself before speaking. And when asked by the prior the reason for this, he shall answer by admitting his fault, saying *Mea culpa domine.* Then, when bidden, let him rise. If he acts in any other wise he shall be deemed guilty. Thus whoever,

---

[4] cf. *Rule* lxxi. 10 f.: 'Si quis autem frater pro quavis minima causa ab abbate vel a quocumque priore suo corripitur etc.'; and *Aix Capit.*, p. 118: 'Ut cum a quocumque priore suo increpatus quis eorum fuerit, Mea culpa primo dicat, etc.'

aliquo reatu, uel si quippiam in officinis [1] [a] excesserit, et non statim ueniam uti regula praecipit [2] postulauerit, *maiori subiaceat uindictae.*[3] Quanto enim quis se humiliauerit seseque *culpabilem* reddiderit, tanto *misericordius ac leuius a priore* debet iudicari; *necesse est enim* ut in omnibus neglegentiis nostris, id est *cogitationum, linguae* uel operum, *in praesenti uita per ueram confessionem* et humilem paenitudinem iudicemur, ne post istius uitae decursum *reos nos* ante tribunal Christi statuant. Finito hoc spiritualis purgaminis negotio quinque psalmos, qui post notantur,[4] pro defunctis fratribus decantent.

22. Ista uero omnia quae diximus post Tertiam his temporibus agenda, dominicis diebus omni tempore ante Tertiam agantur,[5] ita tamen ut fratrum unusquisque suae conscientiae reatum patri spirituali uel eius, si absens fuerit, uicario *per humilem* reuelet *confessionem.*[6] Si autem tanta fuerit multitudo ut ea die omnes ad confessionem uenire nequeant, sequenti die, secunda uidelicet feria, hoc idem impleant. Schola uero nullo modo hoc quamquam puerilis intermittat [b] sed ut senes, licet nondum tentationibus impugnata, consuete peragat. Qui autem aliis indiguerit diebus, tentatione aliqua animi uel corporis stimulatus, ad confessionis salubre remedium [7] deuotus non eo minus uenire differat.

[a] officiis T [b] intermittit F

[1] *officiis,* the reading of T, may be the correct one; the reference would then be to mistakes made in the Office, for which see *Rule* xlv.

[2] *Rule* xlvi. 1 f.: 'si quis . . . aliquid deliquerit aut fregerit quippiam aut perdiderit vel aliud quid excesserit ubiubi, et non veniens continuo ante abbatem vel congregationem, etc.' Cf. also *ibid.* xlv. 4 f.

[3] *Rule* xlv. 4 [4] See 25, 1

[5] That is, the weekday order (Tierce, Morrow Mass, Chapter) was reversed on Sundays (and feasts of twelve lessons, see p. 19 *n.* 1) throughout the year.

[6] cf. *Rule* vii. 134 (St Benedict's Fifth Degree of Humility). Here, in the Concordia, we must understand Sacramental Confession as distinguished from the disciplinary 'confession' connected with Chapter. AE (p. 176) says definitely that each monk makes his confession to the abbot; this is probably the meaning of 'patri spirituali . . . reuelat' in the

when rebuked by a superior for any fault or for anything done amiss in the workshops,[1] does not immediately prostrate himself as the Rule ordains,[2] must undergo the greater punishment.[3] Indeed, the more a monk humbles himself and accepts blame, the more mercifully and gently shall he be dealt with by the prior. For it is meet that in all our negligences, whether of thought, word or deed, we should be judged in this present life by sincere confession and humble penance lest, when this life is over, our sins declare us guilty before the judgment-seat of Christ. When this duty of spiritual purgation has been gone through, the five psalms set forth below [4] shall be said for departed brethren.

22. All that we have ordained to be carried out on week-days after Tierce shall on Sundays be arranged for [5] before Tierce; and this in such wise that each monk shall by humble confession [6] reveal the state of his conscience to his spiritual father or, if he be absent, to whomsoever acts in his place. And if the number of the brethren be such that all cannot make their confession on that day, let them do so on the next, that is, on Monday. Nor shall the *schola* even, on the score of their tender age, ever omit this duty but, although they are as yet untroubled by temptations, let them make their confession in the customary way as the elder brethren do. If, moreover, a brother, urged by some temptation of soul or body, needs to confess at any other time, let him by no means delay to have recourse to the healing remedy [7] of confession.

Concordia for, according to the *Rule* (xlix. 22) the abbot was the spiritual father of his monks.

[7] *Salubre remedium* is found in the various forms of the prayer used for the Blessing of Ashes at the absolution of penitents on Ash Wednesday. See, e.g., the prayer ' Precibus devotissimis om. s. Deus ' in the *Canterbury Benedictional* (HBS, p. 16). The expression occurs again below (27, 7) in connection with the *Confiteor* at Compline.

23. In diebus autem [a] festis,[1] ob taciturnitatis studiique obseruantiam, ita protendatur [2] Prima ut Capitulo facto matutinalique Missa celebrata, quae die dominica de Trinitate [3] celebranda est nisi alia festiua dies fuerit, si dies dominica fuerit mox accedant ad consecrationem conspersionis,[4] si alia quaelibet sollemnitas mox ad Tertiam. Interim enim dum ea Missa agitur, sequentis Missae ministri se induant et, Tertia peracta, mox signorum motu fidelem aduocantes plebem [5] missam incohent. Post pacem [6] fratres cotidie, nisi qui crimine se aliquo uel carnis fragilitate reos cognouerint, regulari studio prorsus intenti, Eucharistiam accipere [7] non renuant, attendentes illud quod ait beatus Augustinus in libro *De Verbis Domini*,[8] Quod, uidelicet, in oratione dominica non annotinum sed cotidianum deposcimus panem et, ut ipse inibi testatur, tam facile christianum posse carere ne unquam uitae pabulum, corpus uidelicet ac sanguinem Christi, accipiat quam non crebrius quam semel in anno degustet; *Sic*, inquiens, *uiue ut cotidie merearis accipere; qui cotidie non meretur accipere non meretur post annum accipere.*[9] Videant tamen ad cenam inuitati dominicam ne, crimine aliquo turpiter infecati, sine [b] confessione et paenitentia praesumant accedere et uitae alimenta sibi in damnationem conuertant, ut ait beatus apostolus, *Non diiudicantes corpus Domini.*[10]

[a] *om.* F [b] siue in T

[1] That Sundays as well as feasts of twelve lessons are to be understood here appears from the context and from AE (p. 176). Sundays and feasts of twelve lessons were given up to silence and reading. See p. 20 *n. b.*

[2] cf. AE, p. 176: 'Dominicis tamen diebus protendatur Prima et sedeat abbas in claustro' (the monks then go to Confession to him). For 'protendatur' cf. *Rule* xx. 10.

[3] See *Trèves*, p. 15 (cf. *Eins*, p. 103): '[The Morrow Mass] dominicis agitur de Trinitate, diebus exceptis sanctorum.'

[4] A procession through the cloister with blessed water: the modern *Asperges*. See 36, 2.

[5] i.e., the lay congregation

[6] The kiss of peace, given first to the deacon by the celebrant of the Mass, just before the Communion.

[7] These and further instructions towards the end of the paragraph

23. Now on feast days,[1] on account of the observance of silence and study, Prime shall be prolonged [2] so that when the brethren have finished the Chapter, and have celebrated the Morrow Mass—which on Sundays, if no feast day falls thereon, should be of the Trinity [3]—they shall go straightway to the blessing of holy water [4] on Sundays or to Tierce on any other solemnity. And while the Morrow Mass is being said the ministers of the following Mass shall vest and then, Tierce being said, the bells shall ring to call the faithful [5] together and the Mass shall be begun. When the *Pax* has been given,[6] the brethren, except those who are conscious of the guilt of sin or of weakness of the flesh, shall not hesitate, in their fervent practice of the exercises of the monastic state, to receive the Eucharist daily.[7] Let them bear in mind the words of the blessed Augustine in his book *Of the sayings of the Lord*,[8] namely, that in the Lord's Prayer we ask for daily not yearly bread. There also he declares that it is as easy for a Christian never to receive the food of life, that is the Body and Blood of Christ, as to receive it no more than once a year. *So live*, he says, *that you may be worthy to receive daily; he who is not worthy to receive daily is not worthy to receive once a year.*[9] Nevertheless, let those who are invited to the Lord's Supper beware lest, stained with the filth of sin, they dare to draw nigh to it unconfessed and unrepentant, and so turn the food of life into damnation unto themselves, *not*, as the blessed apostle says, *discerning the Body of the Lord.*[10]

---

are based on a sermon attributed to St Augustine: *In Dedic. Eccl.*, *PL* xxxix. 2166 f.

[8] So known to the authors of the Concordia. The attribution was general, but see following note.

[9] St Ambrose, *De Sacramentis*, v. iv. 25 (paraphrased in the previous sentence). AE (p. 176) cites this passage, from the Concordia, but would seem to enjoin Communion on Sundays and feasts only. See *Sources*, p. 157 f.

[10] 1 Cor. xi. 29

24. Finita Missa detur spatium quo ministri fratres [1] *propter communionem sanctam mixtum* [2] *accipiant*, ceteris omnibus interim in ecclesia residentibus; et facto signo agant orationem,[3] deinde Sextam: post Sextam eant ad mensam. Hoc semper attendendum ut sexta feria de cruce, sabbato de Sancta Maria, nisi festiua aliqua dies euenerit, Missa celebretur principalis.[4] Omnibus namque diebus, festiuis siue cotidianis, Missa finita dicatur pro rege psalmus *Exaudiat te Dominus*,[5] et pro [a] regina *Ad te leuaui*,[6] consequentibus precibus [7] et oratione congrua; uidelicet, ut post Missam eorum agatur memoria uti in Missa [8] et in omnibus aliis agitur horis. Tota enim die sollemni silentium [b] teneatur in claustro.

25. *Surgentes* [9] *a Capitulo* canant quinque psalmos pro defunctis: *Verba mea, Domine ne in furore tuo* [c] (*i*), *Dilexi quoniam, Credidi propter*,[d] *De profundis* [10]; post quos pulsetur tabula,[11] et si opus [12] non habuerint ad agendum dicatur tantum a priore *Benedicite*, ceteris respondentibus *Dominus;* si uero opus habuerint pulsata tabula prior auxilium prius inuocet diuinum dicens tertio *Deus in*

[a] *om.* F [b] cf. *Warnfrid*, p. 238 and *Vita Odonis PL* cxxxiii. 57
[c] *om.* T [d] *om.* T

[1] The weekly servers and readers (*septimanarii, hebdomadarii*): cf. *Rule* xxxv. 20–23: 'Septimanarii autem ante unam horam refectionis accipiant super statutam annonam singulos biberes et panem ut hora refectionis sine murmuratione et gravi labore serviant fratribus suis.'

[2] cf. *Rule* xxxviii. 23: 'Frater autem lector hebdomadarius *accipiat mixtum* priusquam incipiat legere, *propter communionem sanctam*.'

[3] This and similar expressions recur nine times (25, 18, 25 and 36; 27, 6; 29, 25; 33, 6; 34, 20; 35, 2; 36, 9), in connection with Tierce, Sext, None, Vespers and Compline. The prayer may have been the *Pater* only; cf. 33, 17 below: 'dicant orationem dominicam; dehinc sequatur Tertiam'; *Trèves*, p. 24: '[before Compline] intrant oratorium summo silentio . . . conventus flexis genibus dominica oratione studeant pariter humiliari'; *ibid.* p. 20 '[before None] oratio dominica.' But see *Eins*, p. 108: '[before Sext] dominicam orationem et alias preces.'

[4] See Alcuin, *Lib. Sacr. PL* ci. 445. The custom of celebrating the principal Mass on Fridays and Saturdays in honour of the Holy Cross and of Our Lady was probably traditional in the Anglo-Saxon Church. See Bishop, *Lit. Hist.*, p. 226, *n.* 1.

24. After the Mass there shall be an interval during which the ministers[1] shall partake of the *mixtum*,[2] on account of Holy Communion, while the rest of the brethren remain in the church. Then, when the bell is rung, there shall be a space for prayer[3]; Sext shall follow, after which they shall go to the refectory. It must always be borne in mind that the principal Mass[4] shall be of the Cross on Fridays and of St Mary on Saturdays, unless a feast day occurs. Every day, whether feast day or feria, after Mass there shall be said the psalm *Exaudiat te Dominus*[5] for the King, and the psalm *Ad te levavi*[6] for the Queen, with the *preces*[7] and the appointed prayer; so that after the Mass they may be remembered as they are in the Mass[8] and at all the other hours. Moreover there shall be silence in the cloister throughout the day on solemn feasts.

25. Rising[9] up from the Chapter the brethren shall sing five psalms for the dead: *Verba mea, Domine ne in furore tuo* (*i*), *Dilexi quoniam*, *Credidi propter*, and *De profundis*[10]; then the *tabula*[11] shall be struck, and if there is no work[12] to be done the prior shall say *Benedicite* only, to which they shall answer *Dominus*. But if there is work to be done, as soon as the *tabula* is struck the prior shall first of all call upon the divine assistance saying three times the *Deus in*

---

[5] Ps. xix [6] Ps. cxxii

[7] No *preces* are mentioned in 18, 1 f. above.

[8] That is, probably, the Morrow Mass, which was usually said for the Royal House.

[9] Here the weekday order is resumed. This section, down to the words 'agant orationem,' is based mainly on OQ (pp. 32–33).

[10] Pss. v, vi, cxiv, cxv, cxxix

[11] A wooden instrument used to give the signal for manual labour (here, 32, 19 and 55, 3), for the Maundy (26, 8), and in connection with deaths (65, 23 and 68, 3 and 21).

[12] i.e., manual labour. See Introd., p. xxxiv.

adiutorium meum intende,[1] fratribus hoc idem respondentibus, et *Gloria, Pater noster* et *Adiutorium nostrum*. Tunc cum decantatione canonici cursus et psalterii [2] operentur *quod eis iniungitur* usque dum audiunt [a] signum ad induendum. Quod cum audierint *disiungant se singuli* [b] ab operibus suis festinantes ad *Opus Dei*,[3] uenientesque ante oratorium benedicant Dominum qui eis adiutorium praestitit dicentes *Benedictus es Domine Deus*,[c] *qui adiuuasti me et consolatus es me* [4] ter, et *Gloria, Pater noster*, et *Adiutor⟨ium⟩* [d] et *Propitius sit nobis omnipotens Dominus*. Ingredientes autem ecclesiam agant orationem,[5] dehinc eant ad induendum se ministri; induti uero introeant chorum et pulsatis signis celebrent Sextam; finita Sexta canant psalmos [e] *Deus misereatur nostri* [6] et *Domine exaudi* (*i*),[7] pro rege reginaque et familiaribus, cum praescriptis collectis; sequitur letania [8] qua finita cantor [9] ad hoc more solito indutus Missae Officium incohet. Finita Missa pulsetur primum signum Nonae et agatur oratio. Post orationem eant fratres hebdomadarii[10] accipere mixtum,[11] sedentibus interim ceteris fratribus in ecclesia psalmodiae deditis donec iterum dato signo Nonam [f] agant; peracta Nona dicant pro rege reginaque et familiaribus psalmos *Qui regis Israhel* [12] [g] et *De* [h] *profundis* [13] cum praenotatis collectis; dehinc pergant ad mensam.[14] Surgentes

[a] audiant T

[b] cf. *Rule*, xlviii. 26–29: '. . . usque nonam omnes in opus suum laborent quod eis iniungitur. Facto autem primo signo nonae horae, deiungant (*disiungant se*: *Text. Recept.*) ab opera sua *singuli*. . . .'

[c] *om* T [d] adiutor . . . (erasure) F; adiutor T [e] psalmum F T

[f] See *Eins*, p. 99: '. . . celebrata missa, *pulsetur primum signum horae nonae*, et intervallo parvo facto, *dato* alio *signo*, cantent *nonam*.'

[g] *om*. F [h] *om*. F

[1] Ps. lxix. 2. In the *Rule* this verse is found before the day hours (xvii. 5), possibly before Matins (xi. 27: 'data benedictione') and, three times repeated, when the incoming server of the week enters on his duties (xxxv. 33 f.). It came to be used as a blessing before every action, spiritual or temporal (see p. 11 *n*. 4); above all it was used, as here, before the manual labour, when it was said thrice as in the *Rule, loc. cit.* See also 55, 15.

[2] See *Eins*, p. 108: '. . . post hos [the five psalms after chapter] vero incipiant *Romanum cursum per ordinem*, quo completo *psalterium* per

adiutorium meum intende,[1] which the brethren shall repeat after him, with the *Gloria*, *Pater noster* and *Adiutorium nostrum*. The brethren shall then perform the work laid upon them, reciting as they do so the Office of Canons and the Psalter[2] until the sound of the bell for vesting. At this, all shall cease from their work and hasten to the *Opus Dei*.[3] When they reach the oratory they shall bless the Lord for his assistance saying *Benedictus es Domine Deus, qui adiuvasti me et consolatus es me*[4] three times with the *Gloria*, *Pater noster*, *Adiutorium* and *Propitius sit nobis omnipotens Dominus*. On entering the church there shall be a space for prayer,[5] after which the ministers shall retire to vest: when vested they shall enter the choir and, the bells being rung, Sext shall be said. After Sext the brethren shall chant the psalms *Deus misereatur nostri*[6] and *Domine exaudi (i)*[7] for the King, Queen and benefactors, with the appointed collects. The Litany[8] follows; after which the cantor,[9] vested, as is customary for this, shall give out the Introit of the Mass. After Mass the first bell for None shall be rung and there shall be a space for prayer. The ministers of the week[10] shall then go to partake of the *mixtum*[11] while the rest of the brethren, intent on the psalms, remain in the church until None which shall be recited when the second bell has rung. After None they shall say for the King, Queen and benefactors the psalms *Qui regis Israel*[12] and *De profundis*,[13] with the collects as before, and shall then go to table.[14] Rising up from

---

totum.' The *canonicus cursus* was the Roman or Secular Office as distinguished from the Monastic. For the use of the Roman Office in Holy Week, etc., see p. 36 *n.* 3.

[3] St Benedict's term for the Divine Office

[4] In the *Rule* (xxxv. 30) this verse is said three times when the outgoing server has completed his week's duty.

[5] See p. 20 *n.* 3 [6] Ps. lxvi [7] Ps. ci [8] See p. 15 *n.* 12

[9] This officer is mentioned again (36, 21; 50, 12; 52, 7). See also 48, 25.

[10] See p. 20 *n.* 1 [11] See p. 20 *n.* 2 [12] Ps. lxxix [13] Ps. cxxix

[14] The one fasting meal *ad nonam*. See Introd., p. xxxv

a mensa *uacent lectioni aut psalmis* iuxta praeceptum regulae,[1] aut si aliquid fuerit agendum pulsetur tabula et cum benedictione quod agendum est incipiatur. Temperius [2] agatur Vespera cuius signa dum sonant, fratres post orationem in choro, iuniores quidem spiritualis lectionis studio singuli semotim occupati, seniores uero orationibus diuinis intenti, cum Domini gratia nusquam uagantes sedeant. Vesperam uero canentes duos, post *Miserere mei Deus*,[3] pro rege reginaque et familiaribus addant psalmos, id est, *Benedixisti Domine* [4] et *Domine exaudi* (*ii*).[5] Vesperi, sicut diximus superius [6] agendum de antiphonis post Matutinas, ita agatur post Vesperam ; et Vesperae De Omnibus Sanctis et Mortuorum, et Vigilia [7] usque Kalendas Nouembris; quibus peractis eant fratres ad exuendos [8] diurnales calceos induantque nocturnales.

26. Si sabbatum fuerit singuli pedes suos lauent, sintque uasa huic operi congrua singulis designata. Post pedum lauationem lauent etiam calceos [9] quibus expedierit; post haec, tintinnabulo a priore percusso, accedant cum gratiarum actione ad haurienda pocula.[10] Surgentes uero prior hunc uersum dicat, *Adiutorium nostrum:* ceteri respondeant *Qui fecit caelum* [*et terram*].[a] Inde pulsata tabula eant ad Mandatum secundum regulae edictum [11] quo peracto, facto signo, in ecclesia

[a] [ ] *om.* F

[1] *Rule* xlviii. 30 f.: 'post refectionem autem *vacent lectionibus suis aut psalmis.*' See Introd., p. xxxiii.

[2] 'Punctually' or even 'early,' in view of the additional Offices that followed Vespers

[3] Ps. l, see p. 14 *n.* 6 [4] Ps. lxxxiv [5] Ps. cxlii [6] See 19, 12

[7] i.e., Nocturns Of the Dead; cf. 29, 18 and 31, 13. For these Offices see Introd., p. xxxii. [8] See 20, 1.

[9] These 'washings' are the *munditiae* of the *Rule* (xxxv. 13 f.). See also 64, 2.

[10] Not to be confused with the *potus* after None, for which see p. 26 *n.* 3. Here the *poculum* is a measure of drink allowed, not only on Saturdays after the *munditiae* which followed Vespers, but on all week days, before the reading (*collatio*) with which Compline began, from September 14th

the meal, they shall give themselves to reading or to the psalms, according to the ordinance of the Rule[1]; if, however, there is work to be done, the *tabula* shall be struck, the blessing be given and the work begun. Vespers shall be celebrated punctually[2]; and while the bells are ringing the brethren shall not, by God's grace, wander about after the prayer has been said but shall sit in choir, the juniors apart, busily occupied with spiritual reading, the seniors intent on divine prayer. When Vespers have been sung they shall say, in addition to the *Miserere mei Deus*,[3] two psalms for the King, Queen and benefactors, namely, *Benedixisti Domine*[4] and *Domine exaudi* (*ii*).[5] Moreover,[6] they shall say after Vespers the same antiphons as those appointed to be said after Matins. There shall follow Vespers Of All Saints and Of the Dead and, until the Calends of November, Vigils[7] Of the Dead. When all these have been said, the brethren shall retire to exchange[8] their day shoes for night ones.

26. On Saturdays the brethren shall wash their feet, for which purpose each shall have a suitable basin. Having washed their feet, those who need to shall wash their shoes also.[9] Then the prior shall strike the little bell and all shall assemble with thanksgiving to draw their measure of drink.[10] When all have risen, the prior shall say this verse: *Adiutorium nostrum*, to which the brethren shall answer *Qui fecit coelum et terram;* whereupon, at the sound of the *tabula*, they shall go to the Maundy prescribed by the Rule.[11] After this the bell is

---

to Lent, when one fasting meal was taken *ad nonam* (and perhaps also from Lent to Easter, when the one meal was *ad vesperam*). See *Aix Capit.*, p. 118: 'Si necessitas poposcerit . . . post refectionem vespertinam (i.e., when the one meal was *ad nonam* or *ad vesperam*) etiam in Quadragesima . . . priusquam lectio Completorii legatur, bibant.' Cf. also *Eins*, p. 109.

[11] The weekly Maundy performed by the incoming and outgoing ministers of the week. See *Rule* xxxv. 15: 'pedes vero tam ipse qui egreditur quam ille qui intraturus est omnibus lavent.'

initietur collatio [1] rursumque dato tintinnabuli signo refectorium introeant caritatis gratia.[2] Quotiescumque fratribus caritas interim dum collatio legitur praebetur, lectione finita omnibusque surgentibus, dicat prior uersum [a] *Sit nomen Domini benedictum* [b] et *Benedicamus Domino*,[c] ceteris ut mos est respondentibus.[d]

27. Reliquis uero diebus post mutationem calceamentorum cum signo refectorium petant.[3] Exhinc similiter cum signo collationem adeant, quae prout tempus permiserit utque priori uisum fuerit [e] legatur, et sic accedant ad Completorium.[4] Signo namque Completorii pulsato agatur oratio; qua finita facto signo a priore inuicem sibi dent confessionis salubre remedium.[5] Finito Completorio et ad ultimum more solito *Miserere mei Deus* [6] decantato, addantur duo psalmi, *Deus in adiutorium meum* [7] et *Leuaui*,[8] pro rege ac regina et benefactoribus. Finito Completorio, ut in ultima hora canonica, uti in exordio, sanctae Trinitatis ac indiuiduae Vnitatis reuerentia legitime a seruulis exhibeatur catholicis, agant primum pueri tres orationes: post pueros agant fratres. In prima oratione canant psalmos: *Vsquequo Domine* [9] et *Iudica me Deus*, [10] [f] *Kyrie eleison, Pater noster* [g]; preces [11]: *Auerte faciem tuam, Cor mundum, Ne proicias me*,[h] *Redde mihi laetitiam;* oratio⟨nem⟩ [i]: *Gratias* [12] *tibi* [j] *ago Domine sancte Pater omnipotens aeterne Deus, Qui me dignatus es in hac die custodire*

[a] *om.* T [b] *om.* F [c] *om.* F
[d] cf. II Mach. i. 23: '*ceteris* autem *respondentibus*.'
[e] *om.* T [f] + et discerne F [g] + et T [h] *om.* T [i] *om.* T [j] *om.* F

[1] The reading which preceded Compline; cf. *Rule* xlii. 6 and 13

[2] The *caritas* was a special Saturday indulgence. It was probably carried out here much as on Maundy Thursday (42, 21 f.). *Trèves*, pp. 26 and 65 (cf. *Eins*, p. 98), comes very close to the Concordia.

[3] i.e., for the drink before collatio. See p. 22 *n.* 10.

[4] cf. Rule xlii. 13–15

[5] See OQ, p. 48: 'Tunc . . . intrent ad Completam et orent cum intentione mentis et *dent confessiones suas* alterutrum.' For *confessiones* as

rung and *collatio* [1] is begun in the church. When the little bell rings again, the brethren shall enter the refectory for *caritas*.[2] As often as *caritas* is provided for the brethren during the reading of the *collatio*, they shall all rise when the reading is finished, and the prior shall say the verse *Sit nomen Domini benedictum* and *Benedicamus Domino*, the brethren answering in the usual way.

27. On the remaining days of the week the brethren shall go to the refectory [3] when the bell is rung, having first changed their shoes. Thence, again at the sound of the bell, they shall go to the *collatio*, at which the length of the reading shall be as time allows and as seems good to the prior; and so to Compline.[4] When the bell is rung for Compline there shall be a space for prayer after which, at a sign from the prior, the brethren shall offer to one another the healing remedy of confession.[5] When Compline is over and the psalm *Miserere mei Deus* [6] has been said as usual, the brethren shall add two psalms, *Deus in adiutorium meum* [7] and *Levavi* [8] for the King, Queen and benefactors. Then, in order that God's faithful servants shall duly show their reverence for the Holy Trinity and Undivided Unity after the last canonical hour of the day as after the first, the *Trina oratio* shall be said, first by the children and then by the brethren. For the first prayer they shall say the psalms, *Usquequo Domine* [9] and *Iudica me Deus*,[10] *Kyrie eleison*, *Pater noster*, the *preces*,[11] *Averte faciem tuam*, *Cor mundum*, *Ne proiicias me*, *Redde mihi laetitiam* and this collect [12]: *I give Thee thanks O Holy Lord, Almighty Father, Eternal God, Who hast*

---

meaning the *Confiteor* at Compline see the *B Life* of Dunstan (*Memorials*, p. 15): '. . . post voces orationum iungentes capita sua in unum, quo *confessiones suas* solita consuetudine vicissim proderent.' See p. 18 *n.* 7.

[6] Ps. l. See p. 14 *n.* 6. [7] Ps. lxix. [8] Ps. cxx.

[9] Ps. xii. [10] Ps. xlii.

[11] Verses 11 to 14 from Ps. l [12] This prayer is from OQ, p. 48.

per tuam sanctam clementiam; concede mihi hanc noctem mundo corde et casto corpore sic peragere qualiter mane surgens gratum tibi seruitium persoluere possim. Per Dominum. In secunda oratione: *Deus misereatur nostri* [1] et [a] *Nisi Dominus,*[2] *Kyrie eleison, Pater noster,* easdem preces quas supra, collectam: *Deus,*[3] *cui omne cor patet et omnis uoluntas loquitur, et nullum latet secretum, purifica per infusionem Sancti Spiritus cogitationes cordis nostri ut perfecte te diligere et digne laudare mereamur. Per Dominum.* In tertia oratione: *De profundis,*[4] *Kyrie eleison, Pater noster,* easdem preces, collectam: *Omnipotens* [5] *mitissime Deus, qui sitienti populo fontem uiuentis aquae de petra produxisti, educ de cordis nostri duritia compunctionis lacrimas, ut peccata nostra plangere ualeamus remissionemque, te miserante, mereamur accipere. Per Dominum.* Alia: [b] *Omnipotens* [6] *mitissime Deus, respice propitius ad preces nostras et libera cor nostrum de malarum tentatione cogitationum, ut Spiritus Sancti dignum fieri habitaculum mereamur.*[c] *Per Dominum.* Quibus peractis, conspergantur [d] a sacerdote hebdomadario [e] benedicta aqua et sic pergant ad requiem suam cum summae tranquillitatis [f] reuerentia. Si quis uero post haec, deuotionis suae forte feruore, his diutius incumbere uoluerit, agat quidem haec; sed audito signo aeditui quo resides ad egrediendum uocat nil moretur. Omni etiam nocte post Completorium aspergatur domus requietionis eorum recumbentibus eis, *propter illusiones diabolicas.*[7]

[a] *om.* F [b] *om.* T [c] + inueniri T

[d] See *Eins,* p. 109: ' . . . et presbiter spargit singulos aqua benedicta sicque revertentur ad lectulos '; cf. *Trèves,* p. 25.

[e] See *Eins,* p. 82: ' Officium hebdomadarii . . . est . . . Post Completorium vero super fratres aquam benedictam spargere et per omnes illorum lectulos '; cf. *Trèves,* p. 48. [f] + uoce et T

[1] Ps. lxvi [2] Ps. cxxvi

[3] See collect from the ' Missa de gratia Sancti Spiritus postulanda ' in Alcuin, *Lib. Sacr., PL* ci. 446; cf. *Leofr* (A).

[4] Ps. cxxix

[5] See collect from ' Missa pro petitione lacrymarum ' in Alcuin, *op. cit.,* 448; cf. *Jumièges* and *Leofr* (A).

graciously deigned to protect me this day; grant me this night so to bear myself with cleanness of heart and chastity of body that when I rise in the morning I shall be enabled to pay worthy service to Thee. Through our Lord. For the second prayer let them say the psalms *Deus misereatur nostri*[1] and *Nisi Dominus*,[2] the *Kyrie eleison*, *Pater noster* and *preces* as before, with this collect: *O God*[3] *to whom every heart is open, every desire speaks and from Whom no secret is hid; cleanse by the outpouring of the Holy Ghost the thoughts of our hearts that we may deserve to love Thee perfectly and praise Thee worthily. Through our Lord.* For the third prayer let them say the psalm *De profundis*,[4] the *Kyrie eleison*, *Pater noster* and *preces* as before, with this collect: *Almighty*[5] *God, most lovingkind, Who didst bring forth from the rock a fountain of water for Thy thirsting people, do Thou bring forth from the hardness of our hearts tears of repentance that we may be able to weep for our sins and, by Thy mercy, deserve to obtain their forgiveness. Through our Lord.* Another collect: *Almighty God,*[6] *most lovingkind, hearken graciously to our prayers and deliver our hearts from the temptation of evil thoughts that we may deserve to become the dwelling place of the Holy Ghost. Through our Lord.* When these prayers are finished, the brethren shall be sprinkled with blessed water by the *hebdomadarius* and shall then go to their rest with reverence and the utmost quiet. If perchance a brother, in the fervour of his devotion, wishes to remain longer at his prayers, let him do so. But as soon as he hears the sacrist ring the bell to call forth those who have remained behind let him delay no longer. Moreover, every night after Compline, when the brethren are in bed, the dormitory shall be sprinkled, on account of the illusions of the evil one.[7]

---

[6] See collect from 'Missa pro tentatione cogitationum' in Alcuin, *op. cit.*, 450; cf. *Jumièges*, p. 257, and *Leofr* (A), p. 188.
[7] *Rule* liii. 10–11 (but in another context)

CAPVT II

QVALITER ORDO HYMNORVM TEMPORE HIEMALI CVSTODIATVR, ET CETERA QVAE REGVLARITER[1] AGENDA SVNT QVALITER AGANTVR

28. A Kalendis Nouembris [2] usque in Caput Quadragesimae [3] unus teneatur ordo hymnorum scilicet, ut in diebus breuioribus breuiores [4] dicantur hymni et in longioribus productiores etiam hymni psallantur; id est ut dominica uespera [5] *O Lux beata*,[6] ad Completorium *Christe qui lux es*, ad Nocturnas uero *Primo dierum*, et ad Matutinas dicatur *Aeterne rerum Conditor*. Omni uero tempore ad Nocturnam, ad Matutinam, ad Vesperam, exceptis dominicis et festiuitatibus sanctorum, feriales more solito teneantur; praeclaris uero et festiuis solemnitatibus, hymni competentes usu celebrentur consueto. Aduentus autem Domini, Quadragesimae ac Passionis tempore, hymni eiusdem cultus legitime decantentur ita tamen ut non hymni de ieiunio, sed hi qui per totum annum [7] currunt, dominicis diebus siue noctibus tempore quadragesimali [8] celebrentur.

29. Ab eisdem Kalendis concedatur fratribus accessus ignis dum necessitas compulerit et frigoris nimietas incubuerit; quod tamen sub silentio fiat; in refectorio

[1] i.e., according to the *Rule* [2] November 1 [3] Ash Wednesday

[4] 'Diebus breuioribus . . . longioribus' is obscure. Evidently the 'unus ordo hymnorum' concerns Sunday hymns only; for below (60, 5), having given a list of Sunday hymns for summer (i.e., from the Octave of Pentecost to the Calends of November), the Concordia directs that, after these Calends, longer hymns shall be said 'ut supradictum est.' Thus it is a question of the length of the Sunday hymns; and in fact the 'night' hymns, *Primo dierum*, *Aeterne rerum Conditor* and *Christe qui lux es* (winter), are longer than *Nocte surgentes*, *Ecce iam noctis* and *Te lucis ante terminum* (summer); while the day hymn, *O lux beata* (winter), is shorter than *Deus*

CHAPTER II

OF THE ORDER OF THE HYMNS IN WINTER; AND OF THE MANNER IN WHICH CERTAIN OTHER MONASTIC[1] DUTIES SHALL BE FULFILLED

28. From the Calends of November [2] until the beginning of Lent [3] one general rule for the distribution of the hymns shall be followed, namely, that on short days shorter hymns [4] shall be sung and on long days longer ones. Thus at the first Vespers [5] of Sunday *O lux beata* [6] shall be sung, at Compline *Christe qui lux es*, at Nocturns *Primo dierum* and at Matins *Aeterne rerum Conditor;* but at Nocturns, Matins and Vespers throughout the year, Sundays and saints' days excepted, the usual ferial hymns shall be said. On very great and festal solemnities proper hymns shall be sung according to custom. In Advent, Lent and Passion-tide hymns of the season shall duly be said, except on Sundays in Lent [8] when the hymns for both the day and the night Office shall be those in use throughout the year [7] and not the Lenten ones.

29. From the Calends of November aforesaid the brethren shall be allowed to have a fire as long as necessity demands and excess of cold lasts: silence, however, must be observed; nor may any such thing

---

Creator omnium (summer). For the Concordia Office hymns see *Sources,* pp. 151 ff.

[5] The First Vespers of the Sunday, as appears from AE, p. 177, and from the words 'Sabbato dominicalis Vesperae' (60, 1).

[6] The text of this and the three following hymns is in Stevenson, *Latin Hymns of the Anglo-Saxon Church* (Surtees Soc., Durham, 1851).

[7] But of course according to the winter arrangement

[8] That is, until Passion Sunday. See AE, p. 178.

uero hoc minime agatur. In huius quoque hiemis tempore propter nimiam imbrium asperitatem locus aptus fratribus designetur, cuius cacumenae [1][a] refugio hibernalis algoris et intemperiei aduersitas leuigetur; si autem temperies tranquilla fuerit claustro,[2] uti libuerit, cum Christi benedictione utantur. Quod si pro necessitate claustro egredientes domum, uti diximus, designatam ingressi fuerint, idem ibi mos in omnibus teneatur qui in claustro solito tenetur; nec quispiam ullo umquam tempore, claustrum deserens, domum praedictam ad commorandum praesumptuosus adeat uel, domum derelinquens, claustrum sine prioris licentia. Secundum uero regulae edictum [3] *temperius ad Vigiliam surgatur* ut, nocturnali peracto officio et psalmis supradictis [4] ac Vigilia Pro Defunctis cum Laudibus suis atque Matutinis De Omnibus Sanctis [5] expletis, fratribus psalmodiae deditis uel lectioni, secundum regulae praeceptum,[6] si qui indiguerint inseruientibus, interuallum usquequo lucescat cum magna uigilantia custodiatur. In lucis crepusculo, dum aedituus signum pulsauerit, ad ecclesiam uniuersi conueniant, factaque oratione Laudes psallant Matutinales quibus finitis dicant antiphonas supradictas [7] usque [b] Aduentum Domini: quas sequatur Prima et speciales psalmi [8] et

[a] caumene T [b] + ad T

[1] There is probably only one reading here, since that of T evidently = *ca⟨c⟩umene*. Though the reading is corrupt, the meaning is clear from T (gloss): 'fyꞃhyses.' For correction of the text, *caminea* (see W. Map, *De Nugis Curial.*, dist. I, ch. 25, where M. R. James translates *camineas suas* as 'their firesides') or *cheminea* (see Baxter and Johnson, *Med. Latin Word List*) may be suggested as useful pointers.

[2] A general term denoting that part of the monastic buildings in which the monk spent his day when not praying, eating or resting. See *Warnfrid*, p. 117.

[3] cf. *Rule*, xi. 1: 'Dominico die *temperius surgatur ad Vigilias*'—though this is Sundays only. The Concordia is freely cited in the *Vita Ethelwoldi auctore Wolstano*, *PL* cxxxvii. 97: 'Tempore quodam hiemali cum fratres

be permitted in the refectory. Thus in winter, when storms are harsh and bitter, a suitable room shall be set aside for the brethren wherein, by the fireside,[1] they may take refuge from the cold and bad weather. When, however, the weather is fair, they shall be free to use the cloister[2] with Christ's blessing. And when it is necessary for them to leave the cloister and to enter the special room of which we have spoken, there let them keep in all things the observance which is kept in the cloister. Nor shall anyone, at any time whatsoever, dare to leave the cloister and go to the aforesaid building in order to dwell therein, nor leave that building and frequent the cloister without the permission of the prior. According to the ordinance of the Rule[3] they shall rise in good time for Nocturns so that when that Office is over, and the psalms aforesaid[4] with Vigils and Lauds Of the Dead and Matins Of All Saints[5] have been gone through, the interval until dawn may be spent with great vigilance, the brethren being intent on psalms or, as they require it, reading, according to the ordinance of the Rule.[6] At early dawn when the sacrist rings the bell the brethren shall come together to the church and, after a space for prayer, shall sing Matins. When this is finished they shall say the antiphons aforesaid,[7] until Advent: Prime shall follow with the special psalms[8] and Litany. They shall then leave

---

secundum regulae edictum temperius ad Vigilias surgerent et nocturno *intervallo psalmodiae* et *lectioni inservirent*.'

[4] See 18, 1 [5] For these Offices see Introd., p. xxxii.

[6] cf. *Rule*, viii. 1–8: 'Hiemis tempore . . . octava hora noctis surgendum est . . . Quod vero restat post Vigilias, a fratribus qui psalterii vel lectionum aliquid indigent, meditationi inserviatur.' For the winter interval see Butler, *Benedictine Monachism*, p. 279. cf. *Eins*, p. 101.

[7] See 19, 8

[8] The Penitential psalms

letania. Post haec egrediantur ecclesiam atque in lectione sacra animae profectum meditentur usque ad tempus supradictum.[1]

30. In festiuitate Sancti Martini,[2] refectis fratribus, ecclesiam intrantibus agatur signum Nonae quod sequatur ipsa laus; quam Nonam non sequitur potus [3] usque ad Purificationem Sanctae Mariae. Sic agitur omnibus sollemnibus diebus; aliis uero diebus iuxta supradictum ordinem [4] faciant ut, uidelicet, facto signo calcient se et reliqua omnia sicut dictum [5] est impleant. In Aduentu Domini pinguedo [6] interdicitur, scilicet lardi, nisi festiuis diebus. Vespera cotidie more solito agatur ut, scilicet, suo tempore post mensam [7] celebretur.

[1] i.e., until *hora secunda*. See 19, 31

[2] November 11

[3] See again 55, 14. The drink after the Office of None took place whenever there were two meals, *prandium* and *cena*, i.e., on all Sundays and feasts of twelve lessons throughout the year, except from the feast of St Martin until Candlemas, and on ordinary days in summer (fast days presumably excepted) until September 14th. See *Epistola Pauli Diaconi ad Carolum Regem*, C.M., iii. p. 56 f. This custom was of general observance in the tenth century.

the church and meditate on holy reading for the profit of their souls until the time spoken of above.[1]

30. On the feast of St Martin,[2] as the brethren enter the church after the meal, the bell shall be rung and None shall follow. This Office is not again followed by *potus*[3] until the Purification of St Mary. This is the order for all solemnities; but on other days let the arrangement be as laid down above,[4] namely, that when the bell rings the brethren shall put on their shoes and carry out all other duties as has been said.[5] In Advent *pinguedo*,[6] that is, lard, is forbidden except on feast days. Vespers shall be said daily in the usual way, that is to say, in its proper place after the meal.[7]

---

[4] The reference is probably to the section beginning 'secundum uero regulae edictum' (29, 16).

[5] See 20, 1 f.

[6] The *Aix Capitula*, p. 142, forbade *pinguedo* only on the last eight days before Christmas. The earliest Cluniac customs, B B_1 C, forbade *adeps* or *sagina* (the corresponding Cluniac terms) only on Mondays, Wednesdays and Fridays in Advent, but *Farfa* agrees with the Concordia. See *Sources*, p. 276.

[7] The one fasting meal *ad nonam*. See Introd., p. xxxv.

CAPVT III

QVALITER VIGILIA NATALIS DOMINI ET AB EADEM SOLLEMNITATE VSQVE IN SEPTVAGESIMAM AGI CONVENIAT

31. Vigilia Natalis Domini, dum eiusdem natalis mentio a lectore recitetur in capitulo, omnes pariter surgentes genua flectent, gratias agentes propter eius ineffabilem pietatem qua mundum a laqueis diaboli redempturus descendit. Sabbato quoque Sancto Paschae, dum a puero *Resurrectio Domini Nostri Ihesu Christi* legitur, quamquam in martyrologio [1] id non habetur, propter eius gloriosissimi uictoriam triumphi qua, destructis Herebi claustris, secum fideles quosque in caelos aduexit, nobis etiam rediuiuis spem ascendendi concessit,[2] uniformiter agatur. Vespere [a] canantur antiphonae congruae de ipsa completione temporis [3] ad psalmos. In cuius noctis Vigilia [4] in quarto responsorio, ut honorificentius agatur, duo simul cantent; euangelium post *Te Deum laudamus* ab abbate [5] more solito legatur; dicta oratione, sub silentio egrediantur ministri ut calcient se, lauent et induant sub festinatione, omnibusque

[a] For the next few sentences cf. CCCC 190 (see Introd., p. lvii), p. 214: 'Vespere natale Domini canantur antiphonae congruae de ipsa temporis completione ad psalmos. In cuius noctis vigiliis evangelium post Te Deum laudamus a sacerdote more solito legatur et oratio dicatur. Omnibusque signis motis agatur missa. Post haec matutinales laudes quas sequatur missa matutinalis cum in crepusculo aurora diei eluxerit.'

[1] The reading of the Martyrology at the daily Chapter (21, 5) began with the announcement of the feast of the following day. The special solemnity here described was of general observance in the tenth century, but the corresponding announcement of the feast of Easter, on Holy Saturday *when the Martyrology itself was not read*, seems to be peculiar to the Concordia and *Fleury*. See *Sources*, p. 278.

[2] cf. the *Benedictio de Resurrectione* in *Greg*, p. 250: '*spem* resurgendi *concessit*.'

CHAPTER III

OF THE MANNER IN WHICH THE VIGIL OF CHRISTMAS SHALL FITTINGLY BE KEPT AND OF THE PERIOD FROM THAT SOLEMNITY UNTIL SEPTUAGESIMA

31. On the Vigil of Christmas, when the feast itself is announced in Chapter by the reader, the brethren shall all rise together and then genuflect, giving thanks for the unspeakable lovingkindness of our Lord Who came down to redeem the world from the snares of the devil. They shall do in like manner on Holy Saturday when one of the children reads out 'the Resurrection of our Lord Jesus Christ'—though this is not laid down in the Martyrology [1]—in honour of the glorious triumph of the victory by which, having overthrown the gates of hell, He drew with Him into the heavens certain of His faithful ones and gave [2] to us, newly restored to life, the hope of ascending thither. At Vespers the psalms shall be sung with proper antiphons suitable to the fullness of time.[3] At Nocturns [4] on Christmas night the fourth respond shall, for extra solemnity, be sung by two cantors. After the *Te Deum laudamus* the gospel shall be read by the abbot,[5] as is usual; and when the prayer has been said the ministers shall go out silently, change their shoes, wash and vest quickly; then all the bells shall

---

[3] The monastic antiphonars of the X-XI centuries vary as to the Vesper antiphons of Christmas. The wording of the Concordia suggests those found in the Worcester Antiphonar : Rex pacificus, Scitote, *Completi sunt* dies, Ecce *completa sunt.*

[4] i.e., Nocturns of the day as in 29, 16. Elsewhere in the Concordia *Vigilia* always refers to Nocturns Of the Dead.

[5] *Rule* xi. 20–23: 'Post quartum autem responsorium incipiat abbas hymnum *Te Deum laudamus.* Quo perdicto, legat abbas . . . de Evangelia.'

signis motis agatur Missa.[1] Post haec, Laudes Matutinales; his finitis incipiant Laudes De Omnibus Sanctis more solito [2] [si nondum diei aurora eluxerit] [a]; si autem eluxerit, post Missam celebrentur matutinalem [3] quae in [b] lucis crepusculo celebranda est. Dehinc tempore opportuno, signo pulsato, canant Primam. Finita Prima uenientes ad Capitulum, post cetera spiritualis aedificationis colloquia,[4] petant humili deuotione omnes fratres ueniam [c] ab abbate, qui *uices Christi* [5] *agit*, postulantes multiplicium indulgentiam excessuum dicentes *Confiteor;* et abbas respondeat *Misereatur.* Demum ipse abbas solotenus se prosternens eadem a fratribus petat.[6] Idem modus confessionis [7] prima Paschalis sollemnitatis die ita agatur. Capitulo facto et psalmis [8] dictis induant se omnes ut sint ornati [9] omnes ad Tertiam. Ad Vesperam ipsius diei dicantur antiphonae *Tecum principium* [10] et reliquae; reliquis uero tribus diebus [11] dicantur antiphonae de ipsis sanctis cum psalmis ipsi sollemnitati competentibus.[12] His peractis rursum repetatur *Tecum principium* usque Octauas Domini.

32. His autem diebus inter Innocentium festiuitatem et Octauas Domini, quia *Gloria in excelsis Deo* ob tantae

[a] [ ] *om.* T [b] *om.* F [c] *om.* T

[1] The first Mass, *in nocte*

[2] *More solito*, Matins Of All Saints would have been preceded by Matins Of the Dead. See Introd., p. xxxii.

[3] The second Mass, *in aurora*

[4] The customary Chapter conference on feast days. See 21, 16.

[5] cf. *Rule* ii. 3–4: '*Christi* enim *agere vices* in monasterio creditur'; and lxiii. 29: 'abbas autem, quia *vices Christi* creditur *agere*.'

[6] See *Trèves*, p. 57: 'In die sancto Cenae Domini abbas ad capitulum sermonem faciat, et ut iterum confessionem de neglegentiis suis faciant admoneat. Deinde ipse surgat et ad pedes se omnium fratrum provolvat ut veniam neglegentiarum suarum a Deo sibi postulent, et idem in vigiliis Natalis Domini faciat.' The parallel is unique.

[7] See previous note and p. 38 *n.* 6. For the apparent discrepancy between the 'first day of the Easter solemnity' (Concordia) and 'Maundy Thursday' (*Trèves*), see *Sources*, p. 283.

[8] The five psalms for the dead. See 25, 1.

peal and the Mass [1] shall be celebrated. Matins shall follow, after which, if day has not yet dawned, Lauds Of All Saints shall be begun in the usual way [2]; if, however, it is already daybreak, that Office shall be said after the Morrow Mass [3] which must itself be said in the early dawn. Then, at the proper time, when the bell rings the brethren shall sing Prime. After Prime they shall assemble for Chapter at which, when words of spiritual edification have been spoken,[4] the brethren shall all, with lowly devotion, beg pardon of the abbot, who takes the place of Christ,[5] and ask forgiveness of their many failings, saying the *Confiteor*. To this the abbot shall answer *Misereatur* and then, prostrate on the ground, he himself shall ask pardon [6] of the brethren. The same manner of confession [7] shall be observed again on the first day of the Paschal feast. When Chapter is over and the psalms [8] have been said, all shall vest [9] in readiness for Tierce. At Vespers of the Day the antiphons *Tecum principium* [10] and the rest shall be said; but on the next three days [11] the antiphons shall be of those saints whose feasts occur and the psalms shall be those appropriate to the solemnity of Christmas.[12] After these days *Tecum principium* shall be repeated until the Octave day of Christmas.

32. On these days between the feast of the Innocents and the Octave of Christmas, since the *Gloria in excelsis*

---

[9] Vested, ready for the third Mass *in die*

[10] *Tecum principium, Redemptionem, Exortum est, Apud Dominum* are the Antiphons given in the Worcester Antiphonar.

[11] St Stephen, St John and Holy Innocents. The feast of St Silvester is not mentioned here or in AE (p. 179). See *Sources*, p. 145 *n.* 2.

[12] The Christmas Vesper psalms if, as is likely, *ipsi sollemnitati* refers to the feast of Christmas (cf. *tantae festiuitatis*, 32, 2). Note that the context refers only to the Vesper Offices.

festiuitatis honorificentiam ad Missam celebratur, ad Nocturnam et ad Vesperam uti ad Missam, sicut in usum huius patriae [1] indigenae tenent, omnia signa pulsentur; nam honestos huius patriae mores ad Deum pertinentes, quos ueterum usu didicimus, nullo modo abicere sed undique, uti diximus, corroborare decreuimus. Ad Matutinas uero ob rem praedictam,[2] licet *Te Deum laudamus* non canatur et euangelium minime festiuo more legatur, cerei tamen accendantur et signa pulsentur omnia et turibulum turificando deportetur. Hinc usque Epiphaniam Domini psalmi ad Vesperam ad feriam pertinentes cum antiphonis dicantur. In Vigilia Epiphaniae Domini ieiunium minime exsequitur. Ad psalmos ipsius Vesperae antiphonae dicantur de eadem sollemnitate. Ceteris diebus post Octauas Domini et Epiphaniorum primum diem, [et post Primam agatur [a] Missa matutinalis] [b] et tabula [3] post Capitulum pulsatur et obedientia [4] agitur et signa simul non pulsantur nec *Gloria in excelsis Deo* canitur, nisi alia festiuitas interuenerit, usque octauum diem qui sollemniter cum duodecim lectionibus celebratur. Ab ea die usque Caput Quadragesimae [5] suprascriptus ordo [6] teneatur.

33. In Purificatione [7] Sanctae Mariae sint cerei ordinati in ecclesia [8] ad quam fratres ire debent ut

[a] for *agitur*, perhaps; cf. context. [b] [ ] *om.* F

[1] Some native custom is indicated here. But only in one particular can the independence of the Concordia be established with certainty: the ringing of all bells at Nocturns. See *Sources*, pp. 144 ff.

[2] The reference is either to the *Gloria in excelsis* at Mass or to the retention of native custom noted above.

[3] See p. 20 *n.* 11

[4] That is, manual labour; cf. 40, 6.

[5] The beginning of Lent

[6] See previous sentence

[7] The Concordia differs from the Cluniac consuetudinaries and from *Eins* on at least three points of detail: the prayer *Erudi* is said when the return procession reaches the church doors; there is no mention of the pealing of bells or of the distribution of cappae; Tierce is said at the end

Deo is said at Mass on account of the solemnity of such a feast, all the bells shall ring at Nocturns and Vespers as at Mass, as is the custom among the people of this country.[1] For we have ordained that the goodly religious customs of this land, which we have learned from our fathers before us, be in no wise cast off but confirmed on all hands. For the same reason [2] candles shall be lit at Matins and all the bells shall peal and the thurible shall be carried round although the *Te Deum laudamus* is not sung nor the gospel read in the manner of a feast day. From the Octave of Christmas until the Epiphany of the Lord the psalms at Vespers shall be the ferial ones with their antiphons. On the Vigil of the Epiphany the fast shall not be observed. At Vespers the antiphons to the psalms shall be of the feast. On other days after the Octave of Christmas and after the first day within the Octave of the Epiphany the Morrow Mass shall be said after Prime, the *tabula* [3] shall be struck after Chapter and work [4] shall be done; the bells, however, shall not peal nor shall the *Gloria* be sung unless some feast occurs; but the Octave day of the Epiphany shall be solemnly celebrated with twelve lessons. From then onwards until Ash Wednesday [5] the order given above [6] shall be observed.

33. On the Purification [7] of St Mary candles shall be set out ready in the church [8] to which the brethren are to

---

of the return procession, immediately before the Mass (see *Sources*, p. 154 f.). CCCC 190 cites the Concordia from 'In Purificatione' to 'post oblationem ea sacerdoti offerant.' *Jumièges* (p. 159) and the *Canterbury Benedictional* (pp. 81 ff.), both contain some of the rubrical directions of the Concordia. The rites of Candlemas are referred to in Bede (*De Rat. Temp.* xii.). For the story of the miracle that took place on Candlemas Day before Dunstan's birth see *Memorials*, p. 54.

[8] For processions to another church, through the streets, etc., see Bede, *loc. cit.*; the *Ordo Officii in Domo S. Benedicti*, C.M., iii. p. 19; the Cluniac consuetudinaries, *Eins* (p. 102), and *Angilbert's Ordo* (see Bishop, *Lit. Hist.*, p. 321 f.).

inde petant luminaria. Euntes autem silenter incedant, psalmodiae dediti, et omnes albis induti si fieri potest uel aeris permiserit temperies; et intrantes ecclesiam agant orationem cum antiphona [1] et collecta ad uenerationem ipsius sancti cui ecclesia ipsa ad quam itur dedicata est. Deinde abbas stola et cappa [2] indutus benedicat candelas et conspergat aqua benedicta et turificet et sic, accepto cereo ab aedituo, psallentibus [3] cunctis, accipiant singuli singulas [a] acceptasque accendant. Inde reuertentes canant antiphonas quae adsunt [4] usquequo ueniant ante portam ubi, decantata antiphona *Responsum accepit Symeon,*[5] dicatur oratio *Erudi quaesumus Domine,*[6] post quam ingrediantur ecclesiam canentes responsorium *Cum inducerent Puerum.*[7] Hoc decantato dicant orationem dominicam [8]; dehinc sequatur Tertia qua finita, si processionem induti non egerunt, induant se et Missam celebrantes teneant luminaria in manibus donec post oblationem ea sacerdoti offerant.[9]

[a] *candelas* is understood

[1] This detail appears to be peculiar to the Concordia.

[2] The cope is mentioned again (51, 6).

[3] The chants accompanying the distribution of candles are given in the *Canterbury Benedictional* as *Puer Iesu, Lumen ad revelationem* and *Nunc dimittis.*

[4] i.e., in the Mass Antiphonar: *Adorna thalamum* with its verses, as in *Lib. Ant., PL* lxxviii. and elsewhere.

[5] From Luke ii. 26; it is found in all versions of this rite.

[6] See *Greg,* p. 22.

go to get their lights. On the way thither they shall walk in silence, occupied with the psalms; and all shall be vested in albs if this is possible and if the weather permits. On entering the church, having prayed awhile, they shall say the antiphon [1] and collect in honour of the saint to whom this same church is dedicated. Then the abbot, vested in stole and cope,[2] shall bless the candles, sprinkling them with holy water and incensing them. When the abbot has received his candle from the doorkeeper, the chanting [3] shall begin and the brethren shall receive and light their candles. During the return procession they shall sing the appointed antiphons [4] until they reach the church doors; then, having sung the antiphon *Responsum accepit Simeon*,[5] with the collect *Erudi quaesumus Domine*,[6] they shall enter the church singing the respond *Cum inducerent Puerum*.[7] Next they shall say the Lord's prayer,[8] and Tierce shall follow; after which, if the brethren were not vested for the procession, they shall vest for the Mass during which they shall hold their lighted candles in their hands until after the Offertory, when they shall offer [9] them to the priest.

---

[7] From Luke ii. 27; found in all versions of this rite.

[8] See 24, 4.

[9] An illustration of the ' offering ' made at Mass: these candles would be used in the church services.

CAPVT IV

QVI REGVLARIS ORDO A SEPTVAGESIMA TOTA QVADRAGESIMA CVSTODIATVR

34. In Septuagesima pinguedo intermittatur usque in Quinquagesimam, a Quinquagesima uero quadragesimalem teneant abstinentiam [1] more solito. A Septuagesima uero [a] finitis tribus lectionibus, sex nocturnae posterioris psalmi, uti priores, cum tribus antiphonis [2] ex ipsorum psalmorum concentu editis, usque ad Cenam Domini cum summa diligentia decantentur. A Capite Ieiunii,[3] quarta et sexta feria processionem [4] custodiant usque in Cenam Domini et ab Octauis Pentecostes usque ad Kalendas Octobris. Cuius ordo processionis ita agatur: quarta feria [5] Capitis Ieiunii, Nona decantata, abbas stola ornatus benedicat cineres; quibus benedictis eat ipse abbas et imponat capitibus singulorum, quia eius est paenitentiam illis imponere, canentes interim antiphonam *Exaudi nos Domine*, psalmum *Saluum me fac Deus* (ii) [6] et *Gloria*, *Kyrie eleison*, *Pater noster*, psalmum *Deus misereatur nostri* [7] [b] et preces [c] et collectam. Tunc uadant quo ire [8] habent canentes antiphonas [9]

[a] autem T [b] *om.* F

[c] CCCC 190 has ‘preces, *Peccavimus Dn̄e ; Adiuva nos*’.

[1] That is, according to AE (p. 181), abstinence from foods made of milk or eggs. It was usual, in the tenth century, for monks to give up *pinguedo* in Septuagesima and to begin the full Lenten abstinence in Quinquagesima; cf. *Eins*, p. 103: ‘In Septuagesima pinguedo . . . dimittatur, in Quinquagesima ova et caseum’; and *Trèves*, p. 54: ‘Multi a Septuagesima . . . abstinent a lacticiniis, nos vero . . . a Quinquagesima abstinere incipimus.’ *Verdun* (p. 115) furnishes an example of the *multi* mentioned by *Trèves*. The *Aix Capit.* (p. 142) forbade *pinguedo* only from Quinquagesima.

[2] AE (p. 181) gives these antiphons for each day of the week.

[3] The beginning of the strict Lenten fast: Ash Wednesday.

[4] The Lenten processions, as well as those on Wednesdays and Fridays from the Octave of Pentecost to October, are found in most of the consuetudinaries of the X-XI and later centuries. They were carried out as on Ash Wednesday, the Concordia alone directing that the *Exaudi* should be said on Ash Wednesday only, and the *Exsurge* on the other days.

CHAPTER IV

OF THE ORDER OF THE REGULAR LIFE FROM SEPTUAGESIMA TO THE END OF LENT

34. From Septuagesima until Quinquagesima *pinguedo* shall be given up, and from Quinquagesima the brethren shall observe the Lenten abstinence[1] in the accustomed way. From Septuagesima until Maundy Thursday, when the three lessons have been read, the six psalms of the second nocturn, like those of the first, shall be most carefully sung with three antiphons[2] taken from the psalms themselves. On Wednesdays and Fridays from the beginning of Lent[3] until Maundy Thursday and from the Octave of Pentecost until the Calends of October processions[4] shall be held. The order of these processions shall be as follows: on Ash Wednesday,[5] when None has been sung, the abbot, wearing a stole, shall bless the ashes and shall then lay the blessed ashes on the head of each brother; for to him it belongs to impose penance on his monks. Meanwhile the antiphon *Exaudi nos Domine* shall be sung with the psalm *Salvum me fac Deus (ii)*,[6] the *Gloria*, *Kyrie eleison*, *Pater noster*, the psalm *Deus misereatur nostri*,[7] *preces* and collect. They shall then proceed whithersoever they should,[8] singing the antiphons[9] which are in

---

[5] i.e., Ash Wednesday. The Concordia differs from other consuetudinaries in several particulars: the ceremonies take place after None; the abbot blesses the ashes; there is no mention of the procession being made barefoot. The chants and prayers during the blessing of the ashes (*Exaudi*, *Saluum*, *Kyrie*, etc.) are as in Martène's ' Mozarabic Missal ', the *Canterbury Benedictional* agreeing with the Concordia. The Litany during the return procession was general. See *Sources*, p. 155. CCCC 190 cites a great part of the Concordia here verbatim.

[6] Ps. lxviii [7] Ps. lxvi [8] That is, to another church

[9] Probably *Immutemur* and *Iuxta vestibulum*, as in, e.g., *Lib. Ant.*, *PL* lxxviii. 657, the *Wulfstan Collectar* and CCCC 190.

quae in Antiphonario[1] continentur; uenientes ad ecclesiam quo eunt iterum[2] agant orationem et, post antiphonam de sancto et psalmum *Ad te leuaui oculos*[3] et preces et orationem, ibi incipientes letaniam reuertantur ad matrem ecclesiam ac dehinc, more solito, agatur Missa. Iste ordo processionis semper teneatur quotiens processio agitur; sed aliis temporibus semper antiphona *Exsurge Domine* dicatur prima cum psalmo et *Gloria*. His peractis induant se ministri altaris postquam ingressi fuerint ecclesiam cum processione, prolongata letania quantum ad hoc sufficiat. Tunc induti casulis[4] sacerdos, diaconus ac subdiaconus peragant ministeria sua; hic autem mos casularum tantummodo tempore quadragesimali et quattuor temporibus, usu praecedentium patrum, obseruetur. Subdiaconus, quotiens casula induitur, exuat eam dum legit epistolam qua lecta rursus ea induatur[5]; diaconus uero, antequam ad euangelium legendum accedat, exuat casulam et duplicans eam circumponat sibi in sinistra scapula, annectens alteram summitatem eius cingulo albae; peracto Communionis Sacramento induat eam antequam collecta finiatur.

35. In supradictis diebus Quadragesimae, completa Missa, pulsetur[a] signum ad Vesperam et agatur[b] oratio; dehinc in interuallo quo signa pulsantur,[c] eant ministri accipere[6] mixtum qui uoluerint; qui

[a] pulsatur F [b] agitur F
[c] cf. 25, 35: 'cuius signa dum sonant.'

[1] The book of Mass Chants. This, in the tenth century, would contain also the processional antiphons for Candlemas, Ash Wednesday, and so forth.

[2] i.e., as on Candlemas; cf. 33, 6.

[3] Ps. cxxii

[4] The use of chasubles by deacon and subdeacon, in Lent and on the Quarter Tense days only, is peculiar to the Concordia.

[5] For this and the following custom see *Sources*, p. 150 f.

the Antiphonar.[1] When they have reached the church to which they are bound, they shall again [2] pray awhile and then, after the antiphon of the saint, the psalm *Ad te levavi oculos,* [3] the *preces* and the collect, they shall there begin the Litany and return to the Mother church where the Mass shall be celebrated as usual. This shall ever be the manner of holding a procession whenever there is one except that, at other times, the first antiphon shall always be *Exsurge Domine* with the psalm and the *Gloria.* On entering the church with the procession, the ministers of the altar shall vest, the Litany being drawn out sufficiently to give them time to do so. Then the priest, deacon and subdeacon, vested in chasubles,[4] shall fulfil their ministry. This custom of wearing chasubles shall be observed only during Lent and on Quarter Tense days as was the practice of our fathers before us. Now whenever the subdeacon wears a chasuble he shall take it off when reading the epistle, and put it on again as soon as he has finished.[5] The deacon, too, before coming forward to read the gospel, shall take off his chasuble, fold it and then adjust it crosswise about his left shoulder, making the lower end thereof fast to the girdle of his alb. When the Sacrament of Communion has been completed and before the collect is ended he shall replace the chasuble.

35. On those same days of Lent when the Mass is ended, the bell shall be rung for Vespers and there shall be a space for prayer. Then, in the interval while the bells are ringing, those ministers who wish to shall partake of the *mixtum* [6]; those who do not wish to shall have permission to forego it. And since we uphold

---

[6] See p. 20 *n.* 1. Note that the one fasting meal in Lent is *ad vesperam* (i.e., after Vespers).

autem [a] noluerint, licentiam habeant dimittendi. Et quia regulae tenemus hortamentum in *his* sanctis *diebus* Quadragesimae *aliquid nobis augendum* diuinae seruituti *ad solitum pensum nostrae seruitutis*,[1] censuimus ut a Capite Quadragesimae usque ad Cenam Domini, festiuis exceptis diebus, cotidie post expletionem uniuscuiusque horae duos psalmos [2] *prostrati solo* [b] *oratorii* peroremus deuoti, eo scilicet ordine ut Matutinis finitis mox dicantur duo psalmi, *Domine ne in furore* (*i*) [3] et *Ad Dominum*,[4] *Kyrie eleison*, *Pater noster* et preces pro peccatis et oratio; ad Primam, *Beati quorum* [5] et *Leuaui* [6] et reliqua ut supra; ad Tertiam, *Domine ne in furore tuo* (*ii*) [7] [c] et *Laetatus sum* [8]; ad Sextam, *Miserere mei Deus* [9] et *Ad te leuaui* [*oculos meos*] [10] [d]; ad Nonam, *Domine exaudi* (*i*) [11] et *Nisi quia Dominus* [12]; ad Vesperam, *De profundis* [13] et *Qui confidunt* [14]; ad Completorium, *Domine exaudi* (*ii*) [15] et *In conuertendo* [16]; ut, uidelicet, per singulas horas unus dicatur psalmus paenitentiae et alter graduum, quo et nos peccatorum nexibus expiati, uirtutum gradibus superna scandamus. In quibus diebus Quadragesimae per tres priores hebdomadas sint inrasi, mediante [17] uero quadragesimali tempore rasurae officio pilorum euellant superfluitatem.

36. Dominica die Palmarum quia maior restat processio agenda, illa [18] quae solet in claustro agi, interim dum matutinalis Missa canitur, agatur a sacerdote tantum, conspersionem et benedictionem agente. Finita illa Missa agatur [e] illa maior processio in qua, sicut in

[a] vero T
[b] sola FT; solo AE; cf. *Rule* lxvii. 7: '*prostrati solo oratorii*' (in another context). AE (p. 183) preserves the correct reading.
[c] *om.* T [d] [ ] *om.* T [e] agitur F

[1] *Rule* xlix. 10: '. . . *his diebus augeamus nobis aliquid* solito penso (*ad solitum pensum—Text. Recept.*) *seruitutis nostrae*.'
[2] These psalms were of general observance.
[3] Ps. vi [4] Ps. cxix [5] Ps. xxxi [6] Ps. cxx
[7] Ps. xxxvii [8] Ps. cxxi [9] Ps. l [10] Ps. cxxii
[11] Ps. ci [12] Ps. cxxiii [13] Ps. cxxix [14] Ps. cxxiv

the exhortation of the Rule that in these holy days of Lent some increase in Divine worship should be added to the accustomed tale of our service,[1] we have decided that from the beginning of Lent until Maundy Thursday, except on feast days, we shall say two psalms [2] every day after each hour, devoutly prostrate on the floor of the oratory. Thus as soon as Matins are over there shall be said the psalms *Domine ne in furore* (*i*) [3] and *Ad Dominum*,[4] *Kyrie eleison*, *Pater noster*, the prayers *Pro peccatis* and collect; at Prime *Beati quorum* [5] and *Levavi* [6] with the rest as before; at Tierce, *Domine ne in furore tuo* (*ii*) [7] and *Laetatus sum* [8]; at Sext, *Miserere mei Deus* [9] and *Ad te levavi oculos meos* [10]; at None, *Domine exaudi* (*i*) [11] and *Nisi quia Dominus*[12]; at Vespers *De profundis*[13] and *Qui confidunt*[14]; at Compline, *Domine exaudi* (*ii*)[15] and *In convertendo*[16]: that is, at every hour one Penitential and one Gradual psalm shall be said, whereby being freed from the bonds of sin we may rise to heavenly things by the steps of the virtues. For the first three weeks of these days of Lent the brethren shall be unshorn; but in the middle of Lent[17] the common duty of shaving shall be carried out and all excess of hair shall be utterly removed.

36. On Palm Sunday, as the greater procession is yet to come, that[18] which customarily takes place in the cloister shall be carried out by a single priest who shall sprinkle with holy water and give the blessing while the Morrow Mass is being sung. When that Mass is over the greater procession shall take place; and it shall be

---

[15] Ps. cxlii [16] Ps. cxxv

[17] This seems to have been the older custom. See *Stat. Murbac.*, C.M. iii. 87. The *Aix Capit.* forbade shaving from the beginning of Lent until Holy Saturday.

[18] The Sunday *Asperges*. See *Eins*, p. 88: 'presbyter hebdomadarius cum cruce tantummodo et aqua benedicta *agat benedictiones* per omnes officinas, dum a ceteris matutinalis missa completur.'

superiori[1][a] diximus agendum, ita agatur[2]: id est, ut ad illam ecclesiam ubi palmae sunt, sub silentio ordinatim eant dediti psalmodiae, omnes, si fieri potest et aura permiserit, albis induti; quo cum peruenerint agant orationem ipsius sancti, implorantes auxilii intercessionem, cui ecclesia dedicata est. Finita oratione, a diacono legatur euangelium *Turba multa* usque *Ecce*[b] *mundus totus post ipsum abiit*,[3] quod sequatur benedictio palmarum; post benedictionem aspergantur benedicta aqua et tus cremetur; dehinc, pueris incohantibus antiphonas *Pueri Hebraeorum*,[4] distribuantur ipsae palmae et sic, maioribus antiphonis[5] initiatis, egrediantur. Venientes ante ecclesiam subsistant donec pueri qui praecesserunt decantent *Gloria laus*[6] cum uersibus, omnibus sicut mos est *Gloria laus* respondentibus; quibus finitis, incipiente cantore *Ingrediente Domino*[7] responsorium, aperiantur portae; ingressi, finito responsorio, agant sicut supradictum est,[8] et teneant palmas in manibus

[a] priori T [b] *om.* T

[1] i.e., when dealing with the Candlemas procession. Note the repetition here of some of the directions for Candlemas.

[2] The Concordia differs from the Cluniac consuetudinaries (B B_1 C and *Farfa*) in the following particulars: general order of ceremonies (procession to another church, blessing of palms, return procession), the position of Tierce (immediately before the Mass, as in Martène's 'Mozarabic Missal' only), no mention of the ringing of bells. For the first procession, 'sub silentio ordinatim eant dediti psalmodiae' (see the Candlemas procession, 33), cf. *Eins*, p. 88: 'cum moderamine et disciplina psalmos canentes.' The *Canterbury Benedictional* (pp. 22 ff.) gives the full ceremonies, citing the greater part of the rubrical directions of the Concordia from 'ad illam ecclesiam ubi palmae sunt' down to 'finito responsorio' (36, 22). See *Sources*, p. 155 f.

[3] John xii. 12–19

[4] *Pueri . . . portantes ramos*, etc., and *Pueri . . . vestimenta prosternebant*, etc. These are found in all forms of the Palm Sunday rites.

[5] The Antiphonar of the Mass would have contained some or all of the following: *Cum appropinquaret*, *Cum audisset*, *Ante sex dies*, *Occurrunt turbae*, *Ceperunt omnes*. See *Eins*, p. 88 f., *Canterbury Benedictional*, p. 25 f., and elsewhere.

[6] The *schola*, or children, went on ahead, entered the church and sang the verses of *Gloria laus* from within the closed doors. The first verse, sung

held, as we have said above,[1] in the following manner[2]: that is, the brethren, vested in albs, if this can be done and the weather permits, shall go to the church where the palms are, silently, in the order of procession and occupied with psalmody. On reaching the church they shall say the prayer of the saint to whom the church is dedicated, imploring the help of his intercession. When the prayer is finished, the gospel *Turba multa* shall be read by the deacon as far as the words *Ecce mundus totus post ipsum abiit*[3]: the blessing of the palms shall follow. After the blessing the palms shall be sprinkled with holy water and incensed. While the children begin the antiphons *Pueri Hebraeorum*[4] the palms shall be distributed. Then the greater antiphons[5] shall be intoned and the procession shall go forth. As soon as the Mother church is reached the procession shall wait while the children, who shall have gone on before, sing *Gloria laus*[6] with its verses, to which all shall answer *Gloria laus*, as the custom is. When this is finished the cantor shall intone the respond *Ingrediente Domino*[7] and the doors shall be opened. When all have entered and the respond is finished they shall do as has been said before,[8] holding their palms in their hands until the

---

by the *schola*, was repeated by those outside the church, and thereafter sung as a refrain to the succeeding verses. The hymn is ascribed to Theodulph of Orleans († 821). Of the thirty-eight verses given in *PL* cv. 308–9 as Theodulph's, a tenth century Pontifical of Poitiers has vv. 1–17 (Martène, *De Ant. Eccl. Rit.* t. 3, l. iv. *c.* xx. p. 74); a tenth century Antiphonar of St Gall (Cod. 339) vv. 1–5; Lanfranc's *Decreta* and the Worcester Antiphonar vv. 1–3; the *Wulfstan Collectar* vv. 3–6 (it may originally have had 1–6) besides three more verses agreeing with vv. 1–3 of the eight peculiar to the *Canterbury Benedictional*.

[7] Found in all forms of the Palm Sunday rites

[8] See 33, 15–20 where, in a like context, Tierce is mentioned. AE (p. 184) is explicit here: 'agantque Tertiam.'

usque dum Offertorium cantetur [a] et eas post oblationem [offerant sacerdoti. Ea [1] die ad passionem] [2] [b] dicitur *Dominus uobiscum*, sed *Gloria tibi Domine* non respondetur; similiter et in reliquis passionibus, excepta Parasceuae passione ubi neutrum dicatur, nec *Dominus uobiscum* nec *Gloria tibi Domine*.

37. Quinta feria, quae et Cena Domini dicitur, nocturnale officium agatur secundum quod in Antiphonario [3] habetur. Comperimus etiam in quorundam reli⟨gi⟩osorum [4] [c] ecclesiis quiddam fieri quod ad animarum compunctionem spiritualis rei indicium exorsum est, uidelicet ut, peracto quicquid ad cantilenam illius noctis pertinet, euangeliique antiphona [5] finita nihilque iam cereorum luminis remanente,[6] sint duo ad hoc idem destinati pueri in dextera parte chori qui sonora psallant uoce *Kyrie eleison*, duoque similiter in sinistra parte qui respondeant *Christe eleison*, nec non et in occidentali parte duo qui dicant *Domine miserere nobis;* quibus peractis respondeat simul omnis chorus *Christus Dominus factus est oboediens usque ad mortem.*[7] Demum pueri dexterioris chori repetant quae supra, eodem

[a] canetur T
[b] [ ] *om.* F
[c] reliosorum F T

[1] This sentence is cited verbatim in *Liber Vitae*, p. 114; cf. also CCCC 190, p. 218.

[2] The Passion according to St Matthew

[3] Here and below (50, 1–4; 59, 1–3) the reference is to the Antiphonar of the Roman Office, or *Canonicus Cursus*, that is, the Secular Office. The occasional substitution of the Secular for the Monastic Office was general at the time of the Concordia; see *Sources*, pp. 18ff. In the Concordia the Secular Office is prescribed for Maundy Thursday, Good Friday, Holy Saturday, Easter Day and the week following (ending with None on Saturday) and for Nocturns on Whit Sunday. For references to the recitation of the Roman Office (*more canonicorum*, etc.) see 38, 3; 39, 2; 39, 14; 47, 17; 49, 18; 50, 2; 52, 10; 53, 18.

[4] cf. 46, 2: 'usum quorundam religiosorum.'

[5] The antiphon to the *Benedictus*

[6] For the putting out of lights during Nocturns and Matins on the last three days of Holy Week see Amalar, *De Eccl. Off.* (*PL* cv. 1202) and

Offertory has been sung, and then offering them to the priest. On that day[1] *Dominus vobiscum* is said at the Passion,[2] but *Gloria tibi Domine* is not given in reply; the same is done at the other Passions except at that on Good Friday when neither *Dominus vobiscum* nor *Gloria tibi Domine* is said.

37. On Thursday, which is called *Cena Domini*, the night Office shall be performed according as is set down in the Antiphonar.[3] We have also heard that, in churches of certain religious men,[4] a practice has grown up whereby compunction of soul is aroused by means of the outward representation of that which is spiritual, namely, that when the singing for the night is over, the antiphon[5] of the gospel finished and all the lights put out,[6] two children should be appointed who shall stand on the right hand side of the choir and shall sing *Kyrie eleison* with clear voice; two more on the left hand side who shall answer *Christe eleison;* and, to the west of the choir, another two who shall say *Domine miserere nobis;* after which the whole choir shall respond together *Christus Dominus factus est oboediens usque ad mortem.*[7] The children of the right-hand choir shall then repeat what they sang above exactly as before and,

---

Ordo Romanus Primus (OR I), 953, 959. AE (p. 184) gives the number of lights as twenty-four, one to be put out at each antiphon and respond. AE and CCCC 190 follow the Concordia here closely down to the words 'uniformiter teneatur,' CCCC 190 giving the verses of the triple *Kyrie* custom as *Qui passurus*, *Qui propheticae* and *Vita in ligno*. The custom was widespread (see Martène, *De Ant. Eccl. Rit.*, t. 3, l. iv, *c.* xxii, p. 82), and the Concordia almost certainly derives it from the version found in *Verdun* (p. 119), the last clause of which runs: 'Qui ordo uniformiter servabitur tribus noctibus,' see *Sources*, p. 284 f. For the corresponding custom of blessing the New Fire on Maundy Thursday, Good Friday and Holy Saturday see 41, 1–9.

[7] Phil. ii. 8

modo quo supra, usquequo chorus finiat quae supra; idemque tertio repetant eodem ordine. Quibus tertio finitis agant tacitas genuflexo more solito preces; qui ordo trium noctium uniformiter teneatur [1] ab illis. Qui, ut reor, ecclesiasticae compunctionis usus a catholicis ideo repertus est ut tenebrarum terror, qui tripertitum [2] mundum dominica passione timore perculit insolito, ac apostolicae praedicationis consolatio, quae [uniuerso mundo] [a] Christum Patri usque ad mortem pro generis humani salute oboedientem reuelauerat, manifestissime designetur. Haec ergo inserenda censuimus ut, si quibus deuotionis gratia complacuerint, habeant in his unde huius rei ignaros instruant; qui autem noluerint, ad hoc agendum minime compellantur.

38. In quarum noctium [3] sequentibus diebus ad nullam dicitur horam *Deus in adiutorium meum*, sed in directum [4] capitula canonici cursus [5] dicantur: dehinc uersus et sequentia. In quinta uero feria eadem capitula altius dicuntur ut ab omnibus audiantur, et Vespera⟨e⟩ et Completorium; ceteris diebus minime. In supradictis noctibus, si Matutinae ante lucem fuerint finitae, fratres qui uoluerint ad suam redeant requiem; qui autem spirituali exercitio noluerint, [agant quidem] [b] cum summo uigilantes silentio quod eorum animabus expediat.[6]

[a] [ ] uniuersum mundum F T
[b] [ ] *om.* T

[1] It is possible that the original text of the Concordia read *tenetur*, *illis* referring to the ' Churches of religious men.'

[2] This expression may be the equivalent of the *triquadrus orbis* found in certain charters and in Aldhelm, who probably obtained it from Orosius. Thus it may mean no more than the ancient division of the world into three parts: Asia, Europe and Africa. See *Times of St Dunstan*, p. 58 and *n*.

[3] Probably only the day hours, from Prime to Compline, are referred to here specifically.

the choir having finished their response, they shall repeat the same thing once again in the same way. When this has been sung the third time the brethren shall say the *preces* on their knees and in silence as usual. The same order of singing shall be observed for three nights by the brethren.[1] This manner of arousing religious compunction was, I think, devised by Catholic men for the purpose of setting forth clearly both the terror of that darkness which, at our Lord's Passion, struck the tripartite [2] world with unwonted fear, and the consolation of that apostolic preaching which revealed to the whole world Christ obedient to His Father even unto death for the salvation of the human race. Therefore it seemed good to us to insert these things so that if there be any to whose devotion they are pleasing, they may find therein the means of instructing those who are ignorant of this matter; no one, however, shall be forced to carry out this practice against his will.

38. At the night Offices on the following days [3] the *Deus in adiutorium meum* is not said at any of the hours, but the divisions of the Office of Canons [5] shall be said straight through,[4] being followed by the verse and the rest. On Maundy Thursday these same divisions, as well as Vespers and Compline, are said loud enough for all to hear; but not on the other days. On the aforesaid nights if Matins are finished before dawn, those who wish may go back to rest; but those who, for the sake of spiritual exercise, do not so wish may do that which is good for their souls,[6] watching in utter silence.

---

[4] i.e., the psalms were sung straight through without the *Gloria Patri* and, in the case of the hours from Prime to None, without antiphons.

[5] The Roman or Secular Office, see p. 36 *n.* 3. *Capitula* is used in the *Rule* (xviii. 5) for the divisions of Ps. cxviii. Here it is used also for Ps. liii.

[6] cf. *Rule* lxvi. 17: 'non *expedit animabus eorum*' (in another context).

39. Mane facto in Cena Domini conueniant ad Primam, qua sonore dicta et canonico more,[1] scilicet, *Deus in nomine tuo*,[2] *Beati immaculati* usque *Legem pone*[3]; tunc, dicto uersu, genuflexo peragant cetera[4] silenter; post *Pater noster* dicitur silenter *Viuet anima mea et laudabit te*[5] usque in finem psalmi. Sed priore perueniente ad confessionis locum facto signo agant confessionem.[6] In ceteris horis similiter residua capitula: ad Tertiam, a *Legem pone* usque *Defecit*,[7] alta uoce, et uersus et cetera silenter; ad Sextam, a *Defecit* usque[a] *Mirabilia*[8]; ad Nonam, a *Mirabilia* usque in finem; Vesperae similiter sonora uoce, unusquisque psalmus cum antiphona, et uersus et euangelium,[9] et cetera silenter; Completorium aeque sonore, et post primum psalmum, canonico more, *In te Domine speraui* (*i*)[10] et euangelium *Nunc dimittis*[11]; post, *Pater noster*, *In pace in idipsum dormiam*.[12][b]

40. His tribus diebus, prima peracta, psallant psalterium[13] ex integro unanimiter[c] in choro; post quod letaniam[14] agant prostrati; deinde lectioni uacent[15] usque dum,[d] facto signo, eant ad calciandum et reliqua more regulari[16] compleant. Facto namque Capitulo discalcient se fratres et intrantes ecclesiam, more oboedientiae,[17] lauent pauimenta ecclesiae, sacerdotibus interim

[a] + ad T [b] *om.* T [c] unianimiter F [d] *om.* T

[1] See p. 36 *n.* 3. [2] Ps. liii [3] Ps. cxviii. 1–32

[4] i.e., the two Lenten psalms (35, 10 f.), Litany (19, 26), etc.

[5] Ps. cxviii. 175–76

[6] This may refer to sacramental Confession (as on Sundays) or, more probably, to the daily Chapter at which the 'confession,' described above (31, 26) as taking place on Christmas Eve and on 'the first day of the Paschal solemnity,' i.e. Maundy Thursday, would have been carried out. See *Sources*, p. 283 f.

[7] Ps. cxviii. 33–80 [8] Ps. cxviii. 81–128 [9] The *Magnificat*

[10] Ps. xxx [11] Luke ii. 29–32 [12] Ps. iv. 9

[13] The recitation of the entire Psalter on these three days would seem to be peculiar to the Concordia.

[14] See p. 15 *n.* 12 [15] See 29, 28

[16] According to monastic usage: in the manner of monks

39. At daybreak on Maundy Thursday the brethren shall assemble for Prime, which shall be said aloud and according to the manner of Canons,[1] namely, *Deus in nomine tuo*[2] and *Beati immaculati* down to *Legem pone*[3]; then, having said the verse, they shall finish the rest[4] in silence and on their knees. After the *Pater noster*, *Vivet anima mea et laudabit te*[5] is said down to the end of the psalm, silently. When the prior arrives at the place for confession, the bell shall be rung and confession shall be made.[6] At the other hours the remaining divisions shall be said in the same way: at Tierce, from *Legem pone* to *Defecit*,[7] aloud, with verse and the rest silently; at Sext, from *Defecit* to *Mirabilia*[8]; at None, from *Mirabilia* to the end. In the same way Vespers shall be sung aloud, each psalm with its antiphon, followed by verse and gospel[9] with the rest silently. Compline, too, shall be said aloud, with *In te Domine speravi* (*i*)[10] after the first psalm, in the manner of Canons, as well as the gospel, *Nunc dimittis*[11]; then the *Pater noster* and *In pace in idipsum dormiam*.[12]

40. On these three days when Prime is over the brethren shall say the entire Psalter[13] together in choir; after this they shall recite the Litany,[14] prostrate; they shall then give themselves to reading[15] until, when the bell is rung, they go to change their shoes and to fulfil the other duties of regular observance.[16] When the Chapter has been held, having taken off their shoes, they shall enter the church and as an act of obedience[17]

---

[17] cf. 'oboedientia agitur' (32, 20). The washing of the pavement and altars of the church took the place of the usual manual labour. The custom was general; cf. *Trèves*, p. 31: 'vadit ad obedientiam universitas congregationis.' CCCC 190 and the *Wulfstan Collectar* (p. 533) cite this sentence with minor differences. The Concordia makes no mention of Tierce, which may have been said before the washing of the altars, as in CCCC 190.

cum ministris altaris benedicta aqua sacra altaria lauantibus; ea enim die non fit celebratio Missae in aliquo altari donec lauetur. Quibus peractis, lotis pedibus, recalcient se. Sexta peracta celebretur Missa,[1] pauperibus ante ad hoc collectis secundum numerum quem abbas praeuiderit; dehinc, collectis in locum congruum, eant fratres ad agendum Mandatum [2] ubi, canentes antiphonas eidem operi congruentes, lauent et extergant pedes pauperum atque osculentur et, data aqua manibus illorum,[3] [a] dentur eis etiam cibaria fiatque secundum abbatis arbitrium in eis distributio nummorum.

41. Dehinc hora congrua agatur Nona. Qua cantata, ob arcanum cuiusdam mysterii [4] indicium, si ita placuerit induant se fratres et pergant ad ostium ecclesiae ferentes hastam cum imagine serpentis,[5] ibique ignis de silice excutiatur [6]; illo benedicto ab abbate, candela, quae in ore serpentis [7] infixa est, ab illo accendatur. Sicque, aedituo hastam deportante, cuncti fratres chorum ingrediantur unusque dehinc cereus [8] ex illo illuminetur igne. Sexta feria eodem ordine agatur et a decano [9] portetur; Sabbato similiter, a praepositoque [10] deferatur. Et post haec celebratio Missae, ad quam *Dominus uobiscum* [11] minime dicatur nisi ab episcopo

[a] eorum T

[1] The Morrow Mass, which could not be said until the altars had been washed. It was attended by those poor who were to receive the Maundy; cf. the *Wulfstan Collectar*, *loc. cit.*

[2] The Maundy of the Poor. cf. *Trèves*, p. 31; *Eins*, p. 90 f.

[3] cf. *Rule* liii. 25: 'aquam in manibus abbas hospitibus det.'

[4] The mystery of the Redemption with, perhaps, special reference to John iii. 14.

[5] This was a candlestick shaped like a serpent and attached to the end of a pole or staff (cf. 'candela . . . in ore serpentis' below); see AE, p. 186: 'imago serpentis . . . hastae adfixa, candelam habens in ore suo.' There is an illustration in Rock, *Church of our Fathers* (ed. Hart and Frere), vol. 4, p. 283. For parallels see *Sources*, p. 26.

[6] For the Blessing of the New Fire see *Sources*, p. 25 f.

[7] See *Fleury*, p. 143: 'in ore draconis.'

[8] This candle, lit from the new fire, was used on these three days to rekindle the lights extinguished at Tenebrae.

wash the pavement thereof while the priests and ministers of the altar wash the sacred altars with holy water. For on that day no Mass shall be celebrated at any altar until it has been washed. When these things have been done the brethren shall wash their feet and then put their shoes on again. At the Mass,[1] which shall be celebrated after Sext, there shall be assembled as many poor men as the abbot shall have provided for. Afterwards, when these have been gathered together in a suitable place, the brethren shall proceed to carry out the Maundy [2] at which, singing the antiphons proper to this ceremony, they shall wash, dry and kiss the feet of the poor men. And when water has been offered for their hands,[3] food also shall be given to the poor men and money, according to the abbot's discretion, distributed among them.

41. None shall be said at the proper time; then, as a secret sign of a certain mystery,[4] if it so please, the brethren shall vest and go to the doors of the church bearing with them a staff with the representation of a serpent[5]; there fire shall be struck from flint[6] and blessed by the abbot, after which the candle which is fixed in the mouth of the serpent[7] shall be lit from that fire. And so, the staff being borne by the sacrist, all the brethren shall enter the choir and one candle[8] shall then be lit from that fire. This arrangement shall be repeated on Friday, when the staff shall be borne by the dean,[9] and on Saturday, when it shall be borne by the provost.[10] At the Mass which shall then be celebrated *Dominus vobiscum*[11] shall not be said except by a

---

[9] This officer appears in the Concordia only here and 57, 2. See Introd., p. xxx f.

[10] The only mention of this officer in the Concordia. See Introd., p. xxx f.

[11] This and the following sentence are cited in the *Wulfstan Collectar*, p. 533.

tantummodo ubi chrisma conficitur; a quo etiam in Eucharistiae acceptione pacis osculum presbyteris, ter *Agnus Dei* decantato, solummodo detur; ab aliis uero minime praesumatur. In qua Missa, sicut et in sequentium dierum, communicatio praebetur tam fratribus quam cunctis fidelibus, reseruata nihilominus ea die Eucharistia quae sufficiat [a] ad communicandum cunctis altera die.

42. Peracta Missae celebratione omnes [1] ad mixtum pergant; post mixtum quos uoluerit abbas ex fratribus secum assumens suum peragat Mandatum,[2] quo peracto Vesperas celebrent. Dehinc refectionem [3] fratrum agant post quam tempore congruo eorundem agatur Mandatum [4]; qui tamen fratres prius pedes suos diligenter emundent; uenientesque ad Mandatum hebdomadarii ministri, secundum morem suum abbatem antecedentes, Mandatum agant, quos subsequitur abbas in concha sua singulorum pedes lauans, ministrantibus sibi quos uoluerit ad hoc obsequium, quos extergat et osculetur. Quo peracto resideat abbas in sede sua ueniantque priores [5] et ei eadem exhibeant; deinde surgens *det aquam in manibus* [6] singulorum rursumque ei eadem seruitus exhibeatur. Interim [b] uero dum manus lauantur [c] diaconus hebdomadarius et reliqui ministri eant et induant se, signoque collationis moto ingrediantur, diacono dalmatica [d] induto cum textu euangelii, praecedentibus cereis et turibulo, legaturque euangelium

[a] sufficit T
[b] Inde T
[c] lauant T
[d] dalmatico F

[1] Since all would have communicated at the principal Mass.
[2] This, the abbot's special Maundy, would seem to be peculiar to the Concordia.
[3] The one Lenten meal *ad vesperam*.
[4] The general Maundy. *Trèves* (p. 33 f.) is very similar.

bishop, and then only when he consecrates the chrism; even as at the reception of the Eucharist he alone gives the kiss of peace to the priests after the threefold singing of the *Agnus Dei*, a thing that can in no wise be done by any other. In this Mass as in those of the next two days, Communion shall be given to the brethren and to all the faithful, a sufficient number of hosts being reserved on Maundy Thursday to allow all to communicate on Good Friday.

42. When Mass has been celebrated, all the brethren[1] shall partake of the *mixtum*, after which the abbot shall carry out his own Maundy,[2] taking with him those of the brethren whom he wishes. When this is finished Vespers shall be celebrated; the brethren shall then have their meal[3] and thereafter, at the proper time, their Maundy[4] shall take place; but they must wash their feet carefully beforehand. When the ministers of the week, preceding the abbot as is their wont, come to the Maundy, they shall perform their part in it, and after them the abbot shall wash the feet of all in his own basin, drying and kissing them, being assisted by those whom he has chosen for this service. When he has done this, the abbot shall sit in his own place and the seniors[5] shall minister to him in like manner, then, rising, he shall offer water for the hands[6] of the brethren and again the like service shall be rendered to him. During the washing of the hands, the deacon and other ministers of the week shall vest; at the signal for *collatio* they shall enter, the deacon wearing a dalmatic and bearing the book of the gospels and preceded by acolytes and thurifer, and the gospel according to St John, *Ante*

---

[5] The seniors or officers of the house
[6] cf. *Rule* liii. 25: '*aquam in manibus* abbas hospitibus *det*.'

secundum Iohannem, *Ante diem festum*,[1] donec tintinnabulum pulsetur. Tunc praecedente processione subsequatur omnis congregatio, cunctisque in refectorio residentibus, idem diaconus stans prosequatur euangelii sequentia, imposito super ambonem euangelio. Interim abbas propinando circumeat fratres cum singulis potibus singulorum osculans manus,[2] qua peracta ministratione, residente abbate, dicatur *Tu autem Domine;* tunc a priore [3] propinetur abbati et reliquis ministris qui assistebant. Euangelio [a] finito potibusque haustis, praecedat [b] processio ut exuant se fratres sintque cum reliquis ad complendum.

43. In die Parasceuae agatur nocturna laus sicut supradictum est.[4] Post haec uenientes ad Primam, discalciati omnes incedant quousque crux adoretur. Eadem enim die, hora nona,[5] abbas cum fratribus accedat ad ecclesiam; qui, dum peracta oratione cum ministris altaris more solito indutus fuerit, ueniens de sacrario ante altare [c] orationis gratia, inde cum silentio ad sedem accedat propriam. Tunc subdiaconus ascendat ad legendum lectionem Oseae prophetae *In tribulatione sua* [6]; sequitur responsorium *Domine audiui* [7] cum quattuor uersibus; postea datur oratio ab abbate, cum genuflectione, *Deus a quo et Iudas.*[8] Deinde legitur alia lectio, *Dixit Dominus ad Moysen* [9]; sequitur tractus *Eripe me Domine* [10]; postea legitur *Passio Domini nostri Ihesu Christi secundum Iohannem.* Ad illam passionem diaconus non dicat *Dominus uobiscum*, sed *Passio Domini* et reliqua,

[a] + que T [b] procedat T [c] altaria T

[1] John xiii. 1–15

[2] See *Eins*, p. 93: '*singulorum deosculans manus.*'

[3] This is the only time that the Concordia uses the word *prior* to denote definitely the chief of the abbot's officers. See Introd., p. xxx.

[4] See 37, 1 f.

[5] This section is derived, with occasional verbal agreements, from OR I, 953 and 962 f. See *Sources*, p. 26 f.

diem festum,[1] shall be read until the small bell is rung. Then the procession shall go forward, followed by all the brethren; and when all are seated in the refectory the same deacon shall place the book on the lectern and, standing, shall continue the reading of the gospel. Meanwhile the abbot shall go round among the brethren drinking the health and kissing the hand[2] of each. Having ministered to all, the abbot shall sit down and *Tu autem Domine* shall be said. Then the prior[3] shall drink to the abbot and to the ministers who assisted him. When the gospel has been read and the healths have been drunk, the procession shall move on so that the brethren may unvest and join the rest at Compline.

43. On Good Friday the night Office shall be performed as has been said already.[4] The brethren shall then come to Prime, walking barefoot until the Cross has been adored. On that same day at the hour of None,[5] the abbot shall proceed with the brethren to the church and, having prayed awhile with the ministers of the altar, and being vested in the usual way, he shall leave the sacristy and come before the altar for prayer before going to his own seat in silence. Then the subdeacon shall go up into the pulpit and shall read the lesson of Osee the prophet, *In tribulatione sua*[6]; there follows the respond *Domine audivi*[7] with its four verses, after which the abbot says the collect *Deus a quo et Iudas*[8] at which there shall be a genuflection. Then is read a second lesson, *Dixit Dominus ad Moysen*,[9] followed by the tract *Eripe me Domine*,[10] and the *Passio Domini nostri Ihesu Christi secundum Iohannem*. At this Passion the deacon shall not say *Dominus vobiscum* but simply *Passio Domini*

---

[6] Osee vi. 1–6
[7] Habac. (versio antiqua) iii. 2 ff.
[8] This prayer is in *Gelas* and *Greg.*
[9] Exodus xii. 1–11
[10] Ps. cxxxix

nullo respondente *Gloria tibi Domine;* et quando legitur in euangelio *Partiti sunt uestimenta*[1] *mea* et reliqua, *statim duo diaconi nudent altare sindone quae prius fuerat sub euangelio posita, in modum furantis.*[2] Post haec celebrentur orationes, et ueniens abbas ante altare incipiat orationes sollemnes,[3] quae sequuntur, et dicat primam sine genuflectione, quasi legendo[4]: *Oremus dilectissimi nobis* [*pro sancta ecclesia Dei*][a].

44. Quibus expletis per ordinem, *statim praeparetur crux ante altare, interposito spatio inter ipsam et altare, sustentata* [*hinc* et *inde a duobus* diaconibus].[5][b] Tunc cantent *Popule meus;* respondentes autem duo subdiaconi stantes ante crucem canant graece *Agios o Theos, Agios Yschiros, Agios Athanatos eleison ymas;* itemque schola[6] idipsum latine: *Sanctus Deus.* Deferatur tunc ab ipsis diaconibus ante altare et eos acolitus cum puluillo sequatur, super quem sancta crux ponatur. Antiphonaque finita, quam schola respondit latine, cantant[c] ibidem sicut prius *Quia eduxi uos per desertum;* [item uero respondeant subdiaconi graece, sicut prius: *Agios,* ut supra; itemque schola latine, ut prius: *Sanctus Deus*].[d] Itemque diaconi, leuantes crucem, canant sicut prius: *Quid ultra;* item subdiaconi sicut prius: *Agios,* ut supra; itemque schola latine: *Sanctus Deus,* ut supra. Post haec, uertentes se ad clerum, nudata cruce, dicant antiphonam *Ecce lignum crucis;* alia: *Crucem tuam adoramus Domine*[e]; alia: *Dum Fabricator mundi;* [versus Fortunati][7][f]: *Pange lingua.*

[a] [ ] et reliqua T [b] [ ] *om.* F [c] canant T
[d] [ ] *om.* F [e] *om.* T [f] [ ] *om.* T

[1] John xix. 24 [2] OR I, 953 and 963

[3] See R. H. Connolly, *Liturgical Prayers of Intercession*, JTS, April 1920, pp. 219 ff.

[4] That is, in a tone akin to that of the Preface of the Mass.

[5] OR I, 954 and 963. The ceremonies that follow are an elaboration of those of OR I; most of them, with the chants that accompanied them, were general in the tenth century. *Ratoldus, Eins* and *Trèves* come nearest to the Concordia. See *Sources*, p. 28 f.

and the rest; nor shall *Gloria tibi Domine* be given in response. When the words *Partiti sunt vestimenta*[1] *mea* and the rest are read in the gospel, straightway and as it were like thieves,[2] two deacons shall strip from the altar the cloth which had before been placed under the book of the gospels. The *Orationes sollemnes*[3] are then sung, the abbot coming before the altar to go through them in order. The first one, at which there is no genuflection, he shall sing to a simple tone[4]: *Oremus dilectissimi nobis pro sancta ecclesia Dei* and the rest.

44. When these prayers have all been said, the Cross shall straightway be set up before the altar, a space being left between it and the altar; and it shall be held up by two deacons,[5] one on either side. Then the deacons shall sing *Popule meus*, two subdeacons standing before the Cross and responding in Greek, *Agios o Theos*, *Agios Yschiros*, *Agios Athanatos eleison ymas*, and the *schola*[6] repeating the same in Latin, *Sanctus Deus*. The Cross shall then be borne before the altar by the two deacons, an acolyte following with a cushion upon which the holy Cross shall be laid. When that antiphon is finished which the *schola* has sung in Latin, the deacons shall sing *Quia eduxi vos per desertum*, the subdeacons responding *Agios* in Greek and the *schola Sanctus Deus* in Latin as before. Again the deacons, raising up the Cross, sing *Quid ultra* as before, the subdeacons responding *Agios* and the *schola Sanctus Deus* as before. Then, unveiling the Cross and turning towards the clergy, the deacons shall sing the antiphons *Ecce lignum crucis*, *Crucem tuam adoramus Domine*, *Dum Fabricator mundi* and the verses of Fortunatus,[7] *Pange*

[6] Either the children of the cloister or, more probably, the *Schola Cantorum*, or official body of singers, as in 48, 22 and 58, 13.

[7] Venantius Fortunatus, Bishop of Poitiers († 600). Like F, the Antiphonar of St Gall (Cod. 339) and *Ratoldus* have 'versus Fortunati.' The eighth verse of the *Pange Lingua* (*Crux Fidelis*, etc.) was commonly used antiphonally before the first and remaining verses, hence this hymn is often referred to as *Crux Fidelis*. The text is in *PL* lxxxviii. 88.

Ilico, ea nudata, ueniat abbas ante crucem sanctam ac tribus uicibus se prosternat, cum omnibus fratribus dexterioris chori, scilicet, senioribus ac iunioribus; et cum magno cordis suspirio septem paenitentiae psalmos [1] cum orationibus sanctae cruci competentibus decantando peroret.

45. In prima quidem oratione, tres psalmos primos [2] cum oratione: *Domine Ihesu Christe,*[3] *adoro te in cruce ascendentem; deprecor te ut ipsa crux liberet me de diabolo percutiente. Domine Ihesu Christe, adoro te in cruce uulneratum; deprecor te ut ipsa uulnera remedium sint animae meae. [Domine Ihesu Christe, adoro te in sepulchro positum; deprecor te ut ipsa mors sit uita mea].*[a] *Domine Ihesu Christe, adoro te descendentem ad inferos liberantem captiuos; deprecor te ut non ibi me dimittas introire. [Domine Ihesu Christe, adoro te resurgentem ab inferis ascendentem ad caelos; deprecor te, miserere mei].*[b] *Domine Ihesu Christe, adoro te uenturum iudicaturum*[c]*; deprecor te ut in tuo aduentu non intres in iudicio cum me peccante, sed deprecor te ut ante dimittas quam iudices. Qui uiuis et regnas.* In secunda, duos medioximos [4][d] sequente oratione: *Domine*[5] *Ihesu Christe gloriosissime conditor mundi, qui cum sis splendor gloriae coaeternus Patri Sanctoque Spiritui, ideoque*[e] *dignatus es carnem ex immaculata uirgine sumere et gloriosas palmas tuas in crucis*[f] *patibulo permisisti configere, ut claustra dissipares inferni et humanum genus liberares de morte; respice et miserere mihi misero, oppresso facinorum pondere multarumque nequitiarum labe polluto; non me digneris derelinquere, piissime Pater, sed*

[a] [ ] *om.* T [b] [ ] *om.* F [c] *om.* F
[d] medioximus T [e] ideo T [f] cruce F

[1] Pss. vi, xxxi, xxxvii, l, ci, cxxix, cxlii
[2] Pss. vi, xxxi, xxxvii
[3] This prayer is found in the eighth century English prayer book, *The Book of Cerne* (ed. Kuypers, pp. 116–17). See *Sources*, pp. 29 and 156 f.
[4] Pss. l, ci

lingua. As soon as it has been unveiled, the abbot shall come before the holy Cross and shall prostrate himself thrice with all the brethren of the right hand side of the choir, that is, seniors and juniors; and with deep and heartfelt sighs shall say the seven Penitential psalms [1] and the prayers in honour of the holy Cross.

45. For the first prayer there shall be said the first three Penitential psalms [2] with this collect: *Lord Jesus Christ,*[3] *I adore Thee ascending the Cross; I beseech Thee that the Cross may free me from the thrusts of the devil. Lord Jesus Christ, I adore Thee wounded on the Cross; I beseech Thee that Thy wounds may be unto the healing of my soul. Lord Jesus Christ, I adore Thee laid in the grave; I beseech Thee that Thy death may be my life. Lord Jesus Christ, I adore Thee descending into hell to set free those in prison there; I beseech Thee not to suffer me to enter there. Lord Jesus Christ, I adore Thee rising from the grave and ascending into heaven; I beseech Thee to have mercy on me. Lord Jesus Christ, I adore Thee Who art to come in judgment; I beseech Thee, at Thy coming not to enter into judgment with me a sinner, but, I beseech Thee, to forgive rather than to condemn. Who livest and reignest.* For the second prayer there shall be said the next two Penitential psalms [4] with the following collect: *Lord*[5] *Jesus Christ, most glorious Creator of the world, splendour of the Father's glory, co-eternal with Him and the Holy Ghost; Who therefore didst deign to take flesh of a spotless virgin and didst allow Thy glorious hands to be fixed to the gibbet of the Cross that Thou mightest overthrow the gates of hell and free the human race from death; look down and have mercy on me, a wretch borne down by the weight of sin and polluted by the stains of my many misdeeds: in Thy mercy forsake me not, most loving Father, but forgive*

---

[5] This prayer is in the Spanish *Liber Ordinum* (ed. Ferotin, Paris 1904), p. 199. See *Sources, loc. cit.*

indulge quod impie gessi. Exaudi me prostratum coram adoranda gloriosissima cruce tua, ut merear tibi mundus assistere et placere conspectui tuo. Qui cum Patre. In tertia, ultimos duos [1] cum oratione [2]: *Deus omnipotens, Ihesu Christe, qui tuas manus mundas propter nos in cruce posuisti et de tuo sancto sanguine pretioso* [a] *nos redemisti; mitte in me sensum et intellegentiam quomodo habeam ueram paenitentiam et habeam bonam perseuerantiam omnibus diebus uitae meae. Amen.* [Et eam humiliter deosculans surgat].[b] Dehinc sinisterioris chori omnes fratres eadem [c] mente deuota peragant. Nam salutata ab abbate uel omnibus cruce, *redeat* ipse abbas *ad sedem* [3] *suam usque dum omnis* clerus ac populus hoc idem faciat.

46. Nam, quia ea die depositionem corporis Saluatoris nostri celebramus, usum quorundam religiosorum,[4] imitabilem ad fidem indocti uulgi ac neophytorum corroborandam, aequiperando sequi si ita cui uisum fuerit uel sibi taliter placuerit, hoc modo decreuimus: sit autem in una parte altaris, qua uacuum fuerit, quaedam assimilatio sepulcri uelamenque quoddam in gyro tensum quo, dum sancta crux adorata fuerit, deponatur hoc ordine. Veniant [5] diaconi qui prius portauerunt eam et inuoluant eam sindone in loco ubi adorata est; tunc reportent eam canentes antiphonas

[a] *om.* T   [b] [ ] *om.* F   [c] eandem F

[1] Pss. cxxix, cxlii

[2] I do not find this prayer outside the Concordia in any liturgical document. The version in Tib. A 3, f. 58*b*, is evidently from the Concordia.

[3] cf. the fragment of an Ordo denoted by Martène as Corbie 663 (*De Ant. Monach. Rit.* iii. *c.* 14, § xxv): 'sacerdos vero *redeat ad sedem suam usquedum omnes* salutent.'

[4] cf. 37, 3: 'in quorundam reli⟨gi⟩osorum ecclesiis.'

[5] The only other example comparable to the custom which follows is that given by Martène from an Ordinarium of Toul (*De Ant. Monach. Rit.* iii. *c.* 14, § xlviii). The Toul version is evidently a late form of the very custom

that in which I have sinned most impiously. Hear me, prostrate before Thy adorable and most glorious Cross that I may deserve to stand before Thee pure and pleasing in Thy sight, Who with the Father. For the third prayer there shall be said the last two Penitential psalms[1] with this collect[2]: *Almighty God, Lord Jesus Christ, Who for our sakes didst stretch out Thy pure hands on the cross and didst redeem us with Thy holy and precious Blood, grant me so to feel and understand that I may have true repentance and good perseverance all the days of my life. Amen.* Then humbly kissing the Cross the abbot shall rise; whereupon all the brethren of the left hand side of the choir shall do likewise with devout mind. And when the Cross has been venerated by the abbot and the brethren, the abbot shall return to his seat[3] until all the clergy and people have done in like manner.

46. Now since on that day we solemnize the burial of the Body of our Saviour, if anyone should care or think fit to follow in a becoming manner certain religious men[4] in a practice worthy to be imitated for the strengthening of the faith of unlearned common persons and neophytes, we have decreed this only: on that part of the altar where there is space for it there shall be a representation as it were of a sepulchre, hung about with a curtain, in which the holy Cross, when it has been venerated, shall be placed in the following manner: the deacons who carried the Cross before shall come forward[5] and, having wrapped the Cross in a napkin there where it was venerated, they shall bear it thence, singing the

---

here borrowed. The early Lotharingian and Cluniac consuetudinaries and AE omit the rite. The three antiphons are taken from the first three of Nocturns for Holy Saturday.

In pace in idipsum,[1] alia: *Habitabit*[2]*;* item: *Caro mea requiescet in spe*,[3] donec ueniant ad locum monumenti; depositaque cruce, ac si Domini Nostri Ihesu Christi corpore sepulto, dicant antiphonam *Sepulto Domino, signatum est monumentum ponentes milites qui custodirent eum.*[4] In eodem loco sancta [5][a] crux cum omni reuerentia custodiatur [6][b] usque dominicam noctem Resurrectionis. Nocte uero ordinentur duo fratres aut tres aut plures, si tanta fuerit congregatio, qui ibidem psalmos decantando excubias fideles exerceant.

47. Quibus peractis, egrediantur diaconus ac subdiaconus de sacrario cum corpore Domini, quod pridie remansit, et calice cum uino non consecrato, et ponant super altare. Tunc [7] sacerdos [8] ueniat ante altare et dicat [uoce sonora] [c]: *Oremus. Praeceptis salutaribus moniti* et *Pater Noster;* inde *Libera nos quaesumus Domine* usque *Per omnia saecula saeculorum. Amen.* Et sumat abbas de sancto sacrificio [9] et ponat in calicem, nihil dicens, et communicent omnes cum silentio. Hoc expleto, Vespertinum Officium canat unusquisque priuatim in loco suo, quo peracto refectorium petant; surgentes autem a mensa cetera [10] more solito peragant. Crucis [d] ueneratione peracta, quibus uacuum fuerit

[a] sancto F
[b] custodiebant F
[c] [ ] *om.* F
[d] + uero T

[1] Ps. iv. 9 [2] Adapted from Ps. xiv. 1 [3] Ps. xv. 9

[4] From the ninth respond of Nocturns of Holy Saturday (cf. Matt. xxvii. 66)

[5] For this reading cf. *sancta crux* 44, 9 and 20.

[6] The reading of F (*custodiebant*) may be the correct one, the subject of the verb being then the 'religious men' from whom the custom was obtained: *sancto* could be read and *crucem* conjectured.

[7] This is the Mass of the Presanctified. The passage, down to the words *refectorium petant* is derived, with occasional verbal agreements, from OR I, 954 and 963.

antiphons *In pace in idipsum,*[1] *Habitabit*[2] and *Caro mea requiescet in spe,*[3] to the place of the sepulchre. When they have laid the cross therein, in imitation as it were of the burial of the Body of our Lord Jesus Christ, they shall sing the antiphon *Sepulto Domino, signatum est monumentum, ponentes milites qui custodirent eum.*[4] In that same place the holy Cross[5] shall be guarded[6] with all reverence until the night of the Lord's Resurrection. And during the night let brethren be chosen by twos and threes, if the community be large enough, who shall keep faithful watch, chanting psalms.

47. When this has been done the deacon and subdeacon shall come forth from the sacristy with the Body of the Lord, left over from the previous day, and a chalice with unconsecrated wine, which they shall place on the altar. Then[7] the priest[8] shall come before the altar and shall sing in a clear voice: *Oremus. Praeceptis salutaribus moniti,* the *Pater noster* and *Libera nos quaesumus Domine* up to *Per omnia saecula saeculorum. Amen.* And the abbot shall take a portion of the holy sacrifice[9] and shall place it in the chalice saying nothing; and all shall communicate in silence. When this has been done the brethren shall say Vespers, each one privately to himself and in his own place, after which they shall go to the refectory. Then, rising up from table,[10] they shall carry out the remaining duties of the day in the usual way. After the veneration of the Cross, those ministers

---

[8] A few lines below we find *abbas.* For a similar confusion see 49, 8 and 14; 58, 13 and 16.

[9] A typical Concordia expansion. OR I has 'sumet de sancta' (954, 963); *Corbie* 663 has 'su*mat* de sancta et po*nat* in calice' (Martène, *loc. cit.* § xlii).

[10] See 25, 32 f.

ministri uel pueri se radant [1] ac balneent,[2] si tanta fuerit cohors societatis ut sabbati crastini ad hoc non sufficiat dies. Completorium uero post collationem unusquisque, in loco suo stans, semotim ac silenter, more canonicorum ut supra diximus [3] decantet et consueto more cetera [4] compleat. His uero tribus diebus in refectorio omnia cum benedictione et in Capitulo more solito agantur.

[1] See 35, 24
[2] cf. *Trèves*, p. 37. This is the only mention of baths in the Concordia.
[3] See 38, 3
[4] The *Trina oratio*, etc., as 27, 13 f.

or children who can shall shave [1] and bath [2] themselves if the number of the community is so great that Saturday, the next day, would not suffice for this. After *collatio* each one shall say Compline in his own place silently and after the manner of Canons, as we said before [3]: the rest [4] shall be fulfilled in the accustomed manner. On these three days everything shall be carried out with a blessing in the refectory and in the usual way in Chapter.

CAPVT V

QVALITER DIVRNA SIVE NOCTVRNA LAVS PASCHALI FESTIVITATE AGATVR

48. Sabbato Sancto hora [1] nona, ueniente abbate in ecclesiam cum fratribus, nouus, ut supradictum est, afferatur [2] ignis. Posito uero cereo [3] ante altare, ex illo accendatur igne; quem diaconus more solito [a] benedicens, hanc orationem quasi uoce legentis [4] proferens dicat: *Exultet iam angelica turba caelorum.*[5] Tunc, uoce sublimiore, dicat *Sursum corda* et reliqua. Finita benedictione accendatur alter cereus, *et tunc illuminantur duo cerei* [6] *tenentibus duobus* acolitis, *unus in dextro cornu altaris et alter in sinistro.*[7] Benedictione peracta ascendat subdiaconus ambonem ⟨et⟩ legat lectionem primam: *In principio creauit* [8]*;* sequitur oratio a priore: *Oremus. Deus qui mirabiliter.* Secunda lectio: *Factum est in uigilia* [9]*;* tractus: *Cantemus Domino* [10]*;* sequitur oratio: *Oremus. Deus cuius antiqua miracula.* Tertia lectio: [*Apprehendent* [11]*;* tractus: *Vinea facta est* [12]*;* sequitur oratio *Deus qui nos ad celebrandum.* Quarta lectio] [b]: *Haec est hereditas* [13]*;* collecta: *Deus qui ecclesiam tuam;* tractus: *Sicut ceruus* [14]*;* sequitur oratio: *Concede quaesumus omnipotens*

[a] cf. Amalar, *De Eccl. Off.*, *PL* cv. 1034: 'Quod a diacono benedicitur morem sequitur Romanum.'

[b] [ ] *om.* T

[1] The ceremonies and rubrical directions of Holy Saturday, down to the words 'nec Agnus Dei nec communio' (towards the end of the section) are mainly taken from or based on those of OR I (955 f., 957, 963 f.). Note that while the first three lessons and the three tracts are in OR I, all four lessons and the four collects are in *Greg*; cf. AE, p. 188: 'lectiones secundum constitutionem Sancti Gregorii Papae cum tractibus et collectis.' See *Sources*, p. 30 f.

[2] See 41, 4 f.

[3] i.e., the Paschal candle

[4] See the very simple form of the *Exultet* melody in a MS of Arezzo (see *Paléograph. Mus.*, ii, *pl.* 26). The *voce sublimiore* refers to the Preface tone of that portion of the *Exultet* which follows the *Sursum corda*, etc.; cf. *Eins*, p. 96, where the blessing is divided into two parts—*in modum legentis* and *in modum praefationis*.

CHAPTER V

OF THE MANNER IN WHICH THE DAY AND NIGHT OFFICE SHALL BE CARRIED OUT ON THE FEAST OF EASTER

48. On Holy Saturday at the hour of None,[1] when the abbot enters the church with the brethren, the new fire [2] shall be brought in, as we said before, and the candle [3] which has been placed before the altar shall be lit from that fire. Then, as is the custom, a deacon shall bless the candle saying, in the manner of one reading,[4] the prayer *Exultet iam angelica turba coelorum.*[5] Presently, on a higher note, he shall sing *Sursum corda* and the rest. When the blessing is finished a second candle shall be lit; these two lighted candles [6] being held each by an acolyte, one to the right and the other to the left of the altar.[7] After the blessing the subdeacon shall go up into the pulpit and shall read the first lesson: *In principio creavit*[8]*:* there follows a collect said by the prior: *Oremus. Deus qui mirabiliter.* Second lesson: *Factum est in vigilia*[9]*;* tract, *Cantemus Domino*[10] followed by the collect: *Oremus. Deus cuius antiqua miracula.* Third lesson: *Apprehendent*[11]*;* tract, *Vinea facta est*[12] followed by the collect: *Deus qui nos ad celebrandum.* Fourth lesson: *Haec est hereditas*[13]*;* collect: *Deus qui ecclesiam tuam;* tract, *Sicut cervus*[14] followed by the collect: *Concede quaesumus omnipotens Deus.* After the prayer the

---

[5] See *Greg* (Suppl.), p. 151. The *Sursum corda et reliqua* is part of the *Exultet* itself.

[6] i.e., the Paschal candle and the *alter cereus.* See Amalar, *op. cit.*, 1038 and *De Ord. Antiph., ibid.* 1293.

[7] OR I, 963 f. [8] Gen. i.—ii, 2. [9] Exod. xiv. 24—xv. 1

[10] Exod. xv [11] Is. iv [12] Is. v. 1–2 [13] Is. liv. 17—lv. 1 f.

[14] Ps. xli

Deus. Finita oratione incohentur letaniae septenae [1] ad introitum ante altare. Postea descendat abbas cum schola [2] canente letanias quinas ad fontes benedicendos. Sequitur oratio,[a] *Omnipotens sempiterne Deus*,[3] et praefatio. His expletis redeunt ad altare cum letania terna; et, antequam cantatur *Gloria in excelsis Deo*, magister scholae [4] dicat alta uoce *Accendite.*

49. Et tunc illuminentur omnia luminaria ecclesiae et, abbate incipiente *Gloria in excelsis Deo*,[5] pulsentur omnia signa; sequitur collecta; *Deus qui hanc sacratissimam noctem.*[6] Deinde legitur apostolus,[7][b] *Si consurrexistis*,[8] et cantatur *Alleluia*, *Confitemini Domino* [9] et tractus: *Laudate Dominum.*[10] Ante euangelium [11] non portantur luminaria in ipsa nocte sed incensum tantum. Finito euangelio dicat abbas [12] *Dominus uobiscum: Oremus.* In ipso die non cantantur [c] Offertorium nec *Agnus Dei* nec Communio; [et pacem non ⟨debent⟩ dare nisi qui communicent] [13][d] sed, interim dum communicantur, *Alleluia* et *Laudate Dominum omnes gentes* [14] canitur, dehinc antiphona: *Vespere autem sabbati* [15] ⟨et⟩ *Magnificat.* Sic sacerdos Missam ac Vespertinalem Synaxim [16] una compleat oratione. Eadem uero die, tempore Mandati,[17] aqua manibus tantum [18] data a

[a] *om.* T [b] epistola T [c] cantatur T [d] [ ] *om.* F

[1] The invocations of the seven, five and threefold litanies would have been repeated seven, five or three times each (Martène, *De Ant. Monach. Rit.* iii. *c.* 15, § xvii). The rubrical directions concerning the three litanies would seem to be, as they stand, peculiar to the Concordia. See again 58, 11 f.

[2] Here, as in OR I, from which the term is borrowed, the official body of singers, the *Schola Cantorum*, is meant.

[3] For this prayer and the Blessing of the Font (*praefatio*) see *Greg* pp. 55 ff.

[4] The reference is to the cantor, as in OR I. Note that AE (p. 189) has 'a magistro scholae sive cantore.'

[5] The Mass follows OR I. [6] This is the collect of *Greg.*

[7] *Apostolus*, the reading of F, agrees with the printed reading of OR I (Appendix, 964); but see 58, 17, where in a like context the reading of F is *epistola.* [8] Col. iii. 1–4 [9] Ps. cxvii [10] Ps. cxvi

[11] *Cum transisset Sabbatum* (Mark xvi. 1 f.), according to CCCC 190.

sevenfold Litanies[1] shall be begun at the entrance to the altar. Afterwards the abbot shall go down with the *schola*[2] to bless the font, singing the five-fold Litanies. There follow the collect, *Omnipotens sempiterne Deus*,[3] and the Preface. When these are finished they return to the altar singing the three-fold Litanies; and before the *Gloria in excelsis Deo* is sung the master of the *schola*[4] shall sing on a high note *Accendite*.

49. And thereupon shall all the lights of the church be lit and, when the abbot has intoned the *Gloria in excelsis Deo*,[5] all the bells shall peal. There follows the collect: *Deus qui hanc sacratissimam noctem*[6]; then the epistle,[7] *Si consurrexistis*[8] is read and *Alleluia, Confitemini Domino*[9] and the tract *Laudate Dominum*[10] are sung. No lights are borne before the gospel[11] on the night itself, but incense only. When the gospel is finished the abbot[12] shall say *Dominus vobiscum: Oremus*. On the day itself neither the Offertory, *Agnus Dei* nor Communion are sung, nor should the *Pax* be given except by those who communicate[13]; and while Communion is being given *Alleluia* and *Laudate Dominum omnes gentes*[14] are sung followed by the antiphon *Vespere autem sabbati*[15] and the *Magnificat*. Thus the priest completes both the Mass and the Office of Vespers[16] with one prayer. On the same day, at the time for the Maundy,[17] the minister shall offer to the brethren, as a token of charity, water for the hands only.[18]

---

[12] A few lines below we find *sacerdos*. See p. 45 *n*. 8.

[13] See *Apparat*. AE, citing this passage, agrees with F in omitting this clause which may not have been in the original text of the Concordia.

[14] Ps. cxvi

[15] Matt. xxviii. 1–7

[16] This form of the Roman or secular Vespers—consisting of one psalm, the Magnificat and collect—is found in *Ratoldus* and *Trèves*, see *Sources*, p. 31. The *Leofric Collectar* (HBS i. 133) cites the Concordia here freely. For *Vespertinalem Synaxim*, cf. *Rule* xvii. 16. See also 56, 4.

[17] See 26, 7. The Maundy had already taken place on the Thursday; cf. *Trèves*, p. 38.

[18] See *Verdun*, p. 123: 'Ad mandatum ea nocte solummodo manus abluent.'

ministro, fratribus caritatis officio praebeatur.[a] Completorium sonoriter[1] celebretur more canonicorum.[2]

50. In die sancto Paschae septem canonicae horae a monachis in ecclesia Dei more canonicorum, propter auctoritatem beati Gregorii papae sedis apostolicae quam ipse Antiphonario dictauit, celebrandae sunt.[3] Eiusdem tempore noctis, antequam Matutinorum[4] signa moueantur, sumant aeditui crucem et ponant in loco sibi congruo. In primis[b] ad Nocturnam ab abbate seu quolibet sacerdote, dum initur laus Dei in ecclesia, dicatur[c] *Domine labia mea aperies*[d] semel tantum[5]; postea, *Deus in adiutorium meum intende* cum *Gloria*. Psalmo autem *Domine quid multiplicati sunt*[6] dimisso, cantor incipiat Inuitatorium; tunc tres antiphonae cum tribus psalmis,[7] quibus finitis uersus conueniens dicatur; deinde tot lectiones cum responsoriis ad hoc rite pertinentibus.

51. Dum tertia recitatur lectio, quattuor fratres[8] induant se, quorum unus, alba indutus ac si ad aliud agendum, ingrediatur atque latenter sepulcri locum adeat ibique, manu tenens palmam, quietus sedeat. Dumque tertium percelebratur responsorium residui tres succedant, omnes quidem cappis induti, turibula

[a] praebetur F
[b] cf. *Trèves*, p. 58: 'Imprimis ad vigilias Domine labia mea dein Deus in adiutorium vocitent.'
[c] dicat: F; dicat T
[d] + et os meum F

[1] i.e., aloud as usual
[2] See p. 36 *n.* 3
[3] This sentence may be a decree taken from some Council. As appears from the context, it covers the entire Office. The Concordia and AE refer here to St Gregory the Great, the Antiphonar in question being that of the Office, that is, the Roman or Secular as distinct from the Monastic. *Eins*, *Farfa* and *Ulrich* prescribe the Monastic Office for Easter; *Trèves*, *Verdun* and Hartker's Antiphonar agree with the Concordia. See *Sources*, pp. 15 ff.
[4] If this is *Nocturns*, as would seem from the context, a unique parallel can be found in a Rheinau MS cited in Milchsack, *Die Oster und Passionsspiel*, p. 48: 'Antequam ad nocturnos pulsantur sublata est crux a custodibus ecclesiae.' That the Concordia passage is related to this is suggested by its mention of *aeditui* (plural) here only.

Compline shall be said aloud[1] and after the manner of Canons.[2]

50. On the holy day of Easter the seven canonical hours are to be celebrated[3] by monks in the Church of God after the manner of Canons, out of regard for the authority of the blessed Gregory, Pope of the Apostolic See, as set forth in his Antiphonar. On that same night, before the bells are rung for Matins,[4] the sacrists shall take the Cross and set it in its proper place. At Nocturns, when the praise of God is begun in the church, *Domine labia mea aperies* shall first of all be said, once only,[5] by the abbot or by one of the priests; then *Deus in adiutorium meum intende* with the *Gloria;* next, omitting the psalm *Domine quid multiplicati sunt,*[6] the cantor shall give out the Invitatory; three antiphons and three psalms[7] shall follow; and when these are finished the proper verse shall be said; and then three lessons with the appropriate responds.

51. While the third lesson is being read, four of the brethren[8] shall vest, one of whom, wearing an alb as though for some different purpose, shall enter and go stealthily to the place of the 'sepulchre' and sit there quietly, holding a palm in his hand. Then, while the third respond is being sung, the other three brethren, vested in copes and holding thuribles in their hands,

---

[5] Instead of thrice as in the Monastic Office; cf. *Rule* ix. 2.

[6] Ps. iii

[7] Nocturns here are substantially as in OR I (958), Amalar (*De Eccl. Off.*, *PL* cv. 1203 and *De Ord. Antiph.*, *ibid.*, 1293), the *Liber Responsalis* (*PL* lxxviii. 769) and other books of the Roman Office down to the present day. Cf. *Trèves*, pp. 39 and 58.

[8] This custom was widespread. AE omits it. It is fully treated in K. Young, *The Drama of the Mediaeval Church* (Oxford, 1933), i. 239 ff. Of all that give both words and actions of this Easter 'play,' the Concordia version is the oldest. It is interesting to compare with this custom details of the illuminated miniatures of the Resurrection in Ethelwold's Benedictional, *Jumièges*, Hartker's Antiphonar, etc.

cum incensu manibus gestantes, ac, pedetemptim ad similitudinem quaerentium quid, ueniant ante locum sepulcri. Aguntur enim haec ad imitationem angeli sedentis in monumento, atque mulierum cum aromatibus uenientium ut ungerent corpus Ihesu.[1] Cum ergo ille residens tres, uelut erraneos ac aliquid quaerentes, uiderit sibi approximare, incipiat mediocri uoce dulcisone cantare *Quem quaeritis?* Quo decantato finetenus,[2] respondeant hi tres, uno ore, *Ihesum Nazarenum.* Quibus ille: *Non est hic. Surrexit sicut praedixerat. Ite, nuntiate quia surrexit a mortuis.* Cuius iussionis uoce uertant se illi tres ad chorum, dicentes *Alleluia. Resurrexit Dominus.* Dicto hoc, rursus ille residens, uelut reuocans illos, dicat antiphonam: *Venite et uidete locum.* Haec uero dicens, surgat et erigat uelum ostendatque eis locum, cruce nudatum[a] sed tantum linteamina posita quibus crux inuoluta erat; quo uiso deponant turibula quae gestauerant in eodem sepulcro, sumantque linteum et extendant contra clerum ac, ueluti ostendentes quod surrexerit[b] Dominus et iam non sit illo inuolutus, hanc canant antiphonam: *Surrexit Dominus de sepulcro*, superponantque linteum altari.[3]

52. Finita antiphona prior,[4] congaudens pro triumpho regis nostri quod deuicta morte surrexit, incipiat hymnum *Te Deum laudamus;* quo incepto una pulsantur omnia signa. Post cuius finem dicat sacerdos uersum [*Surrexit Dominus de sepulcro*][5][c] uerbotenus[6] et initiet

[a] nudata F
[b] surrexit F
[c] [ ] In resurrectione tua Christe T

[1] cf. Matt. xxviii. 1 f.; Mark xvi. 1 f.; Luke xxiii. 54 f. and xxiv. 1 f.
[2] i.e., 'Q. q. in sepulchro O Christicolae.' See the Winchester Troper (HBS).
[3] For an unique parallel here see Fleury MS Bibl. Orleans *n.* 178: 'postea ponant sindonum super altare' (de Coussemaker, *Drames Liturgiques du Moyen Age*, pp. 188 ff.).

shall enter in their turn and go to the place of the 'sepulchre', step by step, as though searching for something. Now these things are done in imitation of the angel seated on the tomb and of the women coming with perfumes to anoint the body of Jesus.[1] When, therefore, he that is seated shall see these three draw nigh, wandering about as it were and seeking something, he shall begin to sing softly and sweetly, *Quem quaeritis*. As soon as this has been sung right through,[2] the three shall answer together, *Ihesum Nazarenum*. Then he that is seated shall say *Non est hic. Surrexit sicut praedixerat. Ite, nuntiate quia surrexit a mortuis.* At this command the three shall turn to the choir saying *Alleluia. Resurrexit Dominus.* When this has been sung he that is seated, as though calling them back, shall say the antiphon *Venite et videte locum*, and then, rising and lifting up the veil, he shall show them the place void of the Cross and with only the linen in which the Cross had been wrapped. Seeing this the three shall lay down their thuribles in that same 'sepulchre' and, taking the linen, shall hold it up before the clergy; and, as though showing that the Lord was risen and was no longer wrapped in it, they shall sing this antiphon: *Surrexit Dominus de sepulchro*. They shall then lay the linen on the altar.[3]

52. When the antiphon is finished the prior,[4] rejoicing in the triumph of our King in that He had conquered death and was risen, shall give out the hymn *Te Deum laudamus*, and thereupon all the bells shall peal. After this a priest shall say the verse *Surrexit Dominus de sepulchro*[5] right through[6] and shall begin Matins saying

---

[4] i.e., the abbot [5] AE and CCCC 190 agree with the reading of F.

[6] Probably 'to the end,' or 'right through,' as *finetenus* (51, 14); i.e., with the response 'Qui pro nobis pependit in ligno.'

Matutinas, dicens *Deus in adiutorium meum intende;* et a cantore ilico incohetur antiphona cum [a] psalmo *Dominus regnauit,*[1] quia *Deus misereatur nostri* [2] hoc non canitur in loco, sed cum *Deus, Deus meus, ad te de luce uigilo* [3] [b] coniunctim, canonicorum more. Quinque psalmis iure peractis cum antiphonis sibi rite pertinentibus, capitulo etiam a presbytero, uersuque *Surrexit Dominus de sepulcro* ut mos est a puero dicto, initietur antiphona in euangelio, qua peracta dicatur collecta. De Omnibus Sanctis [4] more solito his septem diebus non canimus.

53. Ad Primam quattuor psalmi: *Deus in nomine tuo,*[5] et *Confitemini* [6] [c] prima tantum feria, *Beati,*[7] *Retribue,*[8] cum alleluia et capitulo et uersu *Haec dies* directe a puero prolato; deinde *Kyrie eleison* et oratio dominica cum symbolo,[9] nec non et preces, solito ritu, subsequente collecta. Ad Tertiam: psalmus [d] *Legem pone,*[10] *Memor esto,*[11] *Bonitatem,*[12] cum alleluia et [e] *Haec dies* [responsorium graduale] [13] [f] sine capitulo et uersu. Similiter ad Sextam et Nonam. Ad Vesperam [14]: *Dixit Dominus,*[15] *Confitebor,*[16] *Beatus uir,*[17] cum antiphonis [g] sine capitulo; graduale: *Haec dies* sine uersu; *Alleluia* cum uersu et Sequentia.[18] Postea incohetur antiphona in euangelio, et collecta; dehinc eatur ad fontes, psalmum *Laudate pueri* [19] cum antiphona canentes,[h] quem sequatur collecta. Inde uero reuertentes, chorum uel oratorium quod eis

[a] in F; cum AE. [b] *om.* T [c] + dn̄o T
[d] psalmum F T [e] + gradał T [f] [ ] *om.* T
[g] antiphona T; antiphonis AE
[h] CCCC 190 has ' cum antiphona *Sedit angelus* canentes '.

[1] Ps. xcii [2] Ps. lxvi [3] Ps. lxii
[4] See Introd., p. xxxii [5] Ps. liii [6] Ps. civ
[7] Ps. cxviii. 1–16 [8] Ps. cxviii. 17–32
[9] The Athanasian Creed (*Quicumque vult*) according to AE (p. 190).
[10] Ps. cxviii. 33–48 [11] Ps. cxviii. 49–64 [12] Ps. cxviii. 65–80
[13] The Gradual respond from the Mass of the day.

Deus in adiutorium meum intende; and straightway the cantor shall give out the antiphon to the psalm *Dominus regnavit,*[1] for the *Deus misereatur nostri*[2] is not sung at this point, being joined to the *Deus, Deus meus, ad te de luce vigilo,*[3] as in the Office of Canons. When five psalms have been duly sung with their appropriate antiphons and when the chapter has been said by the priest and the verse *Surrexit Dominus de sepulchro* by one of the children, as is the custom, the antiphon to the *Benedictus* shall be intoned and, after it, the collect shall be said. The usual Office Of All Saints[4] is not sung during this week.

53. At Prime four psalms are said: *Deus in nomine tuo,*[5] *Confitemini*[6]—on Sunday only, *Beati*[7] and *Retribue*[8] with *Alleluia* and chapter and verse, *Haec dies*, said on a monotone by one of the children. Then *Kyrie eleison, Pater noster, Credo*[9] and *preces* in the usual way, followed by the collect. At Tierce: the psalm *Legem pone,*[10] *Memor esto*[11] and *Bonitatem*[12] with *Alleluia* and the Gradual respond[13] *Haec dies*, but without chapter or verse. And so in like manner at Sext and None. At Vespers[14]: *Dixit Dominus,*[15] *Confitebor*[16] and *Beatus vir*[17] with antiphons but no chapter; the Gradual, *Haec dies*, without the verse; the *Alleluia* with verse and the Sequence.[18] Then the antiphon of the *Magnificat* is given out and the collect follows. Next comes the procession to the font, during which the psalm *Laudate pueri*[19] with its antiphon is sung, followed by a collect. Returning thence they shall go

---

[14] This is substantially the Roman, or Secular, Vespers given in the *Liber Responsalis* (*PL* lxxviii. 770) and in OR I (965). Cf. *Trèves*, p. 58.

[15] Ps. cix [16] Ps. cx [17] Ps. cxi

[18] The Sequence of the Mass: either *Fulgens Praeclara* or *Victimae Paschali Laudes*. Both are in the Winchester Troper.

[19] Ps. cxii.

competens uidebitur adeant, psalmum *In exitu Israel* [1] decantantes, quem propria sequatur collecta. Completorium more peragatur canonicorum per omnia. Finitis enim psalmis, subsequitur capitulum. et uersus; exhinc *Nunc dimittis* [2] cum antiphona concinitur, consequentibus eius horae precibus cum collecta et benedictione. Hic [a] in reliquis sex diebus [3] teneatur ordo.

[a] *om.* F; his T; þysum T (gloss)

[1] Ps. cxiii. AE (p. 190) adds ' cum antiphona '. CCCC 190 has ' *In exitu* decantantes cum antiphona *Christus resurgens* quam propria, etc.'

[2] Luke ii. 29–32

[3] i.e., until None of the following Saturday, inclusive

to the choir or oratory, as seems best to them, singing the psalm *In exitu Israel*,[1] followed by a special collect. Compline shall be sung throughout after the manner of Canons. When the psalms are finished, chapter and verse follow; then the *Nunc dimittis*[2] is sung with an antiphon and the *preces*, collect and blessing of that hour follow. This order shall be kept to for the next six days.[3]

CAPVT VI

QVALITER SABBATO OCTAVARVM PASCHAE TOTOQVE AESTATIS TEMPORE AGATVR

54. Vespera uero octauarum Paschae ordo iam regularis pleniter incohetur et *una* tantum lectio *memoriter* ac *breue responsorium*, exceptis festiuis diebus, ad Nocturnam uti regula praecipit [1] tota aestate dicantur. In natalitiis tamen sanctorum [2] in quibus ab operis labore [3] non cessatur, tria responsoria et tres lectiones, ad ipsius sancti uenerationem cuius memoriam recolimus pertinentes, prolixe si ita tempus permiserit legantur. In aliis uero festiuitatibus ubi ab operis labore cessatur, duodecim lectiones [4] cum totidem responsoriis et psalmis competentibus, uti diebus dominicis, decentissime aestiuo sicut hiemali tempore legantur. Cotidianis uero noctibus [5] in quibus duodecim responsoria minime canuntur, nocturnis finitis *paruissimum*, uti regula praecipit,[6] fiat *interuallum;* dehinc facto signo canantur Matutinae. Quod si luce diei,[7] ut oportet, Matutinae fuerint finitae, egredientes ecclesiam fratres calcient [8] se, lauent, peractisque in ecclesia tribus oraminibus,[a] sedentes in claustro uacent lectioni [9] usque dum signum

[a] orationibus T

[1] *Rule* x. 3–7: '. . . lectiones in codice, propter brevitatem noctium, minime legantur; sed pro ipsis tribus lectionibus, *una* de veteri Testamento *memoriter dicatur*, quam *breve responsorium* subsequatur.' This is at Nocturns on ferias in summer. AE on the contrary (p. 196) has: 'valde gratum mihi fore quod obedientes mihi consensistis in hoc ut tres lectiones cum totidem responsoriis tota aestate ad Nocturnas sicut hieme iam praeteritis annis tenuimus . . . celebrentur.'

[2] On these lesser feasts of saints, Nocturns were as on ferias except for the three special lessons and responds. The *Rule* (Ch. xiv.: *In natalitiis sanctorum*) deals with an Office of the Sunday pattern with twelve lessons winter and summer alike, as below (' in aliis uero festiuitatibus ').

[3] For manual labour see Introd., pp. xxxiii ff.

CHAPTER VI

OF THE MANNER IN WHICH SATURDAY THE OCTAVE OF EASTER AND THE WHOLE OF SUMMER TIME SHALL BE KEPT

54. The full regular order shall begin with Vespers of the Octave of Easter; and throughout the summer, except on feast days, there shall be at Nocturns one lesson only, said by heart, and a short respond, as laid down in the Rule.[1] On those saint's days [2] on which there is no cessation from manual labour,[3] three proper responds and three lessons in honour of the saint whose memory is being kept shall be read at some length, if time allows. But on those feast days on which there is no manual labour twelve lessons [4] and as many responds with psalms corresponding thereto, as on Sundays, shall very properly be read, winter and summer alike. On weekdays [5] when twelve responds are never sung, there shall be a very small interval after Nocturns, as the Rule ordains [6]; and then, when the bell is rung, Matins shall be sung. And if Matins are ended at daybreak [7] as they should be, the brethren on leaving the church shall change their shoes,[8] wash and, having said the *Trina oratio* in church, then sit in the cloister reading [9]

[4] See p. 19 *n.* 1

[5] i.e., on ferial days

[6] *Rule* viii. 8 f.: 'A pascha autem usque ad supradictas Novembres, sic temperetur hora ut Vigiliarum Agenda *parvissimo intervallo*, quo fratres ad necessaria naturae exeant, mox Matutini, qui incipiente luce agendi sunt, subsequantur.' See p. 14 *n.* 4.

[7] *Rule*, *loc. cit.*

[8] This was done after Prime in winter. See 20, 1.

[9] No provision was made by St Benedict for the period between Matins and Prime in summer; Abbot Butler considered that it was devoted to *meditatio*, i.e., reading or spiritual exercises (*Ben. Monach.*, p. 282). *Trèves* (p. 46) agrees with the Concordia.

Primae auditum fuerit. Si uero dies necdum fuerit, sique priori uisum fuerit, facto signo, qui uoluerint lectulis suis pausent usque dum mane facto agant ut supradictum est.[1]

55. Tota namque[a] aestate, exceptis dominicis et festiuis diebus, Prima decantata Matutinalique Missa celebrata, Capitulo etiam peracto, pulsetur tabula ut supradictum est[2] et quicquid agendum[3] est agatur usque dum primum signum Tertiae sonuerit. Tertia uero peracta Missaque[b] subsequente celebrata, uti regula praecipit[4] sedentes in claustro fratres *uacent lectioni* usque dum, mediante hora quinta, primum signum Sextae fuerit auditum, quo peracto canatur Sexta; dehinc manibus lotis adeant[c] mensam,[5] sicque refecti, *lectulis suis pausent*[6] usque dum, *mediante octaua hora*, primum Nonae auditum fuerit signum, quo audito surgant et se lauent,[d] sicque ecclesiam ingressi Nonam cantent. Nona uero celebrata, poculisque haustis,[7] dicatur uersus *Deus in adiutorium* more solito, et quicquid necesse fuerit etiam tunc operentur.[8]

56. Ceteris enim horis secundum regulae praeceptum,[9] quia tempus lectionis est, lectioni tantummodo uacantes, silentium diligenti cura in claustro custodiant;

[a] enim T [b] missa est T [c] adeunt F [d] saluent F

[1] i.e., in the previous sentence [2] Above, 25, 3

[3] cf. *Rule* xlviii. 5–8: 'a pascha usque Kalendas Octobres a mane exeuntes a prima usque horam pene quartam laborent quod necessarium fuerit.' See Introd., p. xxxiv.

[4] *Rule* xlviii. 8–10: 'Ab hora autem quarta usque hora quasi sexta agente *lectioni vacent*.' See Introd., p. xxxiii.

[5] The midday meal in summer: *prandium*. See Introd., p. xxxv.

[6] *Rule* xlviii. 10–12: 'Post Sextam autem surgentes a mensa *pausent* in lectis (*lectulis suis* A*).' See the account of St Dunstan's death given in the *B Life* (*Memorials*, p. 52): '. . . dum, post horam refectionis, moribunda membra paulatim *ex more aestivi temporis* quieti dedisset. . . .'

until the bell for Prime is heard. But if it is not yet day and if the prior pleases, the bell shall be rung so that those who wish may rest on their beds until daybreak, whereupon they shall do as has been said above.[1]

55. During the entire summer, Sundays and feast days excepted, when Prime has been sung, the Morrow Mass celebrated and the Chapter carried out, the *tabula* shall be struck, as we have said,[2] and whatever work there is[3] shall be performed until the sound of the first bell for Tierce. When Tierce is ended and the Mass which follows has been celebrated, the brethren shall sit in the cloister reading, as the Rule ordains,[4] until at half past eleven the first bell for Sext is heard: Sext is then sung. Thence, after washing their hands, the brethren shall go to table[5] and then, having eaten, rest on their beds[6] until, at half past two, when the first bell for None is heard, they shall rise and wash and so enter the church and sing None. When None is ended and the brethren have taken their measure of drink[7] the verse *Deus in adiutorium* shall be said in the usual way, and again whatever work is necessary shall be accomplished.[8]

56. The remaining hours of the day are times for reading; and therefore, in accordance with the ordinance of the Rule,[9] the brethren shall spend them in reading only, keeping strict silence in the cloister. For

---

[7] See p. 27 *n.* 3.

[8] *Rule* xlviii. 13 f.: 'Et agatur Nona temperius, *mediante octava hora*, et iterum quod faciendum est operentur usque ad vesperam.' See Introd., p. xxxiv.

[9] The allusion is probably to the *summum silentium* prescribed by the *Rule* xlii. 20 f.

nam et omni tempore a primo pulsu Vespertinalis Synaxis [1] silentium [2] teneatur [a] in claustro usquequo Capitulum finiatur alterius diei, excepto auditorii [3] loco, qui et ab hoc maxime eo censetur nomine quod ibi audiendum sit quid [b] a praeceptore iubeatur; non uero fabulis aut otiosis ibi aut [c] alicubi uacari loquelis oportet. Nam dum regulae auctoritas *omni tempore silentio studendum* dicat,[4] opportuno tamen tempore de rebus necessariis pro *taciturnitatis grauitate*,[5] uti patronus noster beatus Benedictus, non alta sed submissa [6] uoce loquendum permisimus; alias autem [d] de Deo et animae suae salute cum silentio meditandum, uti ipse [7] censuit, hortamur; tempus etiam lectionis tempus est taciturnitatis. Vesperae uero et Matutinae De Omnibus Sanctis ab octauis Paschae una canantur antiphona [8] usque octauas Pentecosten; Vigiliaque Pro Defunctis et psalmi, qui pro benefactoribus [9] solent cani, necne [e] letaniae [10] ante Missam, quoniam a genuflectione [11] ordo ecclesiasticus declinari admonet, omni modo intermittantur.[12] [f]

[a] tenetur F [b] quia T [c] *om.* F [d] *om.* F

[e] nec T. *Necne* in the sense of *necnon* is found in English MSS both before and after the Conquest.

[f] intermittatur F

[1] cf. *Rule* xvii. 16

[2] Strict silence from Vespers until after the next day's Chapter was of common observance. The monks of Inda observed two periods of silence, absolute, from the evening *collatio* until the Chapter of the next day, less strict, from the Chapter to *collatio*, during which period necessary conversation was allowed (cf. *Stat. Murbac.*, C.M. iii. p. 91).

[3] The *Stat. Murbac.* (*loc. cit.* p. 89) mention the *auditorium* as the place where the abbot spoke with the brethren, or where guests might be entertained. In the Concordia the *auditorium* and the guesthouse (*hospitium*, see 63, 4 and 16) are separate.

[4] *Rule* xlii. 1 f.: '*Omni tempore* silentium (*silentio : Text. Recept.*) debent *studere* monachi.'

[5] cf. *Rule* vi. 10 f.: '. . . perfectis discipulis propter *taciturnitatis gravitatem* rara loquendi concedatur licentia.'

from the first bell of the Vesper Office [1] silence [2] must always be kept there until after the chapter of the following day. The *auditorium* [3] is excepted from the rule of silence; indeed, it is called by that name chiefly because it is there that whatever is commanded by the master shall be heard; neither is it right that tales or gossip should go on there or anywhere else. And yet, while the authority of the Rule bids us keep silence [4] at all times, we nevertheless permit talking, as also does our patron the blessed Benedict, at the proper time and touching necessary affairs: not indeed in a loud voice but softly,[6] on account of the importance of silence.[5] For the rest we exhort the brethren to meditate on God and on the state of their souls in silence as St Benedict lays down [7]; for the times for reading are also times for silence. Vespers and Matins Of All Saints are sung with one antiphon [8] from the Octave of Easter until the Octave of Pentecost; but Vigils Of the Dead, the psalms which are sung for benefactors [9] and the Litanies [10] before Mass shall all be omitted,[12] since Holy Church admonishes us to refrain from genuflecting.[11]

---

[6] cf. *Rule* vi. 17, f.; vii. 180 f. and *passim*.

[7] See Butler, *Ben. Mon.*, p. 288: 'The general tenor of the Rule suggests not what Abbot Delatte repudiates under the name "mutism," but rather that the monks spoke when reasonable necessity arose.'

[8] The grouping of a number of psalms under one antiphon was a feature of the Office in Paschal time. Thus there would be one antiphon for the psalms of Lauds, one for those of Vespers (and one for each nocturn at Matins); the extra Offices would follow the same plan. Cf. AE, p. 190.

[9] i.e., for King, Queen and benefactors. See 18, 19.

[10] See 25, 23.

[11] cf. *Epist. Pauli Diac. ad Carolum Regem*, C.M. iii. p. 64: 'A pascha quoque usque ad pentecosten similiter ad publicum officium genua non flectimus' and *Ordo Officii in Domo S. Benedicti, ibid.*, p. 24, apparat.

[12] For these omissions see DR, Oct. 1932, pp. 454 ff.

CAPVT VII

[QVALITER FRATER QVI CIRCA VOCATVR SVVM OFFICIVM IMPLEAT][a]

57. Nam[b] et secundum regulae praeceptum[1] constitui debet aliquis frater qui totius claustri sub decano[2] curam gerat; qui ab officio circuitus sui *circa*[3] uocatur. Est enim eius officium saepius circuire claustrum *ne forte inueniatur frater accidiosus*[4] aut alicui uanitati deditus; quod si inuenerit, nullatenus illud debet reticere in Capitulo uenturi diei, nisi si pro leui qualibet culpa frater ille, satisfactione humiliatus, hoc impetrauerit ab illo. Qui etiam *circa* post Completorium circumeat claustrum et si qua inuenerit ibi codicum aut uestimentorum asportet ea ad Capitulum sequentis diei; nullus enim ea ullatenus tollere debet ab eo loco in quo ea posuerit absque eius licentia. Habeatque ille[c] frater laternam qua nocturnis horis, quibus oportet haec agere, uidendo consideret[5]: quique dum lectiones leguntur ad Nocturnos, in tertia uel quarta lectione prout uiderit expedire, circumeat chorum; et si fratrem inuenerit somno oppressum anteponat illi laternam et reuertatur; qui mox excusso somno petat ueniam genuflexo et, arrepta eadem laterna, pergyret et ipse chorum et si quidem[d] eiusmodi[e] morbo somni affectum inuenerit, agat illi sicut et ipsi factum est reuertaturque in locum suum.

[a] [ ] *om.* T [b] Iam T [c] *om.* F
[d] quem T [e] huiusmodi T

[1] *Rule* xlviii. 39 ff.: 'Ante omnia sane deputentur unus aut duo seniores, qui circumeant monasterium horis quibus vacent fratres lectioni, et videant *ne forte inveniatur frater acediosus* qui vacat otio aut fabulis.'

[2] This is the second mention of the dean in the Concordia. See 41, 10.

[3] The *circa* or *circator* appears in *Warnfrid* (pp. 397 and 266), in documents of the Anianian movement, and later in *Eins*, *Trèves*, *Verdun*, *Farfa* and *Ulrich*, but not in the earliest Cluniac books (B B_1 C). *Verdun* (p. 129) comes very close to the Concordia: 'Circator monasterii horis incompetentibus ubique circuiens explorabit; quod si noxium quid offenderit, mane in capitulo suum erit clamare.'

[4] See *n.* 1 above.

CHAPTER VII

OF THE MANNER IN WHICH THE BROTHER WHO IS CALLED *CIRCA* SHALL FULFIL HIS DUTIES

57. Now, according to the ordinance[1] of the Rule, a brother must be appointed to look after the entire cloister, under the direction of the dean.[2] This brother shall be called *circa*[3] from his office of going rounds. For his duty is frequently to go the round of the cloister lest perchance there be found a brother who is slothful[4] or given to some vanity. And if the *circa* finds such a one he should by no means keep silence about the matter at the Chapter on the following day unless, in the case of some slight fault, that brother, humbling himself and giving satisfaction, shall beseech him. The *circa* shall also go round the cloister after Compline, and if he finds there codices or garments he shall take them away and show them at the next day's Chapter; nor may anyone ever remove them without his permission from the place in which he has put them. Moreover, the *circa* shall have a lantern so that he may look about him[5] in the night hours, when it is proper so to do; and when the lessons are read at Nocturns, at the third or fourth lesson, as seems good to him, he shall go about the choir; and if he finds a brother drowsy with sleep he shall put the lantern before him and return to his place. Whereupon this brother, shaking off sleep, shall do penance on his knees and, taking up the lantern, shall himself go round the choir, and if he finds another overcome by the disorder of sleep, he shall do to him as was done to himself and so return to his own place.

---

[5] *Trèves* (p. 7 f.), *Verdun* (p. 129 f.), *Farfa* (p. 147) and *Ulrich* give the same custom with minor variations. Though there is no literary connection between the two early forms (those of *Trèves* and *Verdun*) and that of the Concordia, the close resemblance suggests that the English borrowed their custom from a Lotharingian source.

CAPVT VIII

QVALITER DIVRNALE SIVE NOCTVRNALE OFFICIVM HEBDOMADA PENTECOSTES AGATVR

58. Incipiunt orationes cum lectionibus [1] atque canticis quae dicuntur in uigiliis Pentecostes ante descensum fontis: prima lectio: *Tentauit Deus*,[2] [cum cantico: *Cantemus Domino*] [3] [a]; sequitur oratio: *Deus qui in Abrahae famuli tui*. Secunda lectio: [*Scripsit Moyses canticum*] [4] [b]; canticum: *Vinea* [*facta est*] [5] [c]; sequitur oratio: *Deus qui nobis per prophetarum*. Tertia lectio: *Apprehendent* [6]; canticum: [*Attende caelum*] [7] [d]; sequitur oratio: *Deus qui nos ad celebrandum*. Quarta lectio: *Audi Israel* [8] [e]; canticum: *Sicut ceruus* [9]; sequitur oratio: [*Omnipotens sempiterne*].[f] Finita oratione incohantur letaniae septenae [10] ad introitum ante altare. Postea descendat abbas [11] cum schola canente letanias quinas ad fontes benedicendos. Sequitur oratio et praefatio. His expletis redeunt ad altare cum letania terna; quo finito dicat sacerdos *Gloria in excelsis Deo*; sequitur oratio: *Praesta quaesumus*; postea legitur epistola,[12] *Cum Apollo*,[13] et cantatur *Alleluia, Confitemini Domino*,[14] et tractus: *Laudate* [15]; deinde Missa secundum ordinem. Post

[a] [ ] *om.* T [b] [ ] apprehendent T [c] [ ] coelum T
[d] [ ] Vinea facta T
[e] + sequitur oratio Deus qui incommutabilis T
[f] [ ] Concede quaesumus T

[1] These prayers and lessons are as in *Greg* and Amalar. It is possible that F has reversed the correct positions of the second and third canticles. For *Attende coelum* and *Vinea facta est* would naturally follow the lessons *Scripsit Moyses* and *Apprehendent* of which they are the respective continuations. This seems to have been the order known to Amalar (*De Eccl. Off.*, *PL* cv. 1068 ff.). T is corrupt but supports this conjecture, reading *Vinea coelum* where the second canticle ought to be, and *Vinea facta* after *Apprehendent* (correctly given as *lectio tertia*). *Jumièges* follows F. CCCC 190 follows Amalar. In general cf. the rites of Holy Saturday (48).

[2] Gen. xxii [3] Exod. xv [4] Deut. xxxi. 22 ff.

CHAPTER VIII

OF THE MANNER IN WHICH THE DAY AND NIGHT OFFICE SHALL BE CARRIED OUT IN WHIT WEEK

58. Here begin the prayers, lessons [1] and canticles which are said on the Vigil of Pentecost before going down to the font: first lesson: *Tentavit Deus* [2] with the canticle, *Cantemus Domino* [3] followed by the prayer, *Deus qui in Abrahae famuli tui.* Second lesson: *Scripsit Moyses canticum* [4]; canticle, *Vinea facta est,*[5] followed by the prayer, *Deus qui nobis per prophetarum.* Third lesson: *Apprehendent* [6]; canticle, *Attende coelum,*[7] followed by the prayer, *Deus qui nos ad celebrandum.* Fourth lesson: *Audi Israel* [8]; canticle, *Sicut cervus* [9] followed by the prayer, *Omnipotens sempiterne.* When this prayer is ended, the sevenfold Litanies [10] are begun at the entrance before the altar. The abbot [11] and *schola* shall then go down to bless the font, singing the fivefold Litanies. There follow the prayer and the Preface. When these are ended they return to the altar singing the threefold Litanies. When this is over the priest shall say *Gloria in excelsis Deo.* There follows the prayer, *Praesta quaesumus;* then the epistle,[12] *Cum Apollo,*[13] is read, the *Alleluia, Confitemini Domino* [14] and Tract, *Laudate,*[15] are

---

[5] Is. v. 1–2 [6] Is. iv [7] Deut. xxxii

[8] Bar. iii. 9 ff. (frequently cited as *Lectio Ieremiae* by Amalar and in documents of the period). [9] Ps. xli

[10] These rubrical directions concerning the three Litanies are the same as those of Holy Saturday; see 48, 20 f. Here they are found also in *Jumièges* but, so far as I know, nowhere else.

[11] A few lines below we find *sacerdos*; see p. 45 *n.* 8. Here the same confusion is found in *Jumièges.*

[12] See p. 48 *n.* 7. [13] Acts xix. 1–8 [14] Ps. cxvii.

[15] From Ps. cxvi.

refectionem uero, tempore congruo, Vesperae ceteraque celebrantur more solito.

59. Illa dominica nocte tribus psalmis totidemque lectionibus cum responsoriis agitur Nocturna laus, uti in Antiphonario [1] titulatur; ceteris uero horis diei et hebdomadae sequentis, regularis ordo [2] teneatur. Sed et Vesperae sabbati et ipsius diei [3] sancti normaliter psallantur. Illa hebdomada Pentecostes sollemniter celebratur sicut et Paschalis, excepto quod ieiuniorum diebus [4] *Gloria in excelsis Deo* non canitur; et *Alleluia* pro gradualibus canitur, et Vesperae De Omnibus Sanctis [5] dicuntur. Rursus in octauis Pentecostes [a] dominica [6] non repetitur *Spiritus Domini*, eo quod septem tantum colimus [b] dona Spiritus Sancti, sed agitur illa hebdomada de Sancta Trinitate.

60. Sabbato dominicalis Vesperae [7] canatur hymnus *Deus Creator omnium* [8]; ad Completorium: *Te lucis ante terminum;* ad Nocturnas: *Nocte surgentes;* ad Matutinas: *Ecce iam noctis.* Iste ordo tota aestate teneatur usque Kalendas Nouembris; ab ipsis uero Kalendis longiores ut supradictum [9] est hymni dicantur et, finitis duobus psalmis,[10] qui post Nocturnas dicuntur, agatur Vigilia [11] quae pro breuitate dierum uespere non poterat agi nisi his tantum diebus festiuis [c] quibus cenaturi [12] sunt fratres; tunc enim cena [13] facta agant Vigiliam,

[a] *om.* T [b] colamus F [c] festis T

[1] The Antiphonar of the Roman, or Secular, Office; see Amalar (*De Eccl. Off.*, *PL* cv. 1213 and *De Ord. Antiph.*, *ibid.* 1301), the *Liber Responsalis* (*PL* lxxviii. 782) and other books of the Roman Office down to the present day. Cf. *Verdun*, p. 125.

[2] The Monastic Office; cf. *Verdun, loc. cit.*

[3] First and second Vespers of Whit Sunday

[4] The Quarter Tense days.

[5] For this Office see Introd., p. xxxii.

[6] The First Sunday after Pentecost, later, Trinity Sunday. The Concordia and *Trèves* have the Mass *De Sancta Trinitate; Farfa, Ulrich* and Lanfranc's *Decreta* have the Mass *Spiritus Domini.*

sung and the Mass proceeds on its course. After the meal, at the proper hour, Vespers and the rest are celebrated in the usual way.

59. On that Sunday the night Office shall be carried out with three psalms and a like number of lessons and responds, as laid down in the Antiphonar.[1] At the other hours of this day and of the week following the regular order [2] shall be kept. Vespers, both of the Saturday and of the feast itself,[3] shall be chanted according to the Rule. Whit week, like that of Easter, is kept solemnly except that the *Gloria in excelsis Deo* is not sung on fast days,[4] *Alleluia* is sung instead of the Gradual, and Vespers Of All Saints [5] are said. *Spiritus Domini* is not repeated on Sunday,[6] the Octave of Pentecost, since we honour no more than seven gifts of the Holy Ghost: instead, the Mass that week shall be of the Holy Trinity.

60. On Saturday, at the first Vespers [7] of the Sunday, the hymn *Deus Creator omnium* [8] shall be sung; at Compline, *Te lucis ante terminum;* at Nocturns, *Nocte surgentes;* at Matins, *Ecce iam noctis.* This order shall last throughout the summer until the Calends of November. But after the Calends of November longer hymns shall be sung, as has been said above [9]; moreover, the two psalms [10] which are said after Nocturns shall be followed by Vigils Of the Dead,[11] which cannot be said in the evening, because of the short days, except on those feast days when the brethren have a second meal [12]: then indeed, when supper [13]

---

[7] First Vespers of the First Sunday after Pentecost. The hymn for the Second Vespers of Sundays throughout the year, summer and winter, was *Lucis Creator;* cf. AE, pp. 177 and 191. See p. 25 *n.* 5.

[8] For the text of this and the three following hymns see Stevenson, *Latin Hymns of the Anglo-Saxon Church.*

[9] 28, 4–7 above

[10] See p. 14 *n.* 3

[11] Nocturns Of the Dead. See p. 28 *n.* 4.

[12] i.e., on Sundays and feasts of twelve lessons

[13] Here used of the second meal

ministris interim cenantibus, ut postmodum iuxta regulae dictum [1] omnes occurrant ad Collationem. Hic ordo Vigiliae usque ad Caput Quadragesimae ita teneatur. In Quadragesima uero post cenam [2] et sic demum, in totius longitudine aestatis, uespere custodiatur post cenam [3] aut post Vespertinalem Laudem si cena defuerit.

[1] *Rule* xlii. 15–16: 'omnibus in unum occurrentibus per hanc moram lectionis'

[2] Here used of the one Lenten meal

[3] Here used of the second meal in summer, allowed daily except on certain fast days

is over, Vigils shall be celebrated while the ministers take their meal, so that afterwards, in accordance with the ordinance of the Rule,[1] all shall come together for *collatio*. This arrangement for Vigils Of the Dead shall last until Ash Wednesday. But in Lent, Vigils Of the Dead shall take place after *cena*,[2] and thenceforth, throughout the entire summer, either after *cena*[3] or after Vespers when there is no *cena*.

CAPVT IX

[QVALITER QVATTVOR TEMPORIBVS AGATVR][a]

61. Quattuor temporibus,[1] quae ecclesiastice custodiuntur, ad Missae celebrationem dicitur a diacono *Flectamus genua* quadragesimali more, et eorundem quorum in Quadragesima fit abstinentia ciborum [2] cum magna custodiatur diligentia, excepto dum in Pentecosten hebdomada euenerit; tum enim aliquantulum remissius [3] pro tantae sollemnitatis reuerentia agi opportunum duximus.

[a] [ ] *om.* T

[1] Wednesdays, Fridays and Saturdays in Lent, in or after Whit week, after September 14th and after December 13th. See Egbert's *Dialogue* (Haddan and Stubbs, *Councils and Ecclesiastical Documents*, iii. 410 ff.).

CHAPTER IX

OF THE MANNER IN WHICH THE QUARTER TENSE DAYS SHALL BE KEPT

61. On the Quarter Tense[1] days, which are of ecclesiastical ordinance, the deacon says *Flectamus genua* at Mass in the Lenten manner. Moreover, the same abstinence[2] as that of Lent shall be faithfully practised except when these days fall within Whit week: then, indeed, we have deemed it right that the observance should be less strict,[3] out of reverence for so great a solemnity.

---

[2] For the Lenten abstinence see p. 32 *n.* 1

[3] See *Verdun*, p. 125: 'Quod si ieiunium quattuor temporum in hac sollemnitate evenerit, . . . licet quadragesimaliter prandeant, sollemni tamen cultu habebunt. . . .'

CAPVT X

QVALITER MANDATVM COTIDIANIS[1] DIEBVS A FRATRIBVS EXHIBEATVR PAVPERIBVS, ET QVO ORDINE ABBAS ERGA PEREGRINOS AGAT

62. Mandatum, quod ex dominico tenemus exemplo[2] sacrae etiam regulae[3] monitu, eo excepto[4] quod sibi inuicem exhibent fratres, pauperibus summa cum diligentia praebeatur[a] in quibus *Christus adoretur, qui et suscipitur.*[5] Sint igitur in unoquoque monasterio singula loca[6] ad hoc constituta ubi pauperum fiat susceptio, omnique die[7] sine intermissione tres, ex his qui continuo in monasterio pascuntur, eligantur pauperes quibus eiusdem Mandati exhibeatur obsequium, quique eisdem pascantur uictualibus quibus fratres eadem utuntur die. Hoc ergo modo illuc eundi ordinem prosequantur, scilicet: sabbato pueri dexterioris[b] chori cum uno custode illud peragant; sequenti die dominica residui pueri sinisterioris[c] chori cum altero custode[8]; deinde singulis diebus hebdomadae ad unamquamque feriam tot constituantur fratres ad hoc agendum ut, extra abbatem, nullus ab hoc debito seruitutis excusetur; qui tamen abbas non una tantum feria sed saepius, dum ei uacuum fuerit utque opportunitas dictauerit, sese ad hoc agendum impendat.[9][d]

[a] praebetur F   [b] dextri T   [c] sinistri T   [d] impendit F

[1] i.e., every day, including Sundays. See 62, 14.

[2] John xiii. 1 f.   [3] *Rule* liii. *passim*

[4] For the weekly monastic Maundy of the *Rule* see 26, 8 and 64, 1. AE (p. 192) says: 'Mandatum omni sabbato faciendum fratribus regula sancta satis monet, sed insuper consuetudo docet omni die trium pauperum . . . fratres . . . debere lavare pedes, etc.'

[5] *Rule* liii. 15; cf. *ibid.* 30–32

[6] See the *hospitium* mentioned twice below.

[7] The daily Maundy of the poor was of general observance. It may have been carried out after Vigils of the Dead in winter and after the first signal for None in summer (cf. *Trèves*, pp. 23 and 43 f.).

CHAPTER X

OF THE ORDER IN WHICH THE DAILY[1] MAUNDY SHALL BE OFFERED TO THE POOR BY THE BRETHREN; AND IN WHAT MANNER THE ABBOT SHALL ENTERTAIN STRANGERS

62. The Maundy, in which we follow the Lord's example [2] as also the admonition of the Holy Rule,[3] shall —apart from that [4] which the brethren carry out among themselves—be administered with the greatest care to the poor, in whom Christ shall be adored Who is received in them.[5] Therefore let there be a place set apart [6] for the reception of the poor, where daily [7] and without fail the service of the Maundy may be rendered to three poor men chosen from among those who are wont to receive their support from the monastery; and let the same foods of which the brethren partake that day be given to them. Let this Maundy, then, be attended to in the following manner: on Saturday the children of the right hand choir with their master shall carry it out, and on the following Sunday the other children, those of the left hand choir, with the other master [8]; and thenceforth on each day of the week let so many of the brethren be deputed to this duty that, apart from the abbot, no one shall be excused from the obligation of this service. As for the abbot, let him devote himself to this office not only once but as often as leisure or opportunity suggests.[9]

---

[8] See *Trèves*, p. 24: 'Sabbato pueri de dextro debent hoc facere coro, die dominica de sinistro, sequenti eos uno magistro'; cf. *ibid.* pp. 55–56.

[9] Nothing like this is to be found in any other consuetudinary. See Introd., p. xxxvii.

63. De cetero, superuenientibus peregrinis pauperibus abbas cum fratribus quos elegerit, secundum regulae praeceptum,[1] Mandati exhibeat[a] obsequium. Omnia igitur humanitatis[b] officia in hospitio pater[2] ipse, si quomodo potuerit, uel fratrum quilibet deuotissime praebeat; nec[c] aliquid in eorum obsequio quod regula praecipit, tumoris fastu seductus uel obliuionis naeuo deceptus, insipienter praetermittat; hoc solummodo, quod sancti patres ob animae salutem uirtutumque potius custodiam quam ad regulae contemptum synodali statuerunt[d] concilio,[3] magnopere custodito ut uidelicet in monasterio degens,[4] extra refectorium nec ipse abbas nec fratrum quispiam nisi causa infirmitatis manducet uel bibat.[5] Cetera omnia, uti diximus, cum magna animi alacritate deuotissimus impleat; nec pauperibus aeterni Christi uicarius[6] in hospitio competenti tardus ac tepidus[7] ministrare differendo desistat qui celer ac feruidus diuitibus caducis ministrando occurrere desiderat. Proficiscentibus uero peregrinis, secundum quod loci suppetit facultas, eis impendatur uictualium solatium.

[a] exhibeant T
[b] cf. *Rule* liii. 20: '. . . omnis ei exhibeatur humanitas.'
[c] ne T
[d] statuerant T

[1] *Rule* liii. 25 ff.: 'Aquam in manibus abbas hospitibus det; pedes hospitibus omnibus tam abbas quam cuncta congregatio lavet. . . . Pauperum et peregrinorum maxime susceptioni cura sollicite exhibeatur.'
[2] i.e., the abbot.
[3] The Council of Aix, 817.
[4] cf. *Rule* v. 26: '. . . in coenobiis degentes. . . .'
[5] See *Aix Capit.*, p. 122: 'Ut *abbas vel quispiam fratrum* ad portam monasterii cum hospitibus non reficiant.' This was contrary to the *Rule* (liii. 34: 'Coquina abbatis et hospitum super se sit'; and lvi. 1–4: 'Mensa

63. Moreover, when poor strangers arrive, the abbot and such of the brethren as he shall choose shall render to them the service of the Maundy in accordance with the ordinance of the Rule.[1] Wherefore whenever he can, the father himself,[2] no less than each of the brethren, shall be most zealous in providing every kind service in the guesthouse; nor, seduced by boastful pride or deceived by idle thoughtlessness, shall he foolishly neglect anything commanded by the Rule in this regard. One point, however, must be firmly kept in mind, namely, the decision made by the holy fathers at a Synodal Council[3]—not indeed out of contempt of the Rule but for the good of souls and the safeguard of virtues—that, of those who dwell in a monastery,[4] neither the abbot himself nor any of the brethren shall eat or drink outside the refectory[5] except in the case of sickness. All other duties, as we have said, the abbot shall fulfil most faithfully and with great gladness of heart; nor let him who is the vicar[6] of the eternal Christ be slow and cold[7] in the guesthouse of the monastery nor delay or neglect his ministrations to the poor while in the management of transitory affairs he shows himself swift and fervent in his desire to serve the rich. For the rest, wayfarers shall on their departure be provided with a supply of victuals according to the means of the house.

---

abbatis cum hospitibus et peregrinis sit semper . . . quos vult de fratribus vocare in ipsius sit potestate '). cf. AE, p. 192.

[6] cf. 69, 15: ' cuius uicarii sunt.'

[7] cf. *Rule* v. 34: ' non tarde, non tepide.'

CAPVT XI

QVO ORDINE SABBATO FRATRES MVNDITIAS EXERCEANT ET QVAEQVE OFFICIA[1a] OB ANIMAE SALVTEM PERSOLVANT

64. Sabbato, secundum regulae praeceptum,[2] Mandatum et munditias diligenti cura exerceant; et qualiter fieri debeant qui adhuc nesciunt solliciti[b] discant ⟨et⟩ solito more studiosi compleant. Nullus[c] *quippiam quamuis parum* sua ac quasi propria adinuentione[3] agere praesumat; nec ecclesia, horas celebrando constitutas, nec *claustro* uti regula praecipit[4] *egredi*, nec parum quid sine prioris licentia superbiae tumore inflatus audeat. Calciamentorum unctio, uestimentorumque ablutio et aquae administratio non aspernatur sed ab uniuersis, si Domini gratia uires concesserit, tempore opportuno consuete peragatur. *Coquinae* ac pistrinae ceterarumque rerum *officia*,[d] uti sancta regula praecipit,[5] unusquisque prout uires suppetunt gratulabundus exhibeat, ne regulae praeceptorum minima paruipendendo praetereat, ac sic, dicente apostolo, *omnium* mandatorum quod absit *reus* existat.[6]

[a] officina F T [b] sollicite F

[c] The order of this and the following sentence is reversed in F.

[d] officina F T

[1] For the reading *officia*, here and later in this section, see the corresponding Chapter heading (13, 26). For *officina* see *Rule* iv. 99.

[2] *Rule* xxxv. 12 ff.: 'Egressurus de septimana, sabbato *munditias* faciat.' For the Saturday *munditiae* of the Concordia see 26, 3 and (for the Maundy) 26, 8.

[3] cf. 6, 1: 'ne igitur singuli si suam . . . adinuentionem, etc.'

[4] *Rule* lxvii. 16–18: 'vindictae regulari subiaceat . . . qui praesumpserit *claustra* monasterii *egredi* . . . vel *quippiam quamvis parvum* sine iussione abbatis facere.'

CHAPTER XI

OF THE ORDER IN WHICH THE BRETHREN SHALL CARRY OUT THE *MUNDITIAE* ON SATURDAY; AND OF CERTAIN DUTIES[1] WHICH THEY SHALL FULFIL FOR THE GOOD OF THEIR SOULS

64. On Saturday, according to the ordinance of the Rule,[2] let the brethren carry out the Maundy and the *munditiae* with loving care; and let those who are as yet ignorant of these duties study carefully how they should be performed and so, in the accustomed way, fulfil them conscientiously. Let no one presume to do anything whatsoever, however small, of his own, and as it were personal choice[3]; neither let him leave the church during the celebration of the appointed hours nor the cloister, as the Rule enjoins,[4] nor, puffed up by overweening pride, let him dare to do the least thing without the permission of the prior. Let no one scorn to grease shoes or to wash garments or to minister water; but let these things be done by each, as the grace of the Lord enables him, at the proper time and in the accustomed way. Let each one according to his strength and with thanksgiving fulfil the duties of the kitchen and bakehouse as the Rule commands[5]; lest by careless neglect of the smallest precept of the Rule he become *guilty*, as the apostle says, *of all* the commandments[6]: which God forbid.

---

[5] *Rule* xxxv. 1–2: 'nullus excusetur a *coquinae officio*.'
[6] Jas. ii. 10

CAPVT XII

QVOMODO CIRCA AEGROTVM [FRATREM AGATVR, QVALITERQVE DEFVNCTVM HVMO CONVENIAT REDDI] [a]

65. Dum ad debitum communis fragilitatis exsoluendum quis uocatus fuerit, dum senserit se nimia inualitudine praegrauari [b] ita ut iam non possit portari, ueniat frater ille ante abbatem uel cunctam congregationem et infirmitatis suae causas exponat; et sic omnium accepta benedictione ingrediatur domum infirmorum,[1] omnibus pro eo sollicitis in suis interuentionibus.[c] In ea itaque domo seruitores [2] sint, Dei timore fraternoque amore feruentes, qui ei in quibuscumque indiguerit suppeditent; aut, si necesse fuerit, cum sollicito fratre famulorum [3] adhibeatur obsequium. Frater autem ille infirmus si senserit suam creuisse imbecillitatem, indicetur hoc conuentui a fratre illius custode. Ex eo ergo cotidie [4] post Matutinalem Missam sacerdos casula exutus, cum reliquis ministris illius Missae Eucharistiam ferentibus, praecedentibus cereis et turibulo, cum omni congregatione eant ad uisitandum infirmum canentes psalmos paenitentiales,[5] consequente letania et orationibus ac unctione olei prima tantum die [6]: demum communicetur. Quod si infirmitas leuigata fuerit intermittatur et hoc [7]; sin alias, prosequatur uisitatio usque ad exitum. Eo igitur in extremis

[a] [ ] *om.* F [b] pergrauari T [c] interbenedictionibus F

[1] cf. *Rule* xxxvi. 12–13: 'quibus fratribus infirmis sit cella super se deputata. . . .'

[2] Monks, not laymen; see context ('Dei timore fraternoque amore feruentes') and *Rule* xxxvi. 13–14: 'servitor timens Deum et diligens ac sollicitus.'

[3] i.e., lay servants

[4] The *daily* visitation, after the Morrow Mass, of a monk who is dangerously ill, appears to be peculiar to the Concordia. Most of the consuetudinaries mention the visit itself. See e.g., *Trèves*, pp. 12 and 63.

CHAPTER XII

OF THE CARE OF A SICK BROTHER; AND OF THE MANNER IN WHICH THE DEAD SHALL BE COMMITTED TO THE EARTH

65. When a brother is called upon to pay the debt of our common weakness and feels himself to be weighed down with such exceeding sickness that he can no longer endure it, he shall present himself to the abbot and the whole community and shall set forth to them the state of his sickness. And thus, with the blessing of all, he shall enter the sick-house,[1] all being solicitous in rendering aid to him. Let there be therefore in that house brethren,[2] fervent in the fear of God and love of the brotherhood, who shall furnish the sick brother with everything he wants; if indeed it is necessary, let the help of servants[3] be employed under a careful brother. And if the sick man shall feel that his weakness increases, this shall be made known to the community by the brother who has care of him. Thenceforth daily[4] after the Morrow Mass the celebrant, having taken off his chasuble, and the other ministers of that Mass, bearing with them the Eucharist, preceded by acolytes and thurifer, with the whole community shall go to visit the sick brother, singing the Penitential psalms[5] followed by the Litanies and prayers and, on the first day only,[6] the anointing with oil: the sick brother shall then receive Communion. If the sickness improves, the visiting shall be discontinued,[7] but if not, it shall be kept up until the death of that brother.

---

[5] Pss. vi, xxxi, xxxvii, l, ci, cxxix, cxlii
[6] The Sacrament of Unction was not repeated in the same illness.
[7] The daily visitation ceased

agente, pulsetur tabula conueniantque omnes [1] ad tuendum exitum eius et initient Commendationem Animae: *Subuenite sancti Dei* [2] et reliqua, iuxta Ordinem Commendationis.

66. Exempto autem homine lauetur corpus a quibus iussum fuerit; lotum induitur [3] mundis uestimentis, id est interula, cuculla,[4] caligis, calceis, cuiuscumque sit ordinis; [nisi si uero] [a] sacerdos fuerit circumdatur ei stola super cucullam si ita ratio dictauerit. Inde defertur in ecclesiam, psallentibus cunctis motisque omnibus signis. Quod si ante lucem nocte aut, finitis tenebris, in matutino obierit, si sepulturae impendenda praeparari possunt, ante refectionem fratrum sepeliatur, peractis Missarum celebrationibus; si minus, ordinentur fratres qui sine intermissione psalmodiae uacent, residentes circa corpus die noctuque sequenti, donec mane facto corpus terrae commendetur.

67. Consummatis omnibus quae sepulturae officio debentur, ibidem incipientes septem paenitentiae psalmos reuertantur ad ecclesiam et, prostrati coram sancto altari, finiant eosdem psalmos pro fratre defuncto. Dehinc per septem continuos dies plenarie [5] agatur Vigilia, offerentibus [6] cunctis ad Matutinalem Missam;

[a] [ ] nisi F; nisi si AE. The original text may have been 'cuiuscumque sit ordinis; si uero etc.' Possibly 'nisi' is a confusion arising from 'ordin*is si*.' See, however, 57, 7 for 'nisi si'.

[1] This was of general observance. There is an example in Adelard's account of the death of Dunstan: 'sanctam adesse iubet fratrum congregationem' (*Memorials*, p. 66).

[2] cf. *Jumièges*, pp. 297 ff.

[3] The three indicative readings of the MSS (*induitur . . . circumdatur . . . defertur*) are supported by AE (p. 193).

[4] The monastic outer garment of the *Rule* (lv.). Before the tenth century it was sometimes called *casula* (see *Warnfrid*, p. 426, and the *Ep. Pauli Diaconi ad Carolum Regem*, C.M. iii. p. 59) owing to its ample form, which may then have resembled the Mass *casula*. The various early

When therefore the sick brother is nearing his end, the *tabula* shall be struck and all shall assemble[1] to assist his passing; and they shall begin the *Commendatio animae: Subvenite sancti Dei*[2] and the rest, according to the *Ordo Commendationis.*

66. When the brother has departed this life, his body shall be washed by those appointed to do so: when washed it is clothed[3] in clean garments namely, in shirt, cowl,[4] stockings and shoes, no matter what his rank. But if he is a priest a stole may be placed about him over his cowl, if such be the rule. The body shall then be borne into the church with the chanting of psalms and the tolling of bells. And if the brother died before dawn, in the night or after the dark hours, in the early morning, let him be buried before the brethren have their meal, when the Masses have been celebrated, provided that those things necessary for a burial can be prepared: otherwise let the brethren be appointed by turns to chant psalms unceasingly by the body throughout that day and the following night until early morning when it shall be committed to the earth.

67. When all things proper to the Burial Office have been completed, let the brethren straightway begin the seven Penitential psalms and, returning to the church let them, prostrate before the holy altar, finish those psalms for the dead brother. Thenceforward for seven successive days the Office Of the Dead shall be said in full,[5] and all shall make the offering[6] at the

---

forms of the *cuculla* evolved into a full, pleated garment, sometimes hooded, with long sleeves: the modern Benedictine Choir dress.

[5] i.e., an Office of three Nocturns (nine psalms, nine lessons, nine responds) as distinguished from that of one nocturn (three psalms, etc.) referred to below (67, 9).

[6] See *Verdun*, p. 132: 'omni die matutinalem missam celebrantes et simul offerentes.'

et omnibus horis regularibus finitis unum ex praescriptis [1] prostrati canant psalmum, sequente oratione. Exinde usque ad tricesimum diem, more solito cum tribus lectionibus agatur Vigilia, offerente uno choro ad Missam; tricesimo uero die iterum plenarie. His tamen triginta [2] diebus cotidie sacerdotum unusquisque secretis oratorii locis [3] specialiter pro eo Missas celebret; diaconi uero psalterium ex integro, subdiaconi quoque quinquagenarium deuotissime psallant [4]; si autem occupati una die nequiuerint alia persoluant.[a] Mittitur et episticula [5][b] ad uicina quaeque monasteria [6] eiusdem depositionis denuntiatura diem, ut iste sit sensus: *Domnus ille abbas monasterii illius* [c] *cunctis sanctae ecclesiae fidelibus tam praelatis quam et subditis. Cum cunctos maneat sors irreuocabilis horae,*[7] *notum uobis esse cupimus de quodam fratre nostro,* N,[d] *quem Dominus de ergastulo huius saeculi uocare dignatus est die illa,*[e] *pro quo obsecramus obnixe ut sitis strenui interuentores ad Dominum sentiatque in interuentione quibus fuerat unitus* [f] *in* [g] *ordinis communione.*

[a] personant T; agyldan T (gloss). [b] epistola T

[c] Over the words *abbas monasterii illius* F has the note *uel episcopus ecclesiae Christi.* [d] illo F (*note* only). [e] F illa (*note* only).

[f] With this word F ends; in another hand follow the words *in ordinis communione uat.* On the reverse of the folio is the following variant form of the *episticula*, or breve:

> Gratia Dei archiepiscopus .ill. humilisque Christi Ecclesiae monachorum coetus cunctis in Christo salutem fidelibus. Quoniam quidem karissimi caritatis uinculo iubemur uniri dilectioneque Dei feruere et proximi, et quia apostolo scimus obediendum ita monenti *Orate pro inuicem ut saluemini*, uestrae fraternitati notum cupimus fieri unum e nostris fratribus .ill. sacerdotem (*note* : uel leuitam) et monachum .ill. (*note*: xi Kal. Febr.) ergastulo carnis exemptum uitam finisse temporalem; pro quo petimus ut strenui ipsa compellente caritate interuentores existatis quo omnipotens, precibus complacatus uestris, animam eius gaudiis inserat sine fine mansuris. Viuat ualeatque qui Deum postulat quo spiritus eius requiescat in pace.

[g] With this word F_2 begins.

[1] The Penitential psalms; cf. AE, p. 193: 'unum ex supradictis.' This is peculiar to the Concordia.

[2] See *Verdun*, p. 132: 'Unusquisque igitur fratrum pro defuncto fratre psalterium cantabit et unusquisque sacerdos triginta missas.'

Morrow Mass; moreover, after each of the regular hours they shall sing, prostrate, one of the Penitential psalms [1] followed by a prayer. Thenceforth until the thirtieth day the Office Of the Dead shall be said daily with three lessons as usual, one choir at a time making the offering at Mass. But on the thirtieth day the Office Of the Dead shall again be said in full. During these thirty days [2] each priest shall say a special Mass daily for the dead brother, in the secret places of the oratory [3]; and with all devotion each deacon shall chant the entire Psalter and each subdeacon fifty psalms [4]; and if on account of his work he cannot do this on one day he shall do so on another. Moreover, a breve [5] shall be sent to neighbouring monasteries [6] informing them of the burial of this brother; and it shall be worded as follows: *Dom N, abbot of such a monastery, to all the faithful of Holy Church, both prelates and subjects. Forasmuch as there awaiteth every man the lot of the irrevocable hour,*[7] *we desire to make known to you concerning one of our brethren, N, whom the Lord has deigned to call forth from the prison-house of this world on such a day, for whom we beseech you earnestly that you be strenuous helpers before the Lord, so that he may profit by the help of those to whom he was once united in the fellowship of the monastic life.*

---

[3] This phrase was used 6, 11.

[4] AE (p. 193) has 'alii fratres in psalmodiis in quantum valent illam adiuvent.'

[5] cf. *Trèves*, p. 65: 'Nomen autem eius . . . per omnia nota monachorum et canonicorum monasteria . . . litteris denuncietur.' It was customary for religious communities to join in spiritual 'confraternity' and to ask each other's prayers on the death of a monk. Letters of Confraternity, in some form or other, have survived in abundance, but the *episticula* or breve of the Concordia is one of the few early examples of the death notice itself. For variant forms of the *episticula*, found in F and F_2, see *Apparat. in loc.*, and Introd., p. liii f.

[6] These would be houses of the 'Confraternity' to which the senders of the breve belonged.

[7] The late J. Armitage Robinson pointed out to me that 'cum cunctos . . . horae' is a complete line of hexameter. I have been unable to trace it.

68. Quod si ex alio monasterio noto[1] ac familiari[2] frater quis nuntiatus fuerit defunctus, conueniant pulsata tabula undique fratres et, motis uti praediximus[3] omnibus signis, septem paenitentiae prostrati [in oratorio][a] modulentur psalmos,[4] hac subsequente oratione: *Satisfaciat*[5] *tibi Domine Deus noster pro anima fratris nostri, N, beatae Dei Genetricis semperque uirginis Mariae [et sancti Petri apostoli tui]*[b] *atque Sancti Benedicti confessoris tui omniumque sanctorum tuorum oratio et praesentis familiae tuae deuota supplicatio, ut peccatorum omnium ueniam quam precamur obtineat; nec eum*[c] *patiaris cruciari gehennalibus flammis quem eiusdem Filii tui Domini nostri Ihesu Christi glorioso sanguine redemisti. Qui tecum et cum Spiritu Sancto uiuit et regnat [in saecula saeculorum].*[d] Et agatur pro eo prima, tertia, septima, tricesima[6] dies plenarie, reliquis sub breuitate, et nomen eius notetur[7] in anniuersariis; [at ex ignoto[8] tantum][e] Commendatio Animae et una dies.[9][f] Si autem hi qui ualde necessarii[10] sunt, [siue in spiritualibus][g] siue in corporalibus, nimia praegrauantur infirmitate, dum id a gerulo nuntiatum fuerit,

[a] [ ] *om.* F_2 [b] [ ] et beati Petri apostoli tui F_2 (*note* only)
[c] enim F_2
[d] [ ] Deus per omnia saecula saeculorum F_2 (*note* only)
[e] [ ] ad caticuminum istum F_2
[f] + explicuit liber T [g] [ ] *om.* F_2

[1] See p. 6 *n.* 3. [2] i.e., joined in confraternity

[3] This would probably refer to the manner in which the bells were rung for the dead; i.e., tolled; cf. 66, 6.

[4] This would seem to be peculiar to the Concordia. AE (p. 193) says: 'Quindecim Graduum psalmos.'

[5] The only other examples of this prayer outside the Concordia known to me are those in the twelfth century Customs of Vallombrosa (C.M. iv. 261) and the Sarum Missal (ed. Wickham Legg, p. 450) which, however, form part of the Burial Service. The incipit *Sat. tibi D. Deus* found in the Liber Usuum of Bec and Lanfranc's *Decreta* in connection with the burial of a monk, may refer to the quite different prayer of *Gelas* and *Greg* (Suppl.). AE omits *et sancti Petri apostoli tui.*

[6] For the thirty days' observance of the memory of the dead of another monastery see the *Vita Oswaldi*, p. 454 f.: 'Advenit quidam gerulus ex pretioso Ethelthrithae reginae monasterio qui ei de cuiusdam fratris

68. When news is brought of the death of a brother of another monastery, well known[1] and of the same confraternity,[2] the *tabula* shall be struck and the brethren shall come together from all sides and all the bells shall toll [3] and, prostrate in the oratory, they shall chant the seven Penitential psalms [4] together with this prayer : *May the intercession of the Blessed and ever Virgin Mary Mother of God, of St Peter Thy Apostle, of St Benedict Thy Confessor, and of all Thy saints and the devout beseeching of this Thy present family make satisfaction unto Thee, O Lord our God, for the soul of our brother, N, that he may obtain that forgiveness of all his sins for which we pray; nor do Thou suffer him to be punished with the flames of hell whom Thou hast redeemed by the glorious blood of Thy Son our Lord Jesus Christ Who with Thee and the Holy Ghost liveth and reigneth for ever and ever.*[5] And the Office Of the Dead shall be said for him in full on the first, third, seventh and thirtieth [6] days, but shortly on the remaining days; and his name shall be set down [7] among the anniversaries. But if the death of a brother is announced from a monastery that is unknown,[8] only the *Commendatio animae* and one day's [9] memory shall be offered. And whenever news is brought by a messenger that one of those who are specially connected [10] with the monastery by ties spiritual or temporal is grievously sick, the

repentina morte nuntiaret quos precatus est . . . ut sollicite ter denis diebus Missas et Vigilias pro eo facerent.'

[7] *Eins*, p. 76: '*nomenque eius notetur* in breviario et martyrologio'; cf. *Trèves*, p. 65. [8] See p. 6 *n.* 3.

[9] T's note at this point (*explicuit liber*; see *Apparat*) is not a mere copyist's error. For AE, while rearranging the Concordia text here, omits nothing, from *quod si ex alio monasterio* onwards, except the final sentence of Ch. xii. (*Si autem hi qui ualde necessarii sunt*, etc.) and closes his reference to the Concordia with the words *Finiunt Consuetudines*. It could be argued that the final sentence of T was an addition to the original text were it not that it is found, without remark, in F_2 also.

[10] This may refer to notabilities, benefactors or patrons.

ilico pulsata tantummodo tabula, omnes ad ecclesiam conueniant ac septem paenitentiae psalmos cum letaniis et orationibus congruis [pro eis] [a] cum magna diligentia perorent; de aliis uero infirmis ut supradictum est agatur.[b]

[a] [ ] *om.* F_2

[b] With this word F_2 ends. There follow these two variant forms of the *episticula* or breve:

> Gratia miserationis Dei archiepiscopus .ill. omnisque ⟨congregatio ecclesiae Christi⟩ omnibus senioribus et iunioribus fidelibus in Christo salutem. Sanctitati uestrae uolumus sit notum de obitu fratris nostri .ill. monachi et sacerdotis (*note*: uel leuitae) qui obiit N (*note*: xi Kal. Febr.), pro quo petimus ut intercessores existatis quatinus

tabula shall at once be struck and all shall come together to the church and shall say fervently for him the seven Penitential psalms, the Litanies and appropriate prayers. In the case of other sick brethren all shall be done as has been said above.

---

uestris ⟨sacris suffragiis⟩ ualeat aggregari coetibus sanctorum in caelis. Valete.

Gratia miserationis Dei archiepiscopus .ill. omnisque congregatio Ecclesiae Christi omnibus ecclesiae fidelibus salutem. Cum omnes diem mortis nostrae expectamus et necesse habeamus mutuis saluari precibus, suppliciter petimus ut pro fratre nostro .ill. monacho et sacerdote (*note*: uel leuite), qui carnis ergastulo exiens N (*note*: xi Kal. Febr.) hoc saeculum deseruit, intercedere dignemini quatinus per uestra sacra suffragia ad aeterna spiritus eius perueniat gaudia. Valete.

< *EPILOGVS* >

69. Praefatus equidem rex, ut huius libelluli Epilogum, uti Prooemium fideli ac rationabili exhortationis monitu coepit, orthodoxe concluderet, prudenti discutiens examine cum magno suae regiae potestatis imperio interdicens magnopere iussit ut nemo abbatum uel abbatissarum sibi locellum ad hoc thesaurizaret terrenum ut solitus census, quem indigenae *Heriatua* [1] usualiter uocitant, qui pro huius patriae potentibus post obitum regibus dari solet, unde pro eis saecularium imitatione dari posset haberent et sic, Ananiae et Zaphirae [2] anathemate corruentes, ad magnum suae animae detrimentum sanctae regulae praecepta peculiaria [3] omnia prohibentia adnullarent; sed hoc tam sibi quam cunctis successoribus suis pro abbate uel abbatissa dari in Christi, cuius uicarii [4] sunt, eiusque Genetricis Mariae ac omnium sanctorum nomine, aeterno prohibuit imperio. Hoc autem beniuola intentione hortando suasit ut monasteriorum patres matresque quaecumque super usus necessarios restauerint, per manus pauperum in caelestes cum magna et iugi compunctione recondant thesauros [5] quo, corpore in terra degente, animus ibi conuersando subsequens maneat ubi thesauros ordine praemisit iustissimo. Si quae uero priore [a] obeunte superfuerint, subsequens abbas, ut Sancti Spiritus gratia instinxerit, non propinquis carnalibus uel tyrannis saecularibus, secundum anterioris dictatum,[6] diuidendo sed necessitatibus fratrum ac pauperum subueniendo ordinans, cum fratrum consilio [7] sapienter disponat.

[a] In the sense of ' abbot.' See context (*subsequens abbas*).

[1] The particular form of heriot mentioned here has not, I believe, received attention from writers on Anglo-Saxon law.

[2] cf. Acts v. 1 ff. and *Rule* lvii. 11–15.

[3] cf. *Rule* lv. 34 and 37.

[4] See 63, 16: *aeterni Christi uicarius.*

[5] cf. Matt. vi. 21

[6] See 69, 4 f.

[7] cf. *Rule* iii. 4 and lxv. 34–35

< *EPILOGUE* >

69. Now in order that he might close the Epilogue to this book in a fitting manner, even as he began the Proem with sincere and reasonable exhortation and advice, the King aforesaid, after prudent discussion and examination, with all the might of his royal power strictly forbade abbots and abbesses to gather together an earthly treasure-store to enable them to pay, as secular persons do, the customary tax or *heriot*,[1] as it is commonly called among us, which it is usual to offer to the King on the death of notable persons of this country; for thus falling headlong into the anathema of Ananias and Sapphira,[2] they would, to the great detriment of their souls, bring to nothing the ordinances of the Rule forbidding all private property.[3] Wherefore with an everlasting ordinance he forbade in the name of Christ, Whose place superiors take,[4] and of His Mother Mary and all the saints, the payment of this tax either to himself or to his successors on the death of an abbot or abbess. And, with his mind set on their well-being, he urged and exhorted the Fathers and Mothers of monasteries that, with deep and lasting compunction, they should lay up as treasure[5] in heaven, through the hands of the poor, whatever remains over and above necessary use; so that while they yet live on earth in the body their hearts may dwell now, and hereafter everlastingly abide, there where they have most rightly placed their treasure. And if, on the death of an abbot, there be found any superabundance of goods, his successor, instead of sharing it with relations or worldly tyrants shall, according to the command already given,[6] use it as the grace of the Holy Ghost inspires him, for the needs of the brethren and poor, thus, with the counsel of the brethren,[7] wisely disposing all things.

INDEX

INDEX OF LITURGICAL FORMS

A Collects and Prayers given in full in the Regularis Concordia.
B Forms of which only the incipits are given in the Regularis Concordia. Two nearly complete forms, marked with an asterisk (*), are included here. Items enclosed in square brackets are conjectural.

A

B

[1] Complete in the Greek form only

Printed in Great Britain at the Press of the Publishers